CU00592020

Britain Speaks

J.B. Priestley takes on the Nazi war machine

Austin Mitchell

GREAT NORTHERN

Great Northern Books
PO Box 1380, Bradford, West Yorkshire, BD5 5FB
www.greatnorthernbooks.co.uk

Selection, introduction and editorial apparatus © Austin Mitchell, 2020

Transcripts © J. B. Priestley

Every effort has been made to acknowledge correctly and contact the copyright
holders of material in this book. Great Northern Books Ltd apologises for any
unintentional errors or omissions, which should be notified to the publisher.

All rights reserved. No part of this book may be reproduced in any form or
by any means without permission in writing from the publisher, except by a
reviewer who may quote brief passages in a review.

ISBN: 978-1-912101-28-3

Design by David Burrill

CIP Data
A catalogue for this book is available from the British Library

Contents

Foreword

by Tom Priestley

I never heard any of my father's wartime overseas broadcasts, being only twelve when the war ended in 1945, so it's been both fascinating and moving to read them now in Austin Mitchell's collection.

It had been a time of great change for my family. The success of the publication of *The Good Companions* had provided enough funds for my parents to buy a house in Highgate, north London, where I was born and in May 1933 they acquired Bellingham Manor on the Isle of Wight, so we lived between the two houses. When the war began, Bellingham was requisitioned by the army and when the bombing began, they had to sell the Highgate house, so we became homeless and everything changed.

My mother ran a group of houses for young families evacuated from the big cities, and my father began his wireless broadcasts, the *Postscripts*, which followed the nine o'clock news. The overseas broadcasts went out to the English-speaking world, chiefly the USA and the Commonwealth. Soon after my arrival at boarding school when the Postscripts began, I was invited by my headmaster, Dorian Williams, to his study one evening to hear his first *Postscript*, about the evacuation of Dunkirk, but I never heard the overseas broadcasts.

I had no clear idea at the time where my father was or what he was doing. My mother would arrange holidays in the British Isles to places like Cornwall, Wales, the Lake District, Scotland or the Scilly Isles, but my father was holed up in London and could only join us from time to time.

What I do remember is how busy the broadcasts kept my father on top of all his other work, and how much interest they attracted across the English-speaking world. Letters arrived in large numbers, with postage stamps which swelled my juvenile stamp collection.

The *Postscripts* were too late for me. However it was very clear that they were well liked from the way people came up so eagerly to my father whenever they recognised his voice – a voice that will always be with me.

Tom Priestley

Tom Priestley is one of Britain's most highly acclaimed film editors. He won a BAFTA in 1967 for his work on the now cult classic Morgan: A Suitable Case for Treatment *and was Oscar nominated in 1972 for* Deliverance *directed by John Boorman. He has worked on numerous prize-winning films with many talented film-makers including Karel Reisz, Lindsay Anderson, Bryan Forbes, Michael Radford, Jack Clayton, Blake Edwards and Roman Polanski. He now spends his time more in the world, lecturing on film editing and promoting his father's life and work. He is both President of The Bradford Playhouse and The J. B. Priestley Society.*

Preface

by Austin Mitchell

B*ritain Speaks* is a collection of broadcasts by J. B. Priestley, one of the greatest British writers of the past century, about Britain's most dangerous moment, the 1939–45 war years, when the country faced an overwhelming Nazi threat. Being scripts, they lack the rich timbre of his Yorkshire voice but still provide a fascinating picture of those darkest hours when Britain stood alone, morale high, totally mobilised, and managing to keep some semblance of ordinary life going.

The greatest credit goes to Priestley, along with the BBC, which kept him broadcasting to the world and preserved the scripts of the broadcasts in their archives at Caversham. There I also owe a debt to Jeff Walden, the archivist, who guided me through the mass of material in his custody.

The book was very much a team effort. The editing was done by Olivia Beattie, the best editor in the business. Tom Priestley provided help and advice as well as his agent, Robert Kirby, who restrained my anxious impetuosity and found the publisher for the book, Great Northern Books in Bradford. They added it to their brilliant series of Priestley's books. The director, David Burrill, was enthusiastic and superbly efficient and I was delighted to offer him something more serious than my *Teach Thissen Tyke* and *Yorkshire Jokes* books he'd published from me earlier. Last but far from least, I owe a tremendous debt to my wife, Linda McDougall, for her contribution to bringing the book out.

My thanks to all of them. They made this book possible.

Austin Mitchell

Introduction

by Austin Mitchell

I.

Priestley Becomes a Radio Star

In 1940, as Britain defied the formidable Nazi war machine and faced the threat of invasion and bombing, Winston Churchill famously declared it the nation's finest hour. It was also a peak time for three other groups. American correspondents clustered in London saw it as their Camelot. Radio broadcasters came into their own, as the nation – and a world – desperate for news tuned to the BBC. And J. B. Priestley, bestselling author and playwright, became a radio star as the voice of a beleaguered Britain.

High tension and danger made it an age of national revival for Priestley. He had been depressed and alienated in the Chamberlain years as his warnings of the dangers of appeasement and the brutal rise of Nazism in Germany were ignored. Now, suddenly, he was inspired by the courage and defiant spirit of the British people and began to see in their strength a vision of a new and better Britain, sloughing off the apathy and despair of Auden's 'low and dishonest decade', the 1930s.

All this gave Priestley plenty to say. No politician, but a man of the people made good and wealthy, he retained the socialist faith of his father and the sense of community of the Yorkshire world in which he'd grown up. Instinctively Labourite, he was on the side of the masses, not the classes living luxurious lives on the hard labour and poverty of the producers. As a northerner living in the south, he remained moved by the suffering, the unemployment and the grinding poverty of the world he had left. A natural democrat, he was instinctively repelled by the gangster viciousness of fascism and appalled by the weak readiness of Britain's class-dominated government to compromise with it through appeasement.

Having begun to make money from writing and entertainment in the late 1920s, Priestley had become more political as the Great Depression hit a generation already decimated by the Great War. His anger came out in *English Journey*, the successful revival of the literary tourism genre begun by Defoe. There, he reported on the state of the nation, contrasting the shallow prosperity of the south with the sufferings of the depressed north, where factories and shipyards closed and thousands were left unemployed Appalled by this inequality, he turned to journalism, writing, particularly for the radical *News Chronicle*, about the betrayals of the ruling class and the dangers of Nazism.

'The day war broke out', as comedian Rob Wilton used to begin his monologues, J. B. Priestley began his public service on the radio. Driving up to London, he had not heard Neville Chamberlain's announcement that his hopes for peace had been dashed and that consequently Britain was now at war with Germany. He arrived at Broadcasting House to broadcast his new effort to keep the nation's spirits up, *Let the People Sing*, to find the building sandbagged and guarded.

This was the start of a hugely successful but all too brief broadcasting career. It was followed on 23 April 1940 by a *New English Journey*, a 45-minute programme of vox pops recorded all over the country by D. G. Bridson, with each section topped and tailed by Priestley to demonstrate British feelings about the phoney war of waiting without fighting which had lasted from September 1939 to May 1940. The general tone was optimistic as jobs, money and hope were brought to the depressed areas by war production. Priestley concluded:

> We'll soon be hearing much praise, as we always do in
> a war, of the ordinary English folk. But there should
> go with that praise the most solemn pledges that for
> folk so humorous, patient and fundamentally good,

*a nobler framework of life must be constructed, and
the vistas of mean little streets and ruined landscapes,
the humiliation of bad housing, the heartbreak of long
unemployment must vanish – as Hitler and his crooked
cross must vanish – like an evil dream.*

That became a major theme in all his later broadcasts. In 1940, it produced hope, but soon it was to produce antagonism and the end of his Home Service broadcasts. The immediate reaction, however, was to impress both the BBC and the newly created Ministry of Information, then messily finding its feet.

Nicknamed the Ministry of Disinformation, its role was censorship and propaganda (where the less mealy-mouthed Germans called their equivalent the Ministry of Public Enlightenment and Propaganda). It was a hastily thrown together collection of artists, musicians, civil servants and academics, few of them with any real knowledge of ordinary people. Their initial worry was the impact of Lord Haw-Haw, William Joyce, broadcasting his 'Jairmany calling' propaganda programme from Hamburg. This could be heard all over Britain and alarmed the Ministry when BBC audience research indicated that one in every six adults listened regularly and three more occasionally to his bulletins about German power, British incompetence and upper-class privilege. Fearful that British morale was being undermined and a network of fifth columnists built up, the Ministry began to seek ways to counter such Nazi propaganda.

Their fears were exaggerated. Joyce was valuable to Germany (so valuable that as Nazism crumbled, Goebbels tried to get him smuggled back to Ireland by submarine), but in 1940 his listeners probably regarded the broadcasts of 'Haw-Haw the humbug of Hamburg' as yet another *drôlerie* in what the French were calling the *drôle de guerre*. Listening dropped off once the real war began.

Yet the BBC's attempts to drown him out by broadcasting *Band Waggon* at the same time were deemed inadequate by the Ministry as it was brought to order by Duff Cooper, appointed by Churchill as the third minister in the department's first eight months. Cooper realised that the only solution was better news and comment (things the BBC was doubtful about as propaganda). This needed to work on two levels: domestic, where morale had to be kept up, and overseas, where German propaganda had to be countered and American support garnered. There, as Harold Nicolson, the new second in command at the MOI, was warned by Walter Lippmann, 'the American people want us to win but wish to keep out. Thus there is a conflict in their desires.' That gap between the two desires, Nicolson noted, was being exploited by German propaganda.

Priestley became an answer to both problems, domestic and overseas. The Ministry urged the BBC to make use of 'eminent figures' as well as 'the fullest reasonable use of Priestley', who was picked out as a good broadcaster and a man well known both in Britain and overseas in America and the English-speaking world. He had passed his auditions with *Let the People Sing* and the *New English Journey*. The door was open. Priestley confidently walked through it.

The first result was the *Britain Speaks* broadcast to the United States and the Commonwealth. Priestley later recalled that these broadcasts began after, and because of, his *Postscripts* on the Home Service. In fact, it was the other way round. His first *Britain Speaks* broadcast went out on 24 May 1940, a patriotic evocation of 'the spirit of England'. It became the launch for his long series of overseas broadcasts.

Next came his takeover of the already existing *Postscripts* on the Home Service. Priestley later claimed to have offered what he called 'a testing sample' on the evacuation of British forces from Dunkirk. This was broadcast on 5 June 1940.

Going out two days after the last British soldiers were rescued from Dunkirk, it immediately established Priestley's reputation as a brilliant broadcaster, with a style and a theme that he maintained through two series of *Postscripts*. In the first, he lauded the courage and determination of the British people and expressed his faith in their ultimate victory over the barbarism of fascism:

> *This Dunkirk affair was also very English (and when I say 'English' I really mean British) in the way in which when apparently all was lost, so much was gloriously retrieved. Bright honour was almost 'plucked from the moon'. What began as a miserable blunder, a catalogue*

of misfortunes and miscalculations, ended as an epic of gallantry. We have a queer habit – and you can see it running through our history – of conjuring up such transformations. Out of a black gulf of humiliation and despair rises a sun of blazing glory.

The broadcast concluded with a moving tribute to the little boats that had rescued the troops, becoming a symbol of British courage. He focused it on the *Gracie Fields*, the pride of his local ferry service to the Isle of Wight, called out, like all the other boats, from 'that innocent foolish world of theirs to sail into the inferno', where she was sunk.

Never again will we board her at Cowes and go down into her dining saloon for a fine breakfast of bacon and eggs. She has paddled and churned away – for ever. But now – look – this little steamer, like all her brave and battered sisters, is immortal. She'll go sailing proudly down the years in the epic of Dunkirk. And our great-grandchildren, when they learn how we began this war by snatching glory out of defeat and then swept on to victory, may also learn how the little holiday steamers made an excursion to hell and came back victorious.

Small wonder that Priestley found another broadcaster in tears as he came out of the studio. Even today, the broadcast is moving. Then, it made him master of the airwaves. 'All England listened,' said his American colleague Eric Sevareid. Seventeen million of them clustered round their sets in the way families then listened to the radio. This was almost as many as had listened to Churchill's own 'We shall fight on the beaches' speech on Dunkirk. It became the brilliant start to Priestley's broadcasting career as the voice of a beleaguered people.

Priestley was a man transformed, speaking for a regenerated Britain. The years since 1918 had been for him a 'melancholy period of disappointment, dwindling hope, growing fear' through appeasement and despair at the Chamberlain government's indolence and indecision in the face of the Nazi threat. Now all that was dispelled. New men were taking power. The nation was re-energised.

His faith in the British people was expressed to the home audience in a series of Sunday night *Postscripts* running from that 5 June 1940 broadcast to 20 October, then in a second series from 26 January to 23 March 1941. For audiences overseas in America, the Commonwealth and Europe, his skill was deployed in *Britain Speaks* until late 1943.

The *Postscripts* have been republished in three books. Some, but not all, of the first half-year of the overseas broadcasts were immediately published in America by Priestley himself. Many of the rest, preserved in the BBC Archive, are published for the first time here in a personal selection, possibly idiosyncratic but which is necessary because the preserved scripts in the BBC total around 400,000 words. This selection concentrates on British experience and domestic life, rather than military matters or the wider scene.

The broadcasts bring home the realities of life in the Second World War. Most historians view it from the top down: Churchill's leadership, the strategies of the generals, the debates in Parliament. Priestley's view was from the bottom up, bringing out the realities of wartime life and the reactions and hopes of the people to reveal the hardships and fears of war and the people's courage. Priestley spoke for them, not for ministers, generals or politicians, as he chronicled their work and their lives.

Being a populist, he was an advocate of people power not power politics, and he brought to life the realities of the home front and how Britain continued the fight against fascism, to which France and most European nations had succumbed. The British exception was Priestley personified.

The purposes of his two different broadcast series were distinct, as were their fates. In *Britain Speaks*, Priestley told the rest of the world about British morale and set out to assure it that Britain would do its duty on the front line of democracy. Its people would fight to the end and would eventually defeat the monster of Nazism. Despite the bombing, the rationing and the stringencies, British life was going on; the tides came in at Margate and Blackpool, the dark satanic mills throbbed, and the pubs and football grounds were crowded as the British people got on with their lives in intolerable conditions.

As he put it in September 1940:

> *The marvel to me is how little downright interruption*
> *to our life there is. You contrive to do, somehow, all the*
> *more important things you've undertaken to do. My*
> *wife, for example, has been busy buying the children's*
> *winter clothes this week. The newspapers arrive in the*
> *morning and in the evening. The radio programmes are*
> *in full swing, even if theatrical and film shows are cut*
> *down. You eat and drink as usual, perhaps rather more*
> *than usual, for these are hungry times. You keep most*
> *of your appointments, either for business or pleasure.*
> *In fact, you carry on, happily conscious of the fact that*
> *you are in the midst of a great battle and appear to be*
> *winning it.*

The *Postscripts*, delivered on the Home Service to Britain in its hour of need, reassured the people that Britain was right and would win through the courage and strength of its people. They made an invaluable psychological contribution to the war effort, which deserves to be remembered today when the media build audiences by sensation, alarms and fears.

The role of the overseas broadcasts was, though Priestley didn't admit it, more a matter of propaganda, to show the world that 'the Britain now fighting this war is very far from what some of us called "the weary, rich old man" … Britain is tremendously alive, and at this moment is probably the youngest nation on earth.' It was inspired by a vision of a better Britain and a new world when the war was won:

> *It seems to me that two separate Englands are now*
> *meeting and combining: the old England of large*
> *stately mansions with their vast parks and their*
> *feudal tenantry, and this new England that is busy*
> *improvising its life under the menace of the Blitzkrieg,*
> *an England of eager and ardent young life that is*
> *determined not only to rid the world of this Nazi terror*
> *but also to discover for itself a new way of living, at*
> *once more adaptable, more easy and democratic, and*
> *yet richer and fuller in its quality of experience.*

This was a matter of psychology aimed at building support and keeping alive the ultimate hope of a British victory.

Both programmes sprang from Priestley's long-standing hatred of Nazism and his feeling that the threat would become a time of renewal leading to the birth of a new Britain. Crusty Tory Blimps might see this as a danger, because it involved the rejection of their old world of class rule where the people knew their place and were duly deferential. Priestley was never that.

He was a populist. Today, populism is seen as a threat to conventional politics and the established order, though it's far from being as bad as purists believe. It certainly wasn't in 1940 because populism is really speaking for the people to rouse them against the incompetence and corruption of the elite. That was Priestley's instinct. Good British populism, based on national pride and trust in the people.

Today, nationalism is unfashionable (at least off the football field) and easily dismissed as xenophobia. Then, it was the nobler version: patriotism, Priestley's weapon to weld the British people together against the threat of fascism:

> *We are all the people so long as we are willing to consider ourselves the people ... If, however, you cannot or will not recognise this fact, if you persist in thinking of yourself primarily as a member of a class then you are not one of the people. And you take the consequences.*

Quoting the American poet Walt Whitman, Priestley felt that 'everything comes out of the people': 'They are, simply, our brothers and sisters. They are the children of God.'

Many were coming to feel the same way as war strengthened the bonds of community, weakened those of class and prepared the way for the post-war revolution. That message imbued all his broadcasts at home and abroad. It sprang from the people but also from Churchill, making Priestley the agent of the surge of patriotism that swept Britain as it faced the horrendous Nazi threat. 'These Nazi leaders are the most contemptible figures who have ever taken up so much space on the stage of world history: they are small-minded, malignant, vindictive, spiritually dead and intellectually second rate ... What chiefly distinguishes them is an appalling and truly inhuman ruthlessness.'

Germany he saw not as another nation motivated by the pursuit of national interest but as a threat to civilisation: a gangster state sustained domestically by force and motivated by a lust for conquest which had no bounds. Hitler had been allowed to rise to power by the compromising weakness of the ruling class. Nazism had subverted France by exploiting its every weakness and developing a fifth column of collaborators. It now threatened to do the same in Britain, through covert sympathisers in the Tory Party and the upper classes.

In truth, this view probably exaggerated the threat of any fifth column at the time. There was no way its contribution to the fall of France could be replicated in Britain, and traitors were unlikely to have been as sinister as he described them in his 1942 book *Blackout in Gretley*, in which an upper-class military man emerges as the traitor, a tale which added to the annoyance of his Tory critics. At the time, estimates of the size of any potential fifth column varied wildly – they didn't stand around outside Parliament waving Nazi flags, perhaps because most were locked up – yet Priestley almost certainly overstated their potential impact.

Nevertheless, he was determined to defeat them as part of his wider campaign to counter skilful Nazi propaganda with a powerful British propaganda built on humanity and British values. His overseas broadcasts were crucial to this effort because they put him on the front line of the propaganda war, armed with his typewriter.

Another theme of all his broadcasts was the need to sustain British values and build up the confidence and courage and cheerfulness of the British people as they stood alone in the face of the threat of invasion and bombing. Churchill had come to power almost as a last resort and the government lacked much of his confidence and ability. Its propaganda was expressed in class terms, such as the early slogan 'Your courage, your cheerfulness, your resolution will bring US the victory'. As Priestley said, 'deep down they have the mandarin's contempt for the general public' and 'have not yet understood that this war depends more on public opinion and on morale than anything else'. Governmental insecurity about the state of the people caused them to nervously commission regular opinion surveys by Tom Harrisson's Mass-Observation project to report on morale around the country. These demonstrated more expensively what Priestley was telling them at a smaller cost.

Churchill faced major challenges. The Chiefs of Staff were pessimistic. Halifax and senior officials at the Foreign Office, doing its traditional job of representing foreigners, urged an approach to Hitler via Mussolini for some kind of armistice. Fears that civilian morale would not hold up, particularly under the threat of bombing, were strong. Baldwin had told the nation that 'the bomber will always get through', and military staff were grievously over-estimating the bombing capacity of the German Air Force, warning that the Germans would deliver more bombs in months than in fact they dropped throughout the whole war.

Priestley, like Churchill, was in better tune with the real mood of the people than the timid politicians who had been dragged into war by the failure of their appeasement policy. The difference was clearly brought out by Mass-Observation's report on the public mood on 19 June 1940, when it recorded that 'there is a dogged determination to see the thing through. It should be recorded, however, that in many working-class districts this determination is accompanied by some anxiety about the efficient conduct of the war and about the credentials of those at the top.'

This confidence underpinned another major theme. Priestley's own military experience in the 1914–18 war convinced him that the new war was very different:

> *The whole atmosphere was entirely different from that of the last war, which began almost as if it were part of some hysterical summer holiday, with a great deal of singing and shouting and flag waving … This war opened very soberly, with none of that noise and hysteria. The ordinary people were united and determined.*

The previous war had been an industrial war fought with shells, tanks and bayonets across a static front running through Belgium and northern France. There, conscripted armies had struggled to grind each other down by killing as many of the other side as possible. At its end, the promises held out in order to keep the troops fighting this horror had not been fulfilled. The better world that would make it a 'war to end wars' and the 'homes for heroes' were forgotten. The soldiers were betrayed. 'In our victory was our defeat,' as one army man later said. Priestley, a former soldier himself, was determined that it should not happen again.

This new war could not be allowed to end in the same betrayal. Nor could it be conducted in the same murderous fashion. This was a people's war, fought by the entire population, whether on the bombed and rationed home front, in the deserts of north Africa, in the jungles of south-east Asia or in the air over Britain and Germany. It was a war to defend democracy against tyranny, not a falling-out of monarchs, and without the courage and determination of the British people, it could not be won. 'We here in Britain', he told his Commonwealth listeners,

> *are fighting this war for democracy. And when I say 'democracy' I mean democracy: not some plaster imitation of it, but the real thing. Democracy as you'll find it already existing, in spite of this fault or that, in Canada, in Australia, in New Zealand and in South Africa. In short, this war is going to make our life much more like your life; it's going to bring us all closer together ... This means that the old Mother Country will step out and no longer lag behind her go-ahead children.*

The people needed something to fight for, and they would fight all the harder for a better Britain in a nobler world.

> *They need to be given new hope, faith and courage. It is no use asking them to risk everything simply in order to return to the world before the war, because most of them hated the world before the war. They need to feel that the whole set of conditions that produced slumps and terrible unemployment and poverty ... must be swept away once and for all. That the common man everywhere can come out of the shadows again, that their children will one day live amply and nobly. For such a cause, men will risk everything and gladly die ...*

*and it seems to me, as it does to many of us, a monstrous
weakness that we do not produce a simple programme,
going beyond the mere destruction of Hitlerism, and
proclaim it day and night.*

Building that nobler world meant creating international
structures to bring the nations together and providing a better
life, housing and full employment at home to make it a fight
not to defend property or restore class rule, unemployment and
housing squalor but for a new world. This world would emerge
from the people, liberating their talents, freeing them from fear
and keeping them 'moving forward in fellowship to reconstruct
this house of ours', as he put it in the full exposition of his
populism in his 1941 book *Out of the People.*

The incompetence and selfishness of the ruling class had led
to war. Only the people could win it. They had to be encouraged
and rewarded by a commitment to create 'an infinitely better
Britain' and a statement of war aims. The *Picture Post* developed
this idea in a forty-page Plan for Britain published on 4 January
1941:

*Our plan for new Britain is not something outside the
war or something after the war. It is an essential part
of our war aims. It is, indeed, our most positive war
aim. The new Britain is the country we are fighting
for. And the kind of life we want, the kind of life we
think the good life, will exercise an immense attraction
over the oppressed peoples of Europe and the friendly
peoples of America.*

This view so closely echoed Priestley's that he might have
written it.

Others felt the same way. Attlee made it clear to Harold
Nicolson of the Ministry of Information when Labour entered
the government

*that we should put before the country a definite
pronouncement on government policy for the future.
The Germans are fighting a revolutionary war for very
definite objectives. We are fighting a conservative war
and our objectives are purely negative. We must put*

*forward a positive and revolutionary aim admitting
that the old order has collapsed and asking people to
fight for the new order.*

Nicolson and Cooper, the two heads of the MoI, agreed, admitting that Priestley's 'views on social reform appear to be shared by the great majority'. Nicolson warned that 'if only we could show people some glimmer of light at the end of the tunnel, we could count upon them enduring any ordeal'. Duff Cooper, the Minister of Information, urged the same, but sadly Nicolson noted in January 1941, 'Winston refuses to make a statement on war aims. The reason given in Cabinet is that precise aims would be compromising, whereas vague principles would disappoint.'

This wasn't the real reason, but with Priestley continually raising the issue 'as the common folk of this island rose to meet the challenge and not only saved what was good but began to dream of something better', Churchill became angry. His complaints ultimately contributed to the ending of Priestley's *Postscripts* because he saw the issue as a diversion of effort from the central purpose of winning the war.

The real anxiety was political. We think of Churchill as a strong, dominant leader, as he was later when the tide of war had turned, but in 1940, so soon after his arrival in power, his position was less secure. A sizeable section of the Tory Party, loyal to Chamberlain, who remained the nominal leader of his party, still resented his accession to power, disliked his coalition with the Labour Party and clung to hopes of some accommodation with Hitler. The early string of defeats made Churchill's position precarious and he feared a discussion of war aims because it would open up the conflicts over appeasement, the arguments about responsibility for the war, and the Tory divisions, all of which Churchill was anxious to close down. Why reopen old wounds from the days of Baldwin and Chamberlain? Better to fight the Nazis than fratch with each other.

Churchill was hardly likely to want his closest rival at rousing the nation to go on with 'an argument utterly contrary to my known views'. Particularly he didn't want one who was 'far from friendly to the government'. In fact, Priestley had welcomed Churchill's accession to power, but he was known as a lefty and a critic. His broadcasts scandalised reactionaries by suggesting that the wealthy who had fled to America leaving the rest to defend their property should see it used for public purposes, and criticising the idle rich filling hotels away from the bombing but contributing nothing to the war effort. He even suggested that the rich should pay more in tax to finance the war. Rampant socialism!

All this was a red rag to the reactionaries who had ruled the roost for so long. They were highly placed, as well as backed by sympathetic newspapers like the *Birmingham Post*, the *Evening Standard* (then a serious newspaper, not the celebrity gossip sheet it's become now) and the solidly Tory *Daily Mail*. Priestley's rivals, such as Beverley Baxter, piled into the fight.

By October 1940, Lord Davidson and Colonel Scorgie of the Ministry of Information were complaining, the latter saying that he had received complaints that Priestley's postscript 'was calculated to set the rich against the poor'. A. P. Ryan, the BBC's Controller of Home Programmes, was asked to attend the Ministry of Information's daily meeting. There, he defended Priestley, pointing out that he was broadcasting because the minister had asked for 'outstanding personalities' and that he had received 1,500 letters of appreciation, with only 200 of criticism. Ryan also pointed out that Priestley was very sensitive about political criticisms and if he were to be stopped was certain to raise Cain in the press. 'We cannot treat a prima donna like a third-row chorus girl,' he argued.

With the complaining Lord Davidson absent, the meeting declared itself happy with the position, as did the chief press adviser to the Ministry. Immediately afterwards, the minister, Duff Cooper, met Ryan and told him that he agreed. By December, a report to the War Cabinet indicated that Churchill was beginning to think that bad news was better broken by a popular novelist than by a politician. All that was shattered by the formation, the following January, of the 1941 Committee, a collection of left-wing thinkers which Priestley chaired.

Other warning signals had emerged earlier. In September 1940, as Priestley's first series ended, Sir Richard Maconachie, the Director of BBC Talks, had minuted his concern that Priestley *has definite views which he puts over in his broadcasts and is, I think, exercising an important influence on what people are thinking. These views may be admirable or otherwise, but the question which I wish to raise is one of principle – whether any single person should be given the opportunity of acquiring such an influence to the exclusion of others who differ from him, merely on the ground of his merits as a broadcaster, which are, of course, very great.*

This became a line of criticism opponents now developed. The crusty brigade, whom Priestley called the 'commanders of the Carlton Club', focused on this rather than complaining about Priestley's politics (which was, of course, the real issue). Yet Priestley's audience was still huge at 29 per cent of the listening public, more than the figures for any of those who had filled the gap between his two series, and Harold Nicolson at the MoI still felt that if Priestley were dropped, 'eleven million people would want to know the reason why'.

Proud of its new star, the BBC renewed Priestley's contract for another series of *Postscripts*. Cheered, he wrote to his lover, Mary Hope Allen, a BBC producer then in Manchester, on 8 January claiming to have had 'an enthusiastic telegram from Ryan tonight, so clearly I'm the white-haired boy again'. He was, but on probation. Angered by the renewal, Churchill demanded that Priestley should be removed, or at the very least hit where it would hurt a Yorkshireman and have his fee withdrawn. Duff Cooper was forced to mollify the Prime Minister and break it to him that the new contract for a record payment had already been agreed.

The warning shots had been fired. But in his first broadcast in the second series of *Postscripts* on 26 January 1941, Priestley launched straight back into his campaign, pointing out that the 'ordinary common folk of this country are heroes' and demanding that public men should 'stand up in public and solemnly pledge your word to those same people that you will never rest until you have created for them an infinitely better Britain and, to show that you mean it, do something now, give a sign that a new democratic order is on the way'. He later claimed to have made the series 'more aggressive, democratic in feeling and tone'. In fact, this was the strongest part of it. As the mutter of criticism rose, the rest of the series became more muted.

That didn't stop the anger of reactionary Tories. David Margesson, who had been Chamberlain's Chief Whip and had stayed on as Churchill's, was particularly vociferous. Brendan Bracken, Churchill's PPS, fixer and amanuensis, as well as publisher of the *Financial News* and *The Economist*, encouraged a press campaign against Priestley. Then, in March 1941, a deputation of members of the Tory Party backbench group the 1922 Committee, led by Harry Strauss, went to the minister, Duff Cooper, to demand that Priestley be taken off the air. A. P. Ryan attended the meeting for the BBC and reported back:

> *Mr. Duff Cooper showed me before the meeting a minute he had just got from the Prime Minister complaining that Priestley had been allowed to express views on Sunday in conflict with the Prime Minister's own views on the subject of war aims. Mr. Duff Cooper also showed me his reply to the Prime Minister, which was quite firm and stood up for the importance of allowing criticism of the government to be heard at the microphone.*

In the discussion with 'the loquacious Mr. Strauss and his comrades', three points emerged:

1. *The minister took full responsibility;*

2. *He said he would seriously consider warning Priestley off discussing war aims;*

3. *He gave an informal undertaking that Priestley would be given a rest after his series of six.*

The fat was in the fire. Cooper, an urbane but not a strong minister, was becoming fed up with his job. He defended the independence of the BBC and freedom of expression for its broadcasters but was getting tired of constant arguments and beginning to feel that Priestley was 'a second-rate author who got conceited by his broadcasting success'. Weary of his department, he was soon to be replaced by Brendan Bracken,

Left to right: F.W. Ogilvie (D.G.), Sir G.A. Powell (Chair),
Sir S.G. Talents (Controller overseas), Sir N. Ashbridge (Engineering),
Roger Eckersley (Programme Controller), Patrick Ryan (Controller home
programmes), G. Beadle (Administration), M. Farquharson (Secretariat),
T. Lockhead (Finance).

who had the confidence of Churchill and was in practice a
more effective Minister of Information, though the fourth to
hold the job in sixteen months. Cooper would be transferred to
Singapore as Resident Minister – just in time for Britain's Asian
citadel to fall to the Japanese. But first, he wanted to clear up the
Priestley imbroglio.

Cooper invited Priestley to his club for lunch, fired him
and announced that he had personally replaced him by A. P.
Herbert, an 'independent' MP of conservative inclination.
Priestley listened sullenly and made no immediate protest, but
his anger simmered, particularly since Cooper had told him he
was 'getting tired'. Most of his anger was unfairly directed at
Ryan, who had in fact worked hard to support him. He also

threatened to stop his overseas broadcasts if he couldn't do the Home Service ones, further complaining to Ogilvie, 'You are allowing the most successful talks feature you have ever had to be deliberately wrecked, and this at a time when such a feature is of immense value to the BBC and the nation.' Clearly, Priestley was not lacking in *amour propre*, though he was somewhat mollified when, in May, Norman Collins went down to spend the weekend with him and requested that he should continue his overseas talks for a considerably increased fee. After visiting him, however, Collins reported that Priestley was 'still smouldering – and sometimes blazing – with a perfectly sincere consciousness of an alleged injustice done to him'. Collins went on, 'As Empire Talks is so urgently in need of Priestley's service (and his listening public in the States is so enormously greater than those of any other speaker) I am anxious to do anything I can to secure his return.' Money looks to have achieved this.

Afterwards, he asserted that his dismissal had been engineered by Churchill, which could have been transmitted by the ubiquitous Brendan Bracken, but Nicholas Hawkes, who has written the most thorough study of the matter, concludes that no evidence can be found of any direct order, and nothing can be found in Bracken's papers since he ordered their burning after his death. Yet written orders were hardly necessary. The deed was done in the best Thomas Becket fashion by those lower down the chain of command, anxious to rid the monarch of this troublesome priest.

Cooper had the real responsibility. The BBC reluctantly acquiesced. Priestley thought there might be BBC resignations. None came, and in his anger he rejected Ryan's initial attempt at a compromise promise to bring him back later, claiming that 'with ordinary folk up and down the country I am next in popularity to Churchill' and arguing that he needed a series to develop his argument. Ryan's rejected offer was in any case withdrawn when BBC higher-ups showed all the courage of a jelly out of its mould. So in fact all of those involved carried an element of responsibility. Each placed the blame on the other, but Cooper had wielded the dagger.

Priestley's reaction was anger: 'We'll never get people to fight the Gestapo by asking them to do so for the Eton and Harrow match, Ascot and the boat race.' He appealed to the trade union movement to back him, but their reaction was a request by the Shop Stewards' organisation for one of their members to do a *Postscript*. He had already got the *Picture Post* to produce a piece defending him and criticising the BBC, but no presenter, however big, can prevail against the machine. The BBC had a monopoly on broadcasting. There was no chance of moving, like *Bake Off* on its cake walk to another channel. Press support was minimal. Priestley had no choice.

In his first flush of anger, he had threatened to stop his overseas broadcasts as well, but the BBC and its Controller (Overseas) were too well aware of his value. The controller, a marketing expert, had already written him a flattering letter about his achievements, concluding, 'Please return to the microphone.' Priestley did, but not without pushing his fees up. The chorus of Tory criticism that had attended the *Postscripts* fell silent as he continued overseas efforts, probably because, as Ryan observed after his meeting with the protesters, 'I did not gather that Strauss and Co. had got round to knowing that they were on.'

Meanwhile, the BBC faced difficulties in replacing him on the *Postscripts*. Long lists of alternatives were compiled. T. S. Eliot was deemed 'rather a difficult man', Arthur Bryant 'unattractive', and Cooper, who forced himself onto the airwaves with a programme on Joan of Arc, irrelevant and boring. None of the replacements actually chosen had Priestley's impact or audience ratings.

He nurtured his anger, which grew over the years, but was nonetheless keen to continue his overseas broadcasts, which were a great success. Priestley lamented that he was

> not prevented from broadcasting to anybody and everybody, only to my fellow countrymen. I was not only allowed but encouraged to talk on the air to the rest of the world ... Very soon I must have had one of the largest regular audiences of listeners ever known for those talks, which went out to all the Dominions and colonies and were transmitted by about eighty radio stations in the United States.

Naturally, he took the opportunity to increase his fee to

twenty-five guineas (that old class-conscious currency unit which added one shilling to every pound as a tip for professional services while humble workers were paid in pounds).

Not that this brought better relations with the BBC. Later in 1941, he was brought back on the Home Service to do a non-political series called *From My Notebook*. It was not a success, and he resented the rejection of a play and more programme ideas by Val Gielgud and Basil Nicholls, the Controller of Programmes. Priestley saw both as his enemies, and a minute by Gielgud attacking Priestley as a petulant, spoiled child goes some way to confirm the animosity was mutual, as Priestley recognised in a letter to Mary Allen in January 1942: 'I'd like to stop broadcasting altogether and not go back until the whole place has been cleaned up. I'll certainly not go back on the Home Service while these boys are around ... Don't tell me these boys didn't gang up on me.' He was happier on the overseas service, where their writ didn't run.

Priestley wasn't one to bite the hand that fed him. Though he continued to grumble, he wanted to keep the overseas broadcasts and remained the voice of Britain abroad. There, he gave a wider social view of Britain than that of Mollie Panter-Downes, who spoke for Knightsbridge in her regular articles for the *New Yorker*, or the London-centric reports of Ed Murrow, John Gunther, Eric Sevareid and other foreign journalists reporting on Britain's battle for survival. They sat, like vultures, in London, where Priestley moved around the country, talking to real people. They spoke as journalists to their home audiences, where he spoke for and to the people he identified with. As one Mass-Observation interviewee put it, 'He can put himself in position of Man in Street, so listener does not feel alone.' That was Priestley's achievement both at home and overseas.

The overseas broadcasts were, as Priestley pointed out 'quite different from the *Postscripts*, which had been more or less spoken essays'. *Britain Speaks* was more journalistic. Priestley was freer to speak his own mind and less subject to the inhibitions and timidity of the Ministry of Information. He was still acceptable to them as a spokesman for a beleaguered Britain.

In the overseas programmes, Priestley devoted considerable effort to criticising the technique and skill of German propaganda, which he saw as the Nazis' secret weapon. He saw his own efforts as honest, journalistic reporting. In fact, his aim was propagandist – for how else can one describe putting Britain's case to the world, building up support and commitment to help (and, later, involvement by the United States), and sustaining the efforts the Dominions and colonies were already making? All this was, as his studio manager rightly described it, 'propaganda that wasn't propaganda', skilfully done.

And truthfully, as far as was possible in a war, with a censorship regime breathing down his neck, Priestley always put Britain's case in the best light. Our bombing was always precisely targeted, our bureaucrats always wise and flexible, our pilots braver and our planes better. Yet he was telling the truth as he saw it and was certainly independent-minded rather than merely echoing government policy. As the Director of Empire Services wrote in 1941, 'He wants to discuss controversial issues and agrees that criticism of the government is not necessarily out of place, provided of course that the ultimate moral conclusion of talks is to our general advantage and in no way interferes with our war effort.'

By 1941, the mood in America was becoming more sympathetic. In Priestley's view, that created a new role, which he put to the Director:

> One suggestion he made was that he might speak with more candour about the United States and the war. He has been much interested with conversations with Agate, now returned from the United States, who argued that our propaganda was weak, that we ought to be quite a bit tougher with the United States, saying that she ought to get into the war as soon as possible etc. Priestley suggests for instance that in one talk he might discuss the issue in the form of a report of a conversation between himself and a distinguished journalist in which he would take the line that while he agreed that we should be considerate of American susceptibilities and more candid, he did not think that it was the business of an Englishman to tell America

*when they should come into the war. His view is that
we can do almost anything short of that one thing ... I
think we must do everything we can to help Priestley
to make his views effective at this stage. I think his
difficulties are real and his suggestions sensible and
very seriously intended. After all, he is our star overseas
broadcaster.*

Priestley did begin to speak more boldly, but it would be
wrong to claim, as some have, that he brought the USA into
the war; the Japanese did that. Pearl Harbor followed by
Hitler's declaration of war on America overcame Roosevelt's
prevarications and brought the US in. Priestley merely prepared
the ground.

In doing so, he was much better suited to American
audiences than the upper-class tones of British ambassadors
to Washington Lords Lothian and Halifax, both of whom
were complacent about British superiority and the prospects
of American intervention. In October 1940, just as Roosevelt
was campaigning for re-election on the promise that American
sons would not be sent into foreign wars, Lord Lothian
complacently reported home that events could be relied upon
to bring America in:

*In the early stages America had felt that this was merely
a European war. They had rather despised us for our
muddle in Norway. Then came the collapse of France
and the sudden realisation that the British fleet was
their first line of defence. In July they were terrified
that we should go the same way as France. Then came
Dunkirk, the triumph of the RAF, the abandonment
of invasion and the pact with Japan. These four things
swung American opinion over in six weeks.*

This was excessively optimistic, though Lothian did admit
that isolationism remained strong and that while WASP and
Anglophile opinion was favourable to Britain, 'the large sections
of German and Italian origin definitely were not'. He could
have added Americans of Irish extraction but didn't.

Priestley, in contrast, suffered from neither complacency

nor the aristocratic assumption of British superiority. His ability to speak as a man of the people had a bigger impact on American attitudes than those of passing peers in the embassy. The problem in the United States was the widespread suspicion that Britain was fighting to keep its empire and maintain an outdated aristocratic order. Priestley's role was to demonstrate to the Americans that the fight was for democracy, liberty and a fairer future. Britain was on their front line.

He regarded the two nations as motivated by different but complementary virtues: the British by democracy, the Americans by liberty. Both were threatened by the intolerant brutality of fascism, and Britain was defending both. He didn't directly urge the intervention Churchill was desperate for. Instead, he described the struggles of the British people against the threat of Nazism and asked for help and sympathy in defending the common interest.

When the US did finally join the fight, he switched to teaching them the lessons Britain had already learned and weaning them from their fear of what many Americans saw as socialism:

> *You cannot fight this kind of war without undertaking the most gigantic social experiments. That is one of the most serious mistakes Britain and France made at the beginning of this war ... Britain woke up after Dunkirk and then Britain tore into the job, with most of her people ready to make any changes so long as they were good for the war effort. But of course we had these critics, who said the rest of us were 'playing politics', taking advantage of the national emergency, indulging in class politics etc. etc. ... The Britain of 1942 bears no resemblance to the Britain of 1939. Its whole economic and social structure is being changed. These changes aren't due to the fact that the men who lead Britain are enthusiastic social revolutionaries. On the contrary, most of them are dyed-in-the-wool conservatives whose natural tendency is to resist any attempt at change. But Mr. Churchill and his colleagues have been led to take these measures by the sheer logic of the facts. They are determined to win the war and gradually they have discovered that to win the war you*

must make these changes, just as a boxer must go into strict training to give himself any chance of winning a fight. A system that may be good enough for peacetime – though I have always doubted it – is clearly not good enough for wartime ... You are compelled to bring the social system nearer some sort of equity, not because you have set out to reform the country but simply because the deadly necessities of war demand it. You have to see that men are properly employed now, because manpower is precious. You are compelled to cut down inessential work and concentrate on essential work for the same reason, that materials and manpower must no longer be wasted. If there should be a shortage of essential supplies – food, clothing etc. – then you have to ration these supplies, to make sure everybody gets a fair share of them. So too, you cannot now afford to have large masses of people who are undernourished, suffering from bad health and unfit to cooperate in the common task. Again, you have to make the fullest possible use of the nation's ability without any reference to a social or economic class system. The barriers of class are now seen to be a bad liability so that anything that helps to remove them is contributing to the common effort. As you need everybody's enthusiastic help, you must make it clear to all and sundry that this is their war.

These lessons had been learned in Britain, where they led to Labour's 1945 victory and developed the tools to build the new society. Preaching them to the USA, home of individualism, competition and powerful capitalism, was another matter, but, facing the same pressures, America was compelled to go part of the way down the same road of wartime socialism and collective effort that Priestley had signposted.

The *Postscripts* and *Britain Speaks* both began at the most crucial moment of the war, when Britain stood alone. The great need was to inspire the nation and boost the courage of its people. Humiliated in Norway, defeated in France, the British Army was evacuated from Dunkirk, leaving most of its equipment and tanks behind. The nation needed inspiration and optimism. Priestley added something more: hope.

The need was urgent and Churchill and Priestley both rallied the nation's morale, the Prime Minister in Parliament, Priestley in his *Postscripts* as well as to a watching world. On the BBC's Empire Service, his programme *Britain Speaks* continued for another three years, with occasional breaks, such as in September 1942, when he felt 'talked out'. He recovered and came back until late in 1943, by which time he felt that his job was done. The conflict would be decided by weight of arms and the might of two nations more powerful than Britain.

Context is crucial. The 1939–45 war, like its predecessor, is commemorated by memorials all over the country inscribed 'lest we forget'. But we have. Memories of the Second World War are being lost as the generations pass. A YouGov poll before the 75th anniversary in 2019 indicated that half the population didn't know what D-Day was. A diminishing number of those who lived through the war survive, and now most of those who remain were, like me, too young to fight or remember. I never heard Priestley's broadcasts live, though people who did have told me how compelling they were and how people of all parties came together to listen. I was too young to feel the full horror of the war I grew up in. My only contribution to victory was to guard my grandmother's house (47 Hyde Park Road, Halifax) with my popgun from the German attack which I anticipated daily, even if Halifax Council didn't.

The only experience I shared with Priestley was the bombing of Bradford in September 1940. To be honest, I hardly heard its dull thuds as I sat, gas mask (posh Mickey Mouse type) at the ready in the damp air raid shelter my dad had built in our back garden. The next day, I passed through Bradford because my parents had decided to send me for safety to Halifax, a mini twelve-mile evacuation but considered to be a less likely target. Passing through Bradford on the way, I watched the clearing-up operations but saw neither the main target, Lingard's the drapers (an obvious strategic target to stop supplies of blackout material), nor the pie shop nearby where Bradford's famous big pie still bubbled in the shattered window. The pie – Bradford's major tourist attraction – survived.

My evacuation was unsuccessful. The bombing moved on to Halifax and I had to take cover under my grandmother's bed,

*The author defending his grandmother and
neighbours against the Nazi onslaught.*

less safe than in our shelter, where the main danger was pneumonia. However, this isn't a chronicle of my part in Hitler's downfall but an attempt to put Priestley's broadcasts into the context of a situation very different to today's.

Priestley's role at the start, like Churchill's, was to inspire the nation to fight on and endure the savage bombing. Hope came with the defeat of the Luftwaffe in the Battle of Britain, then with Hitler's disastrous decision to invade Russia in 1941 so Britain no longer stood alone though bombing and defeats still continued as the British Army was driven out of Yugoslavia, Greece, then Crete, which Churchill had promised to 'defend to the death'. Worse, the Japanese declared war and became part of an Axis alliance against Britain. In February 1942, the supposedly impregnable fortress of Singapore surrendered ignominiously. The Japanese swept into Malaya and Burma and towards the jewel in the crown, India.

The consolations were that Japan brought the Americans in and Britain routed the Italians in north Africa, which provided new hope and a crop of jokes about Italian tanks only having a reverse gear. Even that ended when Rommel arrived and drove the British Army back into Egypt.

The war became a battle of attrition as both sides tried to bomb each other into submission. The Royal Navy blockaded Germany, which in turn tried to cut Britain's supply lines by the heavy toll of submarine warfare in the Battle of the Atlantic. Each side struggled unsuccessfully to wear down the other, until two developments, neither of British making, turned the tide. On 22 June 1941, Hitler's invasion of Russia brought its formidable power into the war one the Russians had checked the Nazi onslaught. Suddenly, Britain's Conservatives found themselves in alliance with their bête rouge, having previously been led by their anti-communist prejudice to shun Russian support when it was really necessary to defend Poland and deter Hitler in 1939. Then, on 7 December, the Japanese attacked Pearl Harbor in a day of infamy which ended Roosevelt's long equivocation and brought America in on the British side. To Churchill's relief, the arsenal of democracy became Britain's military partner.

New allies didn't mean immediate support. Russia was struggling to stop the German advance, and America was hardly ready. Though graffiti demanding a 'Second Front Now' appeared all over Bradford (some painted by David Hockney's dad) as well as in lesser places outwith the county, preparations for invasion required more time and a much bigger build-up. Yet the tide was turning against Germany, and Priestley was now talking to a powerful ally engaged in the fight, no longer begging for help from it. The tone of his overseas broadcasts changed appropriately. Less now about Britain's continuing privations, more about building relationships and working together.

By 1943, prospects were improving fast. In February, Priestley told his listeners, 'We of the Allied nations, who really represent the law-abiding world itself, have definitely moved over to the offensive, to the final grand assault.' The German attack on Russia was held at Stalingrad, Italy was invaded in July, Corsica liberated in August and Rommel was defeated in north Africa. There was still no invasion of Europe, the second front that Priestley urged. 'I am, of course, a second front man,' he told the world in March 1943, 'although I have always felt that very loud demands for it shouldn't come from civilians who have no intention of quitting their homes for the sudden hell of the beaches or for parachute jumps behind German forts.' He felt irritated by the long wait, as did much of the nation and the Russians, producing the joke that Stalin would have to fight his way to the French coast and bellow across the Channel, 'You can come over now.'

Yet 1943 was clearly the beginning of the end, even though the actual invasion of Europe was not launched until D-Day, 6 June 1944. Priestley's overseas broadcasts ended well before that. He gave them up to resume home broadcasts, having been allowed back with a new series called *Make It Monday* that was more concerned with problems to come than a continuation of previous themes, which had by now become outdated.

As Britain began to look to the end, Priestley was turning his mind to post-war problems and devoting less thought to the privations of a war which now looked sure to be won. The magical mood of 1940–41 was fading; the nation was tiring. An impoverished and weaker Britain had to be prepared to face the daunting problems of victory and building a new society.

Priestley had done his duty. The end of the Nazi regime was in sight ahead, if not immediately. His morale-boosting was less necessary. He reflected afterwards:

> *I believed we had to fight that war, cost what it might.*
> *I also believed – though this gave me some powerful*
> *enemies – that we could not fight it to restore the rotten*
> *world that had nourished Hitler and the Nazis. On*
> *those beliefs I took my stand whenever I faced the*
> *microphone. The new and better world I dreamt of*
> *may not have taken shape.*

That was a job still to be done.

II.

Style and Structures

To think about the BBC before the war conjures up images of Lord Reith, all stern caution, and announcers in full evening dress speaking in a Received Pronunciation which is really the dialect of the so-called Home Counties of the south east. In these posh tones they talked down to the rest of Britain's regions, who found RP posh. Priestley helped to change that. The warm, homely burr of his northern accent, like the emergence of Wilfred Pickles reading the news, broke the RP monopoly, causing the Corporation to commission audience research on the acceptability of regional accents. To the surprise of many, more than half the respondents had no objection. The reservation was that 'only in Scotland is there any appreciable dislike of them'.

In Priestley's case, he was, the BBC Director of Talks considered, 'in a class by himself, having the artist's power, the journalist's gift, an organisation behind him on which he could rely for ideas and facts and a good voice and virile manner'. In other words, a star. His warm Bradford tones lacked the class overtones and the crisp authority of the usual BBC performers but were more acceptable to the people and to the world overseas. They could identify with him, and their trust in him made his broadcasts more real and credible. Here was a real person, not a broadcasting automaton speaking the language of another class.

Never forget the impact of class. It remains important today, though now criss-crossed by ethnic and regional differences and moving towards the amorphous middle. Then, it was more powerful. People knew their place and were mostly relegated to it. Class accents were clipped and posh – just look at the films of the '30s and '40s. Priestley was high on the class register, a wealthy man with two houses, a car and servants, but his accent and attitudes reflected a different background and made him one of the people, identifying with them and speaking their language. He was the people's friend.

His talks were personal chats, addressed neither to an audience nor to a wider crowd. He never talked down but spoke to individuals, person to person in their own homes, in warm tones which were just right for the nervous days of war. He knew that

> *the tricks of the writing trade are all very well, but what holds the attention of most ordinary folk is a genuine sharing of feelings and views on the part of the broadcaster. He must talk as if he were among serious friends and not as if he had suddenly been appointed as the head of an infants' school.*

This makes his talks jewels in the BBC's crown. So impressive were his broadcasting skills that when Priestley suggested a BBC style book to help people communicate better, the idea was quickly taken up and he was asked to contribute. He did so by emphasising the need to talk directly on a one-to-one basis to equals, not down to some collective 'audience'. His advice was to relax, speak directly and say only what the speaker thinks and feels.

If you can fake sincerity you've got it made, the joke goes, but there was no faking on Priestley's part. He was giving voice to his feelings, articulating the same love of his country and its people that permeated his writing. He won the trust of his audiences, keeping hope alive in the darkest days and sustaining hopes of victory for both home and overseas listeners. Even now, in our age of high-speed gabble, heckling interruptions by opinionated interviewers and the blandising efforts of public relations, there is much to admire in J. B. Priestley's wartime broadcasts.

He later belittled them as 'wireless talks not essays, dashed off in half an hour', but his fellow broadcaster Eric Sevareid, republishing the *Postscripts* in the 1960s, was more realistic: 'They are essays lovingly if quickly constructed, with beginning, middle and end.' In his view, it was Priestley's writing skills that made him such a master: 'What counts is the word. Churchill and Priestley were artists of the spoken word.' His talents as a novelist and perceptive observer gave him such a clear view of people and their feelings. The reservation was that he saw writing as a lonely art, unlike radio, where, as Priestley put it, 'Ten clever persons will meet every day, trying to please a lot of stupid people they have never met.' His own aim was to mobilise his writing skills to appeal to them personally and directly.

The contrast is brought out by a comparison between Priestley and Orwell, who was not exactly a member of the Priestley fan club, regarding him as 'a second-rate novelist' and later reporting him to the security service as a crypto-communist. This could have been simple jealousy from a less commercial author towards a successful mass market writer. Not only had Priestley pioneered the social anthropology of Britain's two nations – north and south, middle and working class – before Orwell, but his reports read better and were more realistic.

The difference was class. Priestley, like a good Yorkshireman, always talked poor, but unlike most of his fellow northerners he was in fact well off. But he came from solid socialist stock and identified with the people, whereas the poverty-stricken public school chap was observing them like a missionary studying a strange tribe. Priestley's style was warm, sympathetic, even flowery; Orwell's, colder and more clinical, an outsider's description of the industrial north from which Priestley had sprung. Orwell was observing another world *de haut en bas*; Priestley felt himself part of it. His books, like his broadcasts, provide a wonderful description of the lives, hopes and fears of real people. He brought them alive. Orwell studied them from a detached perspective and used them as a political symbol.

Talking the Talk

Priestley enjoyed his role as the voice of Britain. He rejoiced in the

> *staggering power and effect of broadcasting. I have been hard at it getting through to the public mind in one way or another for about twenty years, but as a medium of communication this broadcasting makes everything else seem like the method of a secret society. So long as you don't go on too long and the listeners are not tired of you, a mere whisper over the air seems to start an avalanche.*

It was an exacting life, particularly when the *Postscripts* and *Britain Speaks* were being run in parallel, but even afterwards with two or three overseas broadcasts a week in the early hours of the morning, all written and performed on top of his own hard day's work writing novels, plays and articles for the press. It involved advance preparation and usually submission of the script, until the BBC became its own censor. Then he had to attend at Broadcasting House, or a studio outside London, for a broadcast at 2.30 a.m., often twice a week, and in some cases to record not one programme but two or even three. The BBC producer Norman Collins described the task in the period when Priestley was doing both the *Postscripts* and the overseas broadcasts:

> *On Sunday at 2.30 p.m. he'd sit down at his typewriter with cotton wool in his ears and bash out the Sunday Home Service typescript. He'd put the pages of the script together then bash out another of the same length for North America. He'd finish the Home Service script for about 4.30 p.m. and the North American script for about 6.30 p.m. It was almost uncanny to watch. Then he'd have a drink and broadcast the Home Service piece. Then at 2.30 a.m. he'd do the other. I can't remember that there was ever any need to revise the scripts. His attitude towards the finished piece was: 'Why should I read through what I've written? I've written it.*

Priestley himself described it differently: 'They kept me up several nights a week, until two or two-thirty in the morning … and during the periods of heavy air raids it was no joke first getting the pieces written and then finding my way with the script to Broadcasting House, itself a major German target.' (Though he fails to mention that at Broadcasting House he could find solace in drinking the Director General's best whisky with Ed Murrow as they both waited to broadcast.)

On one occasion, Priestley's hotel room in the Langham was demolished by a bomb, though fortunately he wasn't in it at the time. The alarms regularly disturbed both his sleep and his overseas broadcasts, causing him to complain to his audience that he'd been moved into an inferior but more secure studio where the microphones weren't as good. The threat of bombing hung over everything and had him 'wondering if some young idiot 12,000 feet above you is going to press a button and perhaps blot you out, and all for the sake of the greater glory of an ex-paper-hanging Austrian police spy who probably isn't right in his head'. A powerful image, later used by Orwell.

As a workaholic, he relished the intense schedule. But the excitement didn't prevent regular grumbles, which began early on. In December 1940, he complained to his BBC producer, Miss Wade, that

> *my whole relations with the BBC appear to be unsatisfactory. As I have from a broadcasting view done what seemed to me a very satisfactory job both at home and overseas I had always assumed and perhaps rather naively that I was among friends there, but a great many things that have happened during the last two months suggest that this assumption is not correct.*

He specified that his complaints were about the overseas broadcasts, but they were probably intended to apply more generally.

When his first series of *Postscripts* ended, he complained that working on them made him feel like 'walking across a field of glue'. The BBC for its part found him difficult to handle. Perhaps he was only expressing the desire of so many presenters to be loved, but the BBC was never a loving organisation, particularly in wartime. Perhaps he was asserting the privilege of the great to be ornery; Priestley could be as awkward as the best of them.

The most serious of his litany of grumbles was censorship – which was hardly surprising, since the efforts of inexperienced censors were also bringing the press to a state of revolt. The Ministry required scripts in advance and occasionally made objections, though the main censorship was soon taken on by the BBC itself, and his later scripts are mostly stamped by two departments portentously describing themselves as 'BBC Censorship' and 'BBC Policy', both of which were later put to rest in Room 101. Priestley claimed that 'your text is absurdly mutilated on censorship grounds, though many of the corrections are nonsensical'.

The requirement for six scripts in advance and one for *The Listener* was an onerous obligation to which Priestley protested in August 1941:

> *It would sometimes be more convenient – and help the talks to be more topical – if the rule about the script being in so much in advance were relaxed. After all, I used to write it within an hour or two of the talk going on last year. Can you take this up with Monkton [of the MoI]?*

The question was raised, but, although the time constraints were eased, censorship continued nonetheless.

In fact, Priestley was playing the prima donna. His complaints were regular but exaggerated. The censorship was hardly onerous, and most of the time he was ready to comply with whatever was wanted. In March 1941, the minister was alarmed that Priestley's broadcasts were being used by the Germans to tell the US that Britain was 'going Bolshevik'. Priestley tersely replied that it could equally be said that it was going crypto-fascist, but he made the cuts.

He even helped government with its own propaganda, always giving the best possible picture of Britain, always using official figures for gains and losses even though they were often unreliable, always giving a helping hand. In February 1941, former US President Herbert Hoover was campaigning to send food ships to Europe, as he had done in 1919. The Ministry of Economic Warfare was anxious to spike his guns and asked Priestley to demonstrate the necessity for the blockade Britain was imposing on Germany. He did so. In August 1941, the Head of the BBC's Empire Service commented, 'I have been surprised to see how careful he has been. He realises well that the policy decisions in this matter of criticism or discussion of war efforts etc. must lie with the Ministry.'

Yet he also spoke out on anything which irked him. He said of the thing he hated most:

> *'Curse this blackout,' I've muttered as I've left some cheerful interior for this vast wall of darkness ... I don't hesitate to say that of all the restrictions, limitations, irritations and vexations that this war has imposed on us, the blackout is the most unpopular. I have heard it denounced more often than any other feature of our wartime life.*

He also felt a lack of cooperation and help in provincial studios when he broadcast away from London. This reached a retrospective crescendo of self-pity twenty years later, when he wrote, 'I was punctual and reasonably clean and sober. I have arrived in provincial studios and been made to feel I was a bomb with a trembling detonator. When I left the sigh of relief followed me up the street.'

Nothing here to allow for the enormous pressures of wartime on an overstretched BBC, or for the fact that overworked BBC employees, particularly outside London, must have been overawed by such a great man – an awe indicated by some of the introductions read before his broadcasts by regional announcers, who presented him in such reverential terms that he might have been the Archbishop of Canterbury. In any case, working for such an impersonal and cautious institution as the BBC can be frustrating and must have been more so in wartime when the Corporation was not its own master.

Despite the frustrations, *Britain Speaks* was a job worth doing, and Priestley did it well: his broadcasts were not only more accurate but more effective than official efforts and the propaganda coming from the people at the top ('topside', as he called it).

He also knew their worth: 'Apart from the PM himself I am probably the most popular broadcaster on both the home and overseas programmes.' He knew his value and the Corporation was prepared to pay it. The first contributors to *Postscripts* before he came in had been paid ten guineas per programme. Priestley started at that rate, but as his popularity grew, he drove a harder bargain. For the later programmes in the first series and all of the second, he was paid fifty guineas a programme plus expenses, which he meticulously claimed. That's around £2,600 at today's prices, making him one of the Corporation's highest-paid stars at the time.

When Priestley was forced out of the *Postscripts*, A. P. Herbert, his successor, demanded the same. He didn't get it, and most other successors were driven back to ten or fifteen guineas a shot. For *Britain Speaks*, Priestley had initially been paid twenty guineas a programme, but as his value increased he demanded, and got, forty guineas, plus ten in expenses – nearly £2,000 in today's money. Almost up to Jeremy Clarkson or Graham Norton levels. Priestley wasn't a Yorkshireman for nothing. Indeed, he even managed to retain republication rights and fees, outwitting the BBC's desire to have rights for *The Listener* included in the programme fee.

The Reach

Britain Speaks was transmitted by the BBC on the medium wave to Europe and the shortwave service, then the lingua franca of radio and heard all over the world. Despite the crackles, pops and fades, it was widely accepted by listeners as the world's medium until DAB, VHF and Skype were invented to make listening easier and pockets emptier. The overseas broadcasts were received and retransmitted by the national broadcasting systems in Australia, Canada and New Zealand. The Dominion still listened to the BBC's nine o'clock news when I arrived in New Zealand in 1959. Indeed, the NZBC was very like the old BBC transplanted to New Zealand's green and pleasant land, and even carried on the *Postscripts* format in a programme called *Lookout*, transmitted after the news on Saturday night when no one was listening. That started my broadcasting career.

Unlike me on 3YA, Priestley reached the world. His

programmes on the Empire Service were picked up on the short wave in countries across Europe, while in America they were retransmitted by the Mutual Broadcasting System, the smallest and most innovative of the three big networks.

Mutual was at that time a kind of radio cooperative which had built up its network to over 100 affiliates, though not all of them used Priestley's broadcasts at the same time or with the same prominence. He was unhappy with this situation and in 1941, when told by his American friends that the Mutual stations were haphazard in scheduling and in some cases were not using his broadcasts so that he could not be heard everywhere, he suggested to the BBC that they should come to an arrangement with one of the bigger networks, either NBC or CBS, for whom he'd broadcast before the war.

This proposal was scuppered when Mutual made it clear that ratings had fallen under his replacement and Priestley was the only man they would accept. Feeling that Priestley was 'our star man, the only one Mutual will work with', the Corporation persuaded him that Mutual was much improved and would ensure that all its stations would transmit him at the same time. Priestley dropped his proposal to change. Mutual continued to be the only US station giving the Americans the benefit of good Yorkshire sense.

The audience for the Home Service *Postscripts* had been enormous: seventeen million for the first and an average of fourteen million for the later broadcasts. This audience was so big and, according to both the BBC's audience research and Mass-Observation, so enthusiastic that Priestley later claimed:

> *The astonishing popularity of these Postscripts soon brought me more embarrassment than pleasure ... Suddenly with these radio talks I had millions and millions of fans. My mail arrived in bulging postbags. I couldn't ask for a drink in a bar without my voice being immediately recognised and people crowding round me. I like being reasonably well known – we all do – but I soon began to dislike being celebrated on this gigantic semi-hysterical scale.*

The audience for the overseas broadcasts certainly couldn't

buy him drinks, but the BBC was well satisfied with his performance there. A senior official described him as

> an outstanding success with overseas audiences especially, but by no means exclusively, in the USA. During the difficult months of June, July and August 1940 he did a fine job, for he sounded always confident of victory and must have reassured any American listeners who were doubting our resolve and ability to carry on the struggle. Thousands of supportive letters addressed to him and to the BBC ... make this clear.

Letters don't measure audience figures: people have to be seriously motivated to write. Yet they do indicate that many people round the world were listening, even if we don't have precise figures. The state broadcasting systems did little audience research, while the Americans, in their more competitive market, sought only overall figures for advertising purposes. Priestley measured his success by the mail he received, telling his home audience:

> I wish I could read those letters I receive from the Dominions, from all over the world, and most moving of all from tiny groups, often just a man and wife of British folk, far, far away, perhaps high in the Andes or on some tropical island. And I wish you could understand with what real anxiety and now with what pride and joy, what smiles and tears, they listen to this glorious new chapter in our island's history.

He claimed that 'letters by the hundred arrived from overseas to tell me how enthusiastically these talks were being received, particularly in Canada and Australia', but his audience was wider than expats and the English-speaking world. It included occupied Europe and even Nazi Germany, where the regime tried to punish anyone found listening or turned in by their neighbours (a more effective way of silencing than banging on the wall). After the war, Priestley claimed to have received letters from people in occupied Europe 'who had crouched over radio sets turned down to a whisper because of the Gestapo'. To them, he had brought hope and comfort. 'I might have dodged far more bombs than they had done, but they had been called to endure that creeping despair which had to be defied if we are to live like men.'

The Nazi propagandists clearly recognised the importance of Priestley's broadcasts, attributing to him views he didn't hold and amplifying his criticisms of Britain. All their efforts were carefully reported by the BBC Monitoring Service, created to provide a detailed record of Axis propaganda. Half its staff was devoted to German broadcasts, and their reports were relayed every day to Cabinet ministers. This occasionally resulted in instructions to Priestley to steer clear of this or that, though neither he nor the Corporation could do anything about the highest compliment the Nazis paid him: producing fake Priestley broadcasts. A sample faux Priestley is in the appendix, and it's a clever concoction. Yet, clever as Goebbels was, he couldn't find any collaborator with an authentic Yorkshire accent. The only available traitors were Irish or southerners.

III.

The End and After

In August 1942, Priestley asked for and got a break from his overseas broadcasts on the grounds that he was growing stale and needed a rest. He soon returned, but late in 1943 he finally brought them to an end. The world had changed. Britain no longer stood alone but had become the junior partner in a coalition of more powerful nations. The threats of bombing and invasion which had brought the nation together were easing. Under the pressure of Labour ministers, particularly Herbert Morrison, Churchill had been forced to agree war aims and move towards social solidarity, with the Butler education reforms of 1944 assuring free secondary education for all, and the Beveridge Report in 1943 proposing the elimination of the five great scourges which had afflicted pre-war Britain. Priestley was delighted by the keen interest British troops everywhere were showing in these plans for a new world.

With that in hand, he felt it time to give up the overseas

broadcasts, writing to a friend at the BBC in September 1943:

> *I feel uncertain at the moment whether I ought to continue my overseas talks … The job is easy and pleasant enough and does not give me much trouble as we have organised it now. On the other hand there is not much happening on the home front … Further, it is probable that political issues will tend to have more and more importance and I may disagree with our official policy and feel irked because I am prevented from discussing the issue. Further, it is probably not a good policy – either from my view or yours – that I should begin to give overseas listeners the impression of triviality, for that might damage my reputation as a broadcaster.*

He felt he was growing stale and had little interesting to say now that the emotional high of the danger years was becoming the disciplined duty of clearing up the mess. Victory, which had looked such a remote possibility in 1940, was becoming a real prospect in 1943. There was less need to build up morale, and he felt he had little new to say to audiences overseas who were now allies in the war.

Various new projects had been considered, such as sending him to Australia, Canada and New Zealand to interview their leaders, to Russia to interview Stalin, or, toughest of all, to Whitehall to interview Churchill. All these proposals were encouraged by Priestley and welcomed by the BBC. Some were even accepted by the Ministry, but all failed for various technical reasons. The time was not right for a globe-hopping David Frost.

But the way was open to re-admit Priestley to the domestic airwaves. In May 1943, he began his new series of domestic broadcasts, *Make It Monday*, in which he was able to speak again to the home audience he had always wanted to reach.

The *Postscripts* had gone out at peak time to peak audiences. The new series went out at a less popular time and were not national events in the same way. They were popular but lacked the impact of the earlier series. Times had changed and so had Priestley. Now that the immediate danger had receded and the bombing had slackened, his task was less to boost morale and more to temper expectations and warn of the problems that lay ahead on the road to victory and beyond.

This move from encouragement to exhortation was revealed early, in an attack on the celebratory mood of the 1943 song 'I'm going to get lit up when the lights go on in London'. He responded to this premature jollity:

> *Our forces will be invading Europe before long; there will be hard fighting, perhaps heavy casualties; and men should have something better to fight for, to die for, than our getting lit up for months and months. It's true that in the last war stranger songs were sung while men perished by the thousands in the chalk of Picardy and the mud of Passchendaele. But this is not the last war, and many of us deeply resent, for a variety of good reasons, these attempts to turn it into the last war. This is a war fought in a different spirit and, I suggest, brought to an end in a different spirit. Indeed, it will have to end in a different spirit. When the lights go up in London, they will reveal not only a war-damaged London but also a shattered Europe. Whole populations will be crying out for food, for clothing, for the most urgent medical supplies and services. We will realise to the full then – lit up or not lit up – the havoc and wreckage left behind by the Nazi war machine. We shall probably have to rescue a continent from famine and pestilence. Our responsibilities will be immense. Our opportunities will be equally gigantic. Just as we once helped to save the world by our fortitude, so we can help to save it again by our compassion and generosity. If a lot of people here are going to see this reconstruction in terms of being lit up for months and months, they may not understand and accept those responsibilities and opportunities.*

'Don't', he concluded, 'let us go all little again.' Such was the tone of *Make It Monday*, with Priestley lecturing rather than boosting, as he had in the exciting days of 1940. The new series also added to Priestley's already excessive workload, compounding the strain of late hours and heavy effort he was already bearing for his overseas broadcasts. It may, therefore, have been another reason for his decision to give up the *Britain Speaks* programme, as he did in the summer of that year, quietly announcing at the end of his 23 August broadcast that next week the audience would hear the voice of another speaker, ending nearly four years of broadcasts to the wider world. He had talked of giving up before and the only indication of the change was that he was taking a respite to write. In fact, he never came back.

Perhaps Priestley felt that his job was over now that Britain and America were fighting together. Perhaps he had little new to say. Perhaps, too, disillusion was creeping in as the courage and excitement of 1940 faded and America took over a war for democracy which had previously been an exclusively British affair. Certainly, disappointment showed next year when the BBC attempted to lure him back, not as the voice of Britain but as a contributor to a planned new series of broadcasts to America. He declined to take part, worried about the new balance of power between the USA and Britain.

The Americans were the masters now, and Priestley didn't like it. He told the Corporation:

> *It is vital that Britain should be an equal partner in this set-up because fundamentally we are more democratic and progressive than the Americans, where the reactionaries are more powerful, unscrupulous and dangerous than they are here. But because of the Prime Minister's enthusiasm for America and the directions that come about, we are not keeping our end up and are too busy flattering the already high self-esteem of the Americans. Two years ago, they realised that we were far ahead of them. Now they are beginning to patronise us again. I read the signs of this everywhere. No attempt is being made to flood America with English cultural products – plays, books, films etc. – as we are now being flooded with American ones. This is bad. It's as if the Mississippi were being diverted into the Thames. This is bad for both of us. We are taking a wrong line. And may soon pay a heavy price for it.*

Britain had become an American troop carrier. Still fighting hard, still ruinously overstrained, but now a junior partner in its own war. Awed by the task ahead, Priestley saw his country being swamped by American culture and values. Symbolically, a war begun to the strains of Gracie Fields, George Formby, Noel Gay and (hopefully) hanging out the washing on the Siegfried Line was coming to an end to the music of Glenn Miller, Bing Crosby, the Andrews Sisters and Irving Berlin. A new world was coming, and Priestley, seeing it as the rise of what he later called Admass, didn't particularly like it.

Priestley had inspired the many, however much he was disliked by the few. His success was to keep hope alive and develop the prospect of a new, democratic Britain arising from the ashes to serve the people. That vision helped change the mood of the nation. It led to Labour's victory in 1945 and the building of the new Jerusalem.

This new settlement tilted the social balances to the people and away from money and class. The British got the fairer deal Priestley had always wanted: better housing, healthcare and education, underpinned by full employment. But it was a revolution from the top down created through government power, not built from the bottom up. It was done for the people rather than by the people, so its roots were weaker than Priestley had hoped.

As circumstances and moods changed, the new settlement became more fragile and more strained. It lasted until the 1970s, but growing economic difficulties led to a struggle for shares, which in turn led to Thatcherism and neoliberal economics. They demolished the settlement. Money was restored to its throne. Politics degenerated into a quarrelsome stasis, and a meaner, less equal world was the result. The question Priestley's admirers should ask themselves is: why?

Priestley was an artist and a public intellectual, a breed more common in France than in Britain. He saw his job as pointing the way, rather than building the future; his aim was influence, not power.

To an author, writing is doing ... when he has written, he has taken action. Beyond the printed page is another world that most authors – and I am certainly one of

them — enter without confidence and probably with
loathing. It is a world of meetings, for intrigues in a
smoke-filled room corner to committees talking on and
on long after the last oxygen has gone.

Priestley was no politician. Whenever he did get involved, he
soon pulled out. He formed the 1941 Committee of brilliant
talents to plan the better future but dropped out after writing its
manifesto, *Out of the People*. He formed the Common Wealth
Party with Richard Acland to push for a new politics but pulled
out before its run of by-election victories gave the first warning
of Labour's victory in 1945. He endorsed Labour in that year
but found it joyless and unimaginative.

His own verdict came in *Margin Released*:

> *I have never been a member of any political party*
> *... It is true that before the 1945 election I spoke at*
> *scores of meetings on behalf of Labour candidates. It is*
> *also true that a few years later I did a Labour Party*
> *political broadcast on the understanding that Labour,*
> *if returned, would call a great national conference of*
> *the arts. All I did get was the works from the other side*
> *... My natural sympathies move to the Left: I am a*
> *pink, and a pleasant healthy colour it is too.*

Priestley could create moods, but moods are transient, and
the cost of being a politician would have been a loss of the
trust and influence he enjoyed, so by the '50s he relapsed into
grumbling at large. The unity and exhilaration of the crisis years
had faded. The people had been bought off by the new culture
of consumerism, commercialism and affluence, which became
the 'never had it so good' society. Britain was Americanised,
its people drugged by television, their wants stimulated by
advertising. This was a consumer world, not the democracy of
an activist people Priestley had hoped for.

He had warned in 1940, 'There's a danger that as this high mood
passes, apathy will return to some sections of the community,
and selfishness and stupidity to some other sections.' Perhaps
a democracy can only function at a high intensity such as that
of 1940–41, and then only for limited periods. Perhaps a nation

exhausted by war and resenting the rationing and restrictions of reconstruction wanted to enjoy itself and seek relief. Perhaps Priestley's hopes were unrealistic.

One thing is clear. The threat had brought out the best in both Priestley and the British people. He had spoken for the people, comforted them, held out hope and told the world of their lives, their tribulations and their courage. He immortalised a fascinating picture of the last period of British greatness and prepared the ground for Labour's victory in 1945 and the social revolution that followed. As A. J. P. Taylor put it, 'Few even sang "England Arise". England had risen all the same.' Priestley made his contribution to that rise and never abandoned his dream. Reminiscing as an old man, he was unrepentant: 'Though growing old, gouty and grumpy, weary of power mania and propaganda and all their imbecilities, I have not yet abandoned the hope I felt and tried to celebrate in wartime.'

The Transcripts

The Spirit of England

I don't know whether it's the long hard winter we had, one of the worst in living memory, or whether it's the effect of the war, but I never remember England looking lovelier than it's done this month. I've stared at it as if I'd never seen a spring. I have a house down in the Isle of Wight, which is a sort of miniature southern England, and what I've seen around that house lately has taken my breath away. To begin with, it's all greener than ever this year. Everywhere an incredible variety, lushness and tenderness of green. And we've had all the blossom out – apple, cherry and peach – perfectly set out against the weather-stained old walls; a blaze of tulips; and along the little stream by the tennis court the fattest and yellowest primroses I ever remember seeing. Then behind the twinkling new leaves of the old elms you can see the misty green curves and slopes of the downs, almost melting into the blue. Then swallows and martins flashing about, blackbirds singing exquisitely from morning till night, and cuckoos calling around the house – and I'll swear there have never been so many before – those wandering voices that turn the world again into a fairy place. There's been a magical spell over our country, as if we saw it at last, now that we must give up everything to defend its liberty, its traditions, its very life; we saw it in its full enchantment.

One of the most absurd things Shakespeare ever did was to pretend that his *Midsummer Night's Dream* was set in Athens and its neighbourhood. Actually, nothing was ever more English than this *Midsummer Night's Dream*. It's a kind of lovely mad picture of the English scene, of the English tradition, of the English mind and spirit. The whole odd mixture of the thing is so English. What do you get in it? Well, in the foreground a lot of rather cosy domestic stuff, lovers quarrelling and comic characters like Bottom the weaver and Quince and Snug and Starveling all enjoying themselves, all homely and comfortable, nothing grandiose. Now, all that in the foreground is very English and may be said to represent one half of the English tradition – mind and spirit – cosy and comic and domestic: the England of the novelists, of the music halls, of the cricket and football crowds. But the background of the *Midsummer Night's Dream* is different – the broken moonlight in the enchanted wood; the voices of fairy people; a vague loveliness, mystery, magic – occasionally suggested by lines that make your hair stand on end, they have such evocative beauty, lines like 'following darkness like a dream'.

And this, to my mind, is the other half of England, of the English tradition and spirit. It is the England of the lyric poets and of the old watercolour painters and of such odd mystical figures as William Blake. All this is just as much part of us as the cosy domestic comedy in the foreground. 'The Englishman', said the Spanish philosopher Santayana, 'is governed by the weather in his soul.' We are, you see, an instinctive and intuitive people. We don't act from clear-cut first principles. We haven't worked out a logic of living. We distrust the dialecticians. As a nation, we often behave irrationally and so bewilder our friends, just as we baffle our enemies, and our friends begin to imagine that we are a nation of grown babies just as our enemies come to the conclusion that we are a set of cunning, cold-blooded hypocrites. The truth is that both are wrong. What happens is that we fall under the spell of that strange, hazy background, the broken moonlight in the enchanted wood, and we try obscurely to relate everything to something deep inside us, something that is half moral, half mystical, hoping that at last a decision and a plan will grow naturally out of this dear soil, not popping up like a telegraph pole but growing naturally and strongly, adapting itself to all weathers, like a tree.

The strength of English life – political, social, intellectual – is that it has been allowed to grow like a tree. Compared with a telegraph pole – and the totalitarian states are like telegraph poles – of course it looks queer, twisted, ramshackle and probably ready to come down at any moment. But the tree is that shape because it has adapted itself, with every patient adjustment, to meet every stress of wind and weather, and it is alive and fruitful and after centuries of growth can still put out green leaves. This is what the German mind, which is the exact opposite of the English mind, can never understand. The German cannot understand an intuitive political wisdom, a natural sagacity on the part of men who have both to govern and to be governed. There is more sense of political life, of reasonable government, in any English parish council than there is in the whole of the German Reich. Though their achievements in other directions are great enough, in this world of government, the Germans are a set of mad babies. I will quote here some valuable words written recently by a great German, Thomas Mann. He says:

> *The German people cannot, in the last resort, blink their eyes to the fact that England's attitude to power is quite other, and incomparably more natural and straightforward than the German attitude. Both parties understand something quite different by it – it is the same word with a wholly different meaning. To the Englishman, power is in no way the darkly emotional concept as viewed by the Germans: power in English eyes implies no emotion – the will to power is a German invention – but a function; they exercise it in the gentlest and most unobtrusive manner, with the least possible display, and safeguarding as much freedom as is feasible, for they do not believe that power is a proclamation of slavery, and are therefore not slaves to power themselves. This is called liberalism – an old-fashioned word for a very vital thing...*

This liberalism, as Thomas Mann rightly calls it, is probably England's greatest contribution to world civilisation. It has been produced by an odd mixture of peoples, living their own kind of life on a misty island just off the edge of the great European peninsula, a people who have been allowed by circumstances and also by their own passion for liberty to develop in their own way, to grow as a tree grows. It runs through all our political and social life, and not only here in this island but everywhere the English have gone. It runs through our glorious literature, in which there is blended an appreciation of the twists and turns of human character with a sense of the strange mystical background of this life; a blue haze like that we see so often over the English hills. It is there in our everyday life, in which everything on the surface is so illogical and absurd that we are forever laughing at ourselves, but within there is sanity, there is a deep kindness, there is a natural goodness (here we are in sharp contrast with the German, who is all shrewd sense and logic and efficiency on the surface, and bewildered and half mad inside).

I'm not pretending that we're faultless or that everything is perfect here. I doubt if anyone has criticised this country and some of its people more frequently than I have during these past seven years, ever since the publication of my *English Journey*. But if I've shouted for things that I thought wrong to be put right, it's because I know how well worth the trouble this country, its people and its traditions are, how nobly they can repay our passionate care. Here is no rotten old tree waiting for a pull or two to come crashing down. Here is a grand old oak deeply and thickly rooted in its soil, twisted and gnarled if you like, but still giving shade below and still catching the sunlight and moonlight in its upper branches. If this tree were uprooted, if it vanished from the wood of the world, there would be such a terrible emptiness there, such a desolation where there had once been such sweetness and strength, that the world would never be the same again and would have a tale to tell that would break men's hearts. But it will not be uprooted. And what matters in the end – and if it does not then the earth is simply a hell and the sooner we are all out of it, the better – is downright goodness and simple goodwill. Now, I believe this deep natural goodwill to be a notable characteristic of our people. I remember last year a clever foreigner who knows us well saying to me, 'You know, the English are a good people. When you come to know them, you see there is something deeply instinctively religious about them.' By religious he did not mean that the English people are fonder of prayer worship and ritual than other people, for clearly they are not. He meant that the ordinary English folk have an instinctive trust in the moral order of the universe, have a deep respect for everything that is fundamentally personal to other people and are moved by goodwill. This goodwill runs like a golden thread, glinting with humour and poetry through the fabric of our history. And I believe with all my heart that it would be a black, tragic day for the world when that shining thread is seen no more; but I also believe that it will outlast our time.

30 May 1940

Civilisation Can Defend Itself

I've been spending the last few days in my house in the country, only a few miles from the south coast. At odd times we've heard a sound like the distant banging of doors. Which was of course the noise of bombs and anti-aircraft guns. It hasn't worried anybody very much. At the Star Inn just down the road, the regular customers in the tap room, sitting over their half-pints of bitter, have been telling each other that we're all to set about stopping Hitler. We've formed a local detachment of the local defence volunteer 'Parashots', and I've joined them myself, but so far I've not been called on to take a turn at night-watching in the downs. It's not the first time men have kept guard on these downs, for they did it in Queen Elizabeth's time and then in Napoleon's. And everybody's as cool as a cucumber. The Italians are saying, I read, that we're in a terrible panic, but all I can reply to that is that I've seen and heard more fuss and excitement just landing my luggage in Naples than I've seen and heard here since the war started.

Not that we don't see anything. Today I saw a train of our troops just back from Flanders. They were unshaven, their faces were drawn and sunken-eyed, they had just been fighting one of the greatest rear-guard actions in modern history, they had been bombed day and night, but they were still giving us the thumbs-up sign. They looked what they were: undefeated; pushed back for a while by an overwhelming superiority of machines and armaments, but with no respect whatever for the hordes of robots using those machines and armaments.

Later today I had a long talk with an officer who had just returned from the northern battlefield. He was a man of my own generation, who like myself had been all through the last war, and so I was especially interested in what he had to say. The unit he commanded was not really a fighting unit at all, being composed of searchlights. Nevertheless, his men, having been asked to hold a bridge near a coast town, found themselves attacked by a motorised German detachment including three tanks, fought them there for five solid hours, and then headed them off. The officer, though admitting the ferocity of the attack of the German Air Force, which hardly ever stayed to fight our own airmen but of course greatly out-numbered them, had nothing but a cold contempt for these Nazi troops, who, he said, were far worse types than the German soldiers of the last war.

Of all the things that have happened so far in this war, the deliberate harrying and destruction of refugees must rank as the greatest and foulest crime, and our own soldiers, who are if anything too easy-going and very hard to rouse, grew white with anger when they remembered these atrocities. It has been of course a deliberate policy, just as much part of the planned invasion as the movement of airplanes and tanks. Just as the Red Indians often used to stampede herds of wild buffalo before they attacked in order to disturb and hamper their enemies, so the Nazi strategists have deliberately stampeded and slaughtered refugees simply in order to create confusion, havoc and panic.

I don't want to dwell on the horrors of all that, but I do want to point out the significance of this vast crime. For it means that the Nazis have abandoned the last pretence of being a more or less civilised European power that had entered into a conflict with other European powers. If they imagined for a moment they could be a member of the Commonwealth of powers, they would never have dared to accept such hellish tactics. The fact that they adopted them shows that the mask is off, that no compromise is possible with civilisation, that now either they will be destroyed or they will dominate the world. They themselves have furnished the best proof to everybody that this cannot possibly be regarded as just another quarrel among European powers, that now it is a fight to the death between the old civilisation of Christendom and this new evil empire of machines and robots.

There is a good letter from an American living in England that appeared in this morning's *Daily Telegraph*. He says that he refused to take his embassy's advice to leave this country and then goes on to add Americans leaving England at this critical time are deserting their own cause – freedom and liberty. The American frontier is the English Channel.

Well, that's what one American says. For my part, though I agree with him, I'd put it a bit differently. I'd say this isn't a war in the old sense at all. It isn't a quarrel between certain nations. It isn't a matter of frontiers and possessions. It's a desperate battle in which the whole future of the world is involved, between two ways of life. We don't say that one of them, ours, is perfect. We know very well that it isn't. In fact, some of us have spent a lot of our time these last few years criticising the sort of life we were leading. But at least it was worth criticising. Left to ourselves we could improve it, as we were improving it all the time, to give every man, woman and child a chance to lead a full, useful and happy existence. But the other kind of life, which has spread like a foul stain over half of Europe, is simply evil. It isn't German. There isn't a great German of the past who would not have indignantly refused to have any part in it, just as those great Germans of today have all turned their backs on it and are now in exile. It is simply a gigantic, insane gangsterism, a vast power machine built for nothing but brutal conquest. You can't come to terms with it. There's no living peacefully alongside it, because it has no intention of living peacefully itself or allowing you to live at peace. It is no more simply European than typhoid fever is simply European and, like a plague, if it is not stopped here then it will spread all over the world.

But of course it isn't going to be allowed to spread. What is the position at the moment? The battle of the north still continues. Further south and east, the French, along with the other sections of the British Expeditionary Force (BEF), is holding the line of the Somme and strengthening their defence. Here at home we are at last – and of course as usual it is 'at last' – going into strict training for the big fight.

In my opinion, for what it's worth we've probably done more to make ourselves really fit and ready in the last three weeks than we did in the previous eight months. One reason for the delay is that you can't persuade a lot of the English that they don't live on a magic island. They believe, these nice, comfortable, stupid folk, that disasters and tragedies, fire and slaughter, treachery and invasion are things that only happen over the sea to those strange excitable human beings called 'foreigners'. It's only a month or two ago that the girl who works in our kitchen said quite solemnly, 'Does this man Hitler realise what trouble and expense he's putting us to?' The answer is that he does and likes it. But that was the attitude of mind of many of the English up to a few weeks ago. But now that's gone. Not only because the war has been brought nearer these shores but also, I think, because the people feel that this new government of ours means business, that its leaders are determined, vital men. There's none of that sleepy complacency any more.

The temper of the ordinary easy-going English folk is rising. Any attempt at invasion will only send it up a few more degrees. I haven't met anybody yet who's particularly worried about it. Naturally, when your whole world changes so rapidly it isn't easy to make the necessary adjustments. I know it's tough going trying to be an author these days, for you can't settle down to write a book; the theatres are closing not because people are afraid to go to them but partly because they want to listen to the news at night and also they like to get a bit of fresh air after a long day indoors; and even journalism has been cut down. But I for one am in better trim than I was a year ago. I'm no worse mentally and it will certainly do me no harm taking my turn on the downs watching the searchlights sweeping the sky and looking out for parachute troops. I only hope they don't come down in our part dressed as clergymen, because I've a feeling our chaps are going to be very embarrassed chasing every clergyman they see. You know, all this business is the most tragic thing that's ever happened to us – it seems far more tragic to me than the last war, though I was only young then and a soldier – but in spite of it all you find yourself laughing still; there's a lot of absurdity about, as there always will be in this absurd, beautiful and lovable island of ours. And that's something the Germans will never understand. They don't understand us when we laugh, they don't understand us when we're serious. And they won't learn. They'll never learn. But there's a strong feeling about. I read it not in the newspapers but in the faces of all the folks

I see, and I hear it in their voices, that very soon there'll be thought one or two things they haven't quite understood yet. One of them is that civilisation can defend itself as fiercely as barbarism can attack, and can continue to do it, can keep it up, with more patience, for patience like truth-telling and kindness are civilised virtues.

5 June 1940

Never Have We Seen or Enjoyed So Lovely a Spring

The second great battle has begun, and this time in a far more orthodox fashion than the first, with waves of infantry instead of masses of tanks. It is extraordinary how the same old names, familiar during the last war and many a war before that, keep cropping up again – Abbeville, Péronne, Amiens. It was through a ruined Péronne that I travelled when I went up to the front for the last time – I had been there twice before, in 1915 and 1916 – through the dust and heat of early September 1918, and when I returned, a casualty again, I was taken through Amiens, to be attended to afterwards by the way, by an American doctor. We ought to have known that no matter where this war started it would soon return to the old front lines, to that terrible region of the Somme, where in July 1916 so many of my fellow countrymen perished that there was hardly left one man whom I had known as a boy. If there are ghosts then millions of them must be watching this battle now. And we, who are not yet ghosts and feel very much alive, are all watching it too. English troops are in action there, but here at home we are now making a tremendous effort to strengthen all defence against invasion, so that as soon as possible we can augment the forces in France for a military defeat for the Germans that means the end of Hitler, just as it meant the end of the Kaiser and Ludendorff in 1918.

So we are rapidly turning this island of ours into the greatest fortress the world has ever known. We are working fast. Temperamentally, we may be averse to making elaborate long-term plans, and therefore we always begin at a disadvantage when we are faced with an enemy like the cunning and methodical Germans, who set to work to dominate the world years in advance of their first open move, toiling like ants and termites. But on the other hand, we have the gift of rapid and effective improvisation, as we have just seen in the magnificent embarkation at Dunkirk. And now we are applying that gift to the defence of this island. More has been done during the last week than was done during the last hundred years. People who might turn out to be Fifth Columnists have been rounded up by the hundred. If parachute troops are landed here, they're going to find themselves a bit lonely and not among friends. Children have been evacuated from towns on the east and south-east coast. Even the sheep and cattle are being moved from some coastal districts. Strategic areas have been mined. There are hundreds and hundreds of concrete and sandbagged machine-gun posts. All public buildings are guarded. Two men were shot by a sentry the other day when they refused to halt at his command. Large flat open spaces are now our danger points, because troop-carrying planes could be landed on them, and now they are being dug up and wired so that landing is impossible. Even racecourses – those hallowed stretches of turf – are being roughly handled in this fashion.

This, of course, is only the beginning, for I can hardly begin to suggest the thousand and one precautions that are now being taken. The Parashot Corps, which is functioning everywhere, now numbers over 400,000. In addition, there are various home defence services, and now we are to have the Ironsides, General Ironside's new creation, a corps of hand-picked regular soldiers, very mobile and heavily armed. The corps will be specially trained to deal quickly with enemy troops suddenly landed by air and sea. They will, I prophesy here and now, be a tough crowd and more than a match for any half-dozy young fanatics that Goering shovels out of his airplanes. All England will prove a very awkward country for an enemy to manoeuvre in. It's a very different proposition from northern France and Flanders, with their long, straight roads along which motorised units can roar at full speed because they can see miles ahead. Here we have, as Chesterton said in his poem, 'the rolling English road', which goes this way and then that, seems to turn back on itself and meanders all over the place with ditches and hedges everywhere for cover. I don't care how good the German maps of England are, how clever their staff work; they will soon find themselves lost and tangled if they ever do succeed in landing a force of any size, for every sign has been removed from these mazes of winding roads and lanes, and we're beginning to be lost ourselves if we travel too far from home. And God help anyone who asks the way in a thick German accent. This morning coming up from the country I passed half a dozen stout barricades within ten miles of my house.

As an example of what can happen to an enemy from the sky, there is the adventure of my friend Ralph Richardson, the actor. He's a pilot now and not long ago he was compelled to make a forced landing on a village green not far from the south coast. The villagers thought it must be a German plane masquerading as one of ours; but did they run away? They did not. They came charging on with scythes and shovels, and it was lucky for Ralph that he was a film star and so easily recognised. I like to think of those village men who, machine-gun or no machine-gun, were ready to take a crack at anybody who thought he could drop from the sky on them.

It takes an awful lot to rouse the ordinary English folk. They're apt to be an easy, sleepy, good-natured crowd, but once they are aroused – and the terrible tales of mass murder brought back by the BEF are doing that – they'll wade in and never stop. You know how it is with a bulldog – he'll let you tease him and maul him about perhaps for an hour or two, but go an inch too far and he'll sink his teeth into you and never let go. Well, that's the real English, the ordinary quiet folk. They aren't saying much – the 'chatterbug', as the defeatist gossiper is called, is a special case, and there are very few of them among the ordinary working folk – but believe me, they're solidly behind every word that Mr. Churchill uttered in his great speech yesterday. And the nearer the Nazis get, the more that slow but dogged temper is going to rise.

A lot of stuff heard over the air or read in the press about the British public is based on what goes on in London West End clubs or Mayfair restaurants, where you'll find plenty of dismal Jimmies and 'chatterbugs'. But if you want to know what the ordinary folk are thinking and feeling here, you've got to go into the workshops or the pubs, especially the little taverns in the small towns and villages, and when you find these men looking long-faced and repeating the rubbish invented by the German propaganda then it's time to begin worrying. And I haven't found a trace of it yet. The people are glad now to have a government that'll pile some responsibility on them and set them to work and to fight.

Since this war began, many thoughtful and generous American friends have written to me offering to take the children in my family and look after them until the war is over. Others, all the way from New York to San Francisco, have told us how often they're thinking about us and feeling sorry for us here. While I thank them, I also want to say this. Now that the real blitzkrieg has begun, and all hell is let loose, I feel sorrier for these friends in their position than I do for us in ours. And I'll tell you exactly why. If my American friends lived in another world altogether, where they'd never even heard of what's happening here, then I might envy them. But they do not. They're 3,000 miles away, but what does that mean in these days? All the news of these treacheries and mass murders, this hell on earth that one maniac has created, reaches my American friends just as quickly as it reaches us here and, like us, they're pouncing on the latest editions of the newspapers, they're forever turning on the radio to listen breathlessly to the very last reports from the front. Like us, these American friends of mine can't really think about anything else but these invasions and bombings and wholesale slaughter. Confronted by these disasters and threats to the whole civilised world, they can no more get on with their ordinary lives than we can get on with ours. Only there is this difference. Though my American friends feel all the horror and anguish of this time, just as we do, they are really worse off in mind and spirit now than we are because they can only stare at the dreadful scene in terror and pity, like people on the seashore who watch a great ship struggling against a terrible storm. But we who are on the ship and in the storm are now so completely engrossed in action that there comes to us, as a compensation for all our effort, a certain feeling of expansion, a heightening of the spirit, a sense that somewhere in this struggle of free men against drilled and doped slaves there is a moral grandeur. Soon many of us may die, but nobody can say of us now that we are not alive, and it is a fact that while one disaster piles upon another, many have told each other that never have we seen or enjoyed so lovely a spring.

So I say do not pity us.

After talking to our boys just back from Dunkirk, I have been remembering the famous saying of Henry IV of France, when he met a friend of his who had missed the great battle. He said, 'Go hang yourself, brave Crillon. We fought at Arques, and you were not there.' But now all of us are fighting at Arques.

17 June 1940

Letter to Betty Jane Johnson

This broadcast is addressed to Betty Jane Johnson, 139 South Fourth, Alhambra, California.

Dear Betty, you will remember that on 28 March you wrote to me telling that you are in the last year of high school taking an English course, that you had selected me as your English author whose life and work you have to study and write about in an essay at the end of the year. After saying some very nice things about my work, you said that that if I found it convenient to answer your letter you would feel it a very great honour because most of the students don't have living authors to write to. Well, now I'll explain why I haven't replied. In the first place, your letter took a long time to reach me, and in the second place, when it did reach me it caught me at a time when I had so much to do and was moving about so often that I simply couldn't answer letters. And here I apologise for the delay and also, to show how sorry I am, I'm addressing this broadcast to you.

Now, it's no good talking to you about my books or anybody else's books, because you see we are all busy fighting for our very lives against the Nazis, who are out to destroy all the things that are dear to us, so that we've hardly time to think about books these days. You see, if Hitler conquered us, which I tell you here and now he isn't going to, but if he did, then I'd never be allowed to write any more books, unless of course they were in praise of Hitler, in which case they simply wouldn't be my books at all.

British Author Answers Letters From Alhambra Girl In Radio Broadcast; Contrast In Student Life Described

There is no doubt in the mind of Betty Jane Johnson, 17-year-old daughter of Mr. and Mrs. Roy L. Johnson, 139 South Fourth street, that the world is a very small place, after all. Betty, who is a member of the Alhambra High School summer graduating class, elected to write a biography of J. B. Priestley, the English author, as her A-12 English theme.

"Because she picked a living author," she said, "I thought it would be nice to write him a letter and tell him what I was doing."

So Betty wrote a letter to Priestley. She thought perhaps he might answer it. Priestley did answer it, but not in the way Betty thought he might.

J. B. Priestley

The whole United States and Canada heard Priestley's answer to Betty's letter in a short wave broadcast Priestley made early Sunday morning over the British Broadcasting Company's system and which was picked up in this country.

Hear Broadcast

Unfortunately, Betty did not hear the broadcast, but several local residents did, among them Miss Florence Bevington, a teacher at Park School, and also Roger Summers of Pasadena. Both Miss Bevington and Summers got in touch with Betty by telephone and told her about the broadcast.

Miss Bevington said the announcer, in introducing Priestley, referred to the letter and mentioned Betty as a student at Alhambra High School.

BETTY JANE JOHNSON, Alhambra High School girl, wrote a letter to British Author J. B. Priestley. Priestley replied by short wave radio. (Stockton Photo)

He said that because of the urgency of his war work which included watch duty for parachute troops that he was taking the opportunity of the broadcast to answer the letter and hoped Betty would hear it. Then he contrasted the peaceful way in which American boys and girls were able to pursue their studies in contrast to hectic conditions prevailing in English schools because of the war. He said that one of his children was in a school which had been moved far into the interior of the country as a protection against air raids.

Daughter A War Nurse

Priestley said that one of his daughters was a war nurse and that he had turned over his house in London as well as a country estate to the government to use as it saw fit.

He said that if England could know that all of her children were safe in the United States, she would feel much more determined about defending the British Isles to the last ditch against the enemy.

He contrasted the bright neon lights of Southern California cities to the drab appearance of London in the nightly blackouts, referring to heavy black drapes which every resident is required to place over his windows after sundown.

Priestley said, however, that there is one sort of light which may be seen at night in England, the giant searchlight sweeping the skies to spot possible enemy planes.

The Alhambra Post–Advocate June 19, 1940.

So here we are bang in the middle of another great war, probably the most terrible there's ever been or ever will be. I remember the last war very well because I was a soldier for four and a half years, and spent a long time in the trenches, and was a casualty three separate times. But this war is quite different. To begin with, we're all in it, women and children as well as men. I mean, everybody's threatened. I have six children and not one of them is at home. The eldest one has just become an actress, but she had also trained to become a nurse and is expecting to be called up. The next three are away at school, but their school has been moved away from where it originally was, and is now in a big house in the country, and they use the stables for the art room and have turned lofts into bedrooms and so forth. The two youngest children have gone with their nurse into Wales because of the air raids in south England, where our country house is. This house is still ours and when I'm home I live in it, but it's also used as a Red Cross depot, a First Aid post and may soon have convalescent officers in it. I also have a house in London and it's possible that very soon this will be used for nurses to live in.

Everything here is quite different from any kind of life you've ever known. It's all queer. As soon as it's dusk, we have to put thick black curtains and blinds over all the windows, so as not to show the least glimmer of light. All the towns are quite dark. All those neon signs that you are so fond of in California have completely vanished. If we saw them again now, we'd be quite dazzled. On the other hand, we have another kind of illumination, for at night you see dozens and dozens of bright searchlights sweeping the sky. And all the larger towns and cities have hundreds of barrage balloons, which are a silvery colour, and on a fine day often look very pretty indeed, as if somebody had been stitching pearls on to the blue fabric of the sky. Also, in all towns, there are sandbags to protect important buildings, and sometimes a tangle of barbed wire to prevent parachute troops, if they come here, from rushing into those buildings. Then along every street there are public air-raid shelters and notices saying where you can find the nearest First Aid post. The policemen and the thousands of new firemen all wear steel helmets. Really, wherever you go, you feel you are on the edge of a battlefield. And now, unless you know the district, you can't tell where you are because all the road signs and even our milestones have been taken away and even the names of our railway stations have been painted out. Theatres and movie theatres are still open everywhere, and a lot of restaurants and dance places are still open everywhere, but of course not as many people go to them now. In one respect we're better off than we were in the last war because so far there is more food, and more different kinds of food, than there were then, and all the shops still seem packed with goods.

In all the factories where they make things connected with the war – things like airplanes, guns, shells and so on – the people are working terribly hard, harder than they've ever worked before, for these factories now are working day and night, without stopping, so that whatever time you went into them they would look just the same. And then nearly everyone does some extra work connected with the war, in addition to what they do for a living. Men act as air-raid wardens, auxiliary firemen, ambulance drivers or are members of the Observer Corps, which watches day and night for enemy planes, or members of the local defence volunteers – as I am myself – whose duty it is to look out, report and if necessary shoot parachute troops.

Women and girls can also act as air-raid wardens or go on duty at night as telephonists or ambulance drivers or may serve in the various canteens for the soldiers and sailors or may be helping in the hospitals. In addition, nearly every woman in her spare time is sewing or knitting for the soldiers and sailors. Then a great many women and girls are now doing the work of men who have been called up as soldiers – you see them working as conductors on the buses in the munitions factories, and also as cooks, clerks and automobile drivers in the Army, Air Force and Navy. Some girls, and often girls who have been secretaries or assistants in shops, have now been trained to work on farms, to help our farmers, who are now short of labour. Most of them enjoy this new kind of life and they have the satisfaction of knowing they are doing very useful work.

Most of my friends have sons who are in the Army, Air Force or Navy – in some cases they have three or four sons serving with the forces – and though this makes them very proud, it also leaves them very anxious all the time, wondering what has happened to their boys. You see, we are now fighting in so many different places that often it takes news a long time to come through – I mean news of individual soldiers or airmen or sailors. The general news about the war comes through all the time, for during the day there are no less than six news bulletins broadcast by the BBC. In the last war we hadn't this at all, but some people would prefer not to have so much news all the time because they think it makes foolish people far more worried than they would have been in the old days when there wasn't any radio, only newspapers. I disagree with all this because I think it's very important that people should know as much as possible about what's happening. You see, this war, unlike all the others up to now, is all the people's war, everybody's affair. It's not just armies and navies fighting each other while the rest of the people sit about feeling quite comfortable. All the people in Germany and Italy are now fighting all the people in Britain and her empire and France. This is called 'totalitarian war' and it's a rotten idea.

You might think now that everybody is in it, war would be easy going, but actually it's a lot more fierce and bloodthirsty, and a lot more hate is manufactured. The British are poor people at hating – they are too good-natured and easy-going – but I know that soon, when the Nazis turn all their attention to this island and bomb us hard every day and try to invade us, the British people will be very angry and will offer the most stubborn resistance. My own opinion is that they have much better nerves than the German people, who are very hard-working and well disciplined but tend to be hysterical inside, not quite rational. One of the great mysteries is that the Germans, who are not bad people in ordinary life, always seem to behave with great treachery and cruelty as soon as they are at war. In this war they have been worse than ever – deliberately bombing and machine-gunning hundreds of thousands of Belgian and French women and children, and driving their tanks straight over the wounded, not caring at all what happened to the poor creatures lying in the road. I have talked to a lot of our soldiers from Flanders who saw these horrible things done, and it made them very angry, so that they are much angrier with the Germans than we were in the last war.

As you have probably heard, we have now made plans to resist any attempted invasion. Children have been moved away from all the parts of the country nearest to Germany, and you see trainloads of them moving off. A lot of us would like the children to be taken out of the country altogether, really out of harm's way, carried across the sea to places like Canada where they would be safe from the bombs and machine-guns. If this could be done, we should all feel better here, for it is not pleasant to feel that your children might be in terrible danger, and once we had the children out of the way we could settle down and turn this island of ours into a huge combined war factory and fortress where if necessary we could fight on and on, if we should chance to be invaded, while our fleet still blockaded Germany and prevented all the necessary supplies reaching her.

All this is quite possible, but I'll admit to you that we were sadly behind our programme of war manufactures and are only beginning to make up the ground, whereas the Nazis have been preparing for years and years, doing without everything in order to have plenty of bombing planes and tanks so that they could crush everybody else and bully them. It's no use pretending our present position isn't difficult. We know – and our brave Prime Minister Winston Churchill has told us more than once – that we have a hard and dangerous time ahead of us, but the ordinary people, who are very brave and cheerful, just as your ordinary people would be in the same circumstances, are ready to face everything. But we badly, terribly, need your help, not for men – we can do all the fighting ourselves – but for munitions and above all for airplanes. As you probably know, our government is making plans for huge extra armaments – for the Navy, the Army and the Air Force – and during the next few years you are going to spend millions and millions of dollars on these armaments. But it would be much cheaper and much more sensible simply to help us now, this minute and for the rest of this year and if necessary next year. Because you see, the really dangerous enemy, as we all know, is Nazi Germany. If Hitler beats us then very soon he will attack you, and believe me it doesn't matter that you're a long way off because in these days the world is a very small place, so then you'd find yourself fighting him, possibly at a great disadvantage, as we're fighting him now. In addition, you'd feel bad because two old friends – Britain and France – were no longer important, and might be suffering terrible hardships. But if you'd give us all possible help now, would arrange to manufacture thousands and thousand thousands of planes as soon as possible – and nobody can do it quicker than your people because they're especially clever at manufacturing things at full speed – then we'd beat him once and for all, and there could be a decent Germany instead of this nightmare Nazi Germany, and the newspapers, instead of being filled with horrible tales of persecution and mass murder by these Nazis, could return to pleasant and sensible things again, and I'd be able to write some more books and plays, and you... well, I don't know what you want to do after you've finished with high school, because you didn't tell me, but whatever it was, you'd feel a lot better about it. And I do hope you think this as good as a letter. Good luck and goodbye, Betty Jane.

28 June 1940

What Chances of an Invasion?

The raids we've had this week, not yet on the blitzkrieg scale but for all that fairly big raids, some of them must be giving the German Air Staff a bigger headache than they've given us, because, unless they've been trying out a lot of new pilots and observers, they have been a failure. To begin with, they haven't done much damage, to military targets or to anything else. Some civilians have been killed and wounded, though far less than are killed and wounded by road accidents in the same number of days, and against that must be set the fact that the Germans have lost, by death or capture, the services of a number of trained men, whose services they can ill afford to lose. Again, the effect of the raids on morale here has been to raise it and not lower it. The ordinary people seem to be much livelier than they were last winter, when they found it – as indeed I did – all rather boring. Now they're full of beans, and also enjoying the presence everywhere of soldiers. London streets are filled with Dominion troops, seeing the sights – big tough guys, most of them, and spoiling for a fight. I'm told that the very rich are a bit gloomy, but the few times I've come in contact with the very rich, they always seemed gloomy; and I think the kindest thing to do with the very rich is to stop them from being very rich, which we're now doing good and hard. The typical Whitehall officials are not exactly full of fun and gusto, but that's not because they're afraid of anything but because they're Whitehall officials and superior persons, and they feel they have to behave like mandarins. But the people, on whom I pin my faith, are all right.

So is Mr. George Bernard Shaw, with whom I lunched today. He looked more robust and twinkling than I've seen him look these last two or three years, and never stopped talking. He said he'd always advised the world never to rouse the English because once they were aroused they were capable of more heroism and atrocities than anybody else. He also said that the way to settle the Irish difficulty was to start a cry in Eire that the awful English were not giving that protection to Eire that they were giving to the other members of the Commonwealth, that the English were denying poor old Ireland her airplanes, battleships and tanks, that it was just another big grievance and faith robber. They'll be holding meetings demanding that British forces be sent over.

I've never seen Bernard Shaw in better spirits, and here he is in London waiting, like the rest of us, for the next chapter in the blitzkrieg. We're promised it next week, and news comes from Zurich this morning that Hitler is planning a triumphal entry into Berlin on 1 August after victory over Britain. Orders have already been given for the erection of stands for this victory parade in Berlin. The publication of this stuff has a triple purpose: to hearten the Germans, who apparently must need it very badly in spite of their victories; to impress the neutrals; and to try to panic the people of this island, who are a kind of people that Goebbels simply doesn't understand.

It's worth noticing that in case this programme miscarries, the Nazis are already preparing their big propaganda for the period after the blitzkrieg has failed. The object of this will be to persuade all the people in the countries conquered by Germany that they will go hungry simply because the wicked British are blockading the continent. The real truth being that they will go hungry because the Nazis are now busy stealing all the produce of these countries in order to feed the Nazi armies and munition workers. And no matter how much food you or ourselves or anybody else pours into these countries, it will still be taken by the Nazis to feed their armies.

There's a very good cartoon in tonight's *Evening Standard* by my friend David Low – one of the best cartoonists in the world – and in it we see a ragged woman, France, and five ragged children, Belgium, Poland, Holland, Norway, Denmark, who have a large placard around their necks. Behind them is the immense figure of Goering, who has a sack over one shoulder and a pig in one hand, while the other hand grasps the shaft of a cart that is piled high with sacks and boxes labelled 'Looted Food'. Goering is saying to these ragged and wistful figures, 'I gave you a nice placard in exchange, didn't I?' And this placard that he gave them hangs round their necks and says, 'Appeal to kind hearts in the USA. Please send food to the women and children of starving Europe and help to beat the wicked British blockade.'

Please remember that it was Goering, and not any British politician, who used to say, 'Guns before butter.' Well, this wicked blockade trick is the next on the list for the German propaganda machine if the blitzkrieg against us fails to land Hitler on his triumphant entry into Berlin on 1 August.

What are the chances of this blitzkrieg against us? I've been collecting cautious official opinion about invasion. In the first place, it's possible, of course, that the German General Staff have in hand methods as surprising to us as the methods in Flanders and France were to them. It's possible, but it's not likely. I suspect most of the surprises have already been sprung – though no doubt they've one or two new tricks up their sleeves. And it's very important to remember that the methods in Flanders and France depended upon a good deal of Fifth Column co-operation, on a lot of successful undercover work in advance. How many times during that campaign, from the first invasion of Holland to their armistice in France, did it happen that something of the highest military importance – such as the blowing of a bridge already mined – was somehow forgotten to be put into operation against the Germans? I was reading only this morning about a certain Monsieur Amouralle, who was no less a person than the secretary to the French Senate and was sentenced to death by the Reynaud government for having conveyed much valuable information to German agents. I can't believe that sort of thing is going to happen on any scale in this island. Whatever happens, it's going to be a fight and not half a fight and half a sell-out.

But apart from this Fifth Column danger, we've learnt a lot from what happened in the Low Countries and France. There aren't going to be a number of nice aerodromes left for them to land on – or any other large open spaces – or any convenient supplier of petrol to loot. And now that all our aircraft are back from France, this place is bristling with fighting planes, and large, slow troop-carrying planes will have an awfully bad time against our Hurricanes and Spitfires. They may attempt to gain complete superiority in the air over one area, for purposes of large-scale invasion, but they tried and failed to do that at Dunkirk, where we couldn't have carried out the evacuation unless we'd thoroughly established local air supremacy. Our whole system of aerial reconnaissance, Observer Corps work, searchlight and anti-aircraft defences, plus the fighters, is now very formidable, easily the best in the world, with an amazingly intricate network of communications between all these various defences, and the cost of large-scale penetration of these defences is going to be terrific to the Germans in both machines and men. In Flanders and France, our Air Force worked under grave disadvantages because they were continually compelled to move back their aerodromes, but here at home, working under familiar and friendly conditions, with every facility for repairs and so on, they are at immense advantage. If the German pilots didn't enjoy meeting the RAF in France, they're certainly not going to have a happy time with them over England.

So much for the air. Now for the sea. Here we must make an immediate distinction between invading and raiding. Nobody doubts that it is possible for the Germans to raid the shores of this country, perhaps landing several thousands of men. We have an enormous coastline, a great many possible landing places too, so that in spite of all our defences, a few thousand can set foot on these shores. But then what? We have more than a million and a quarter men under arms, and they are being rapidly trained to meet the specific problems of attempted invasion. These raiders can make a great nuisance of themselves, but their chances of either getting very far into Britain or ever seeing their fatherland again are very small. Invasion proper, as distinct from raiding, needs a considerable army, with all the necessary massive equipment and an absolute armada of transport vessels. Please remember that even with full command of the sea it took weeks and weeks to transport the BEF across the Channel to France, without any hindrance of any kind. It is more than likely that if this large-scale invasion is tried, it will be across the narrowest part of the Channel, with an immense fleet of motor torpedo boats and flat-bottomed boats towed by tugs, and there'll have to be a whale of a lot of them. Now, these boats can only operate successfully in calm water, and there are not many days in the year when the Channel is calm. That was our great stroke of luck at the evacuation of Dunkirk, which wouldn't have been possible at all in rough weather. Landing an army is a very tricky job even when you have complete command of the sea, as our own naval men can tell you. When you haven't complete command of the sea, when at any moment a few destroyers may be let loose among your huge flotilla of tugs and crowded flat-bottom boats, when the wind may blow hard at any moment too, and the hungry seas rise with it, when you are expected at the other side by batteries of artillery and strongly entrenched infantry, bristling with machine-guns, the prospect is not hopeful for the invader.

But, you may say, the invader may ignore the expected places, the narrow Channel, and try elsewhere, across the wider stretches of the Channel or even across the North Sea. But then he has to meet further difficulties. The voyage is too long to be undertaken during the hours of darkness, and an armada in full daylight is a perfect target. Moreover, for this longer voyage across rough seas they must use much larger vessels, and these vessels not only present our warships with better targets but will also find themselves in difficulties among our minefields. But even supposing this fleet of large transport vessels successfully eludes both the Navy and the minefields, it still has to find some kind of harbour, and there is no undefended harbour of any size in this island. Then again, even if this first fleet is transported by a series of lucky chances and arrives here and lands its men, that is only the beginning of invasion, for the invader must keep his forces regularly supplied with food and munitions: he must keep that fleet sailing regularly backwards and forwards to this island, and what chance has he of doing that? Nobody knows better than the authorities in this country of all the difficulties, dangers and expense of maintaining an expeditionary force overseas, and the fact that for once we are freed from that necessity makes our position just now with troops, ships, supplies, immensely strong. We are relatively much stronger, in spite of all these recent disasters to our allies, than we were in the last war, and I still believe that Hitler's Germany, for all its blitzkriegs and triumphant marches, is not as strong as the Kaiser's Germany was. Where it is strongest is where the older Germany was weakest, and that is in its propaganda machine.

27 August 1940

Air-Raid Life Is a Queer Existence

A word on this air-raid life of ours. It's a queer existence. I'm not going to pretend I like it. To a very busy man, it's exasperating, because no matter how you contrive to make the best of these conditions, they do waste your time. Your programme of work and engagements, which may have been planned to a very careful timetable, is broken by these constant raids and warnings, and of course it's a nuisance. But we carry on.

Last night, for instance, I had arranged to see a film producer and his assistant at my house to discuss an important film we're planning, and they arrived just after the alarm went, so instead of talking upstairs, we went downstairs into the basement and held our conference there, and except for the occasional moments when the thudding of bombs seemed near and we gave each other a questioning glance, we simply got on with our job. I have no air-raid shelter in my house, and so we all pop down to the basement floor, which is just below ground level. This may not be as safe as an outside shelter, but at least it has the advantage of being indoors, so that we haven't to go trooping out into the night. My neighbour is an air-raid warden and has quite a large shelter in the garden, and some of the folk in the small houses across the way use this shelter, and immediately after the alarm has gone I hear them hurrying next door carrying their babies. They have music and games down there and do themselves proud.

Yesterday afternoon I looked in at the dress rehearsal of a play of mine that is being revived – it opened tonight – and we hadn't been ten minutes in the theatre before the sirens began wailing. 'What do we do now?' I asked the manager. 'Oh,' he said, 'we keep on until we hear bombs or gunfire very close and then we break off and go down into the green room.' There weren't any sounds of close bombs or gunfire, so they kept on and showed no signs of being worried by the alarm. But then a dress rehearsal is such a desperate business to an actor that I suppose a mere air-raid alarm at the same time makes no difference.

I was very pleased with the story that came out of yesterday afternoon's paper, which described how one of the men who sell little mechanical toys – and his toys were tiny walking mechanical men – somewhere along Oxford Street found that when the alarm went and the crowds on the pavement melted away, he had for once all the space he wanted even if he hadn't any prospective customers, so he set his mechanical little men walking about all over the pavement and said to a passer-by, 'I'm just giving the poor little beggars an outing.' That's a true story, and I liked it because its touch of humour and fancy is like a sudden shaft of warm light in what sometimes feels like a vast gloomy madhouse.

However, to get back to the air-raid life. So far last Saturday was the best example. I'm always wakened in the morning – though actually I'm nearly always awake by then – by the maid bringing in my mail and the newspapers and then drawing the curtains. Well, the timing on Saturday morning was perfect, for the alarm went just as she came in, so I took my letters and papers down to the basement, went through them down there and by the time I had had breakfast and lit my first pipe, the all-clear went and I returned upstairs. After which I settled down to a fruitful morning's work. Good! Then a friend who lives near suggested we might have an hour's tennis at about five o'clock. Excellent! I needed some exercise. But then in the middle of the afternoon the alarm went off again and I thought, 'Bang goes my tennis!' But no, there was some wicked timing again, for the all-clear went just in time for me to change and slip round the corner for my tennis.

A typical incident in this afternoon's raid was that in

the middle of it I became rather bored so came up from the basement and looked out of the dining room window to see what was doing. Outside it was quiet and deserted, all the cheerful bustle of a fine Saturday afternoon having vanished. But then I heard the sound of some approaching vehicle and was curious to know what kind of fire engine or ambulance this majestic vehicle might be, so waited to see it pass my window. It was an enormous load – the biggest I've seen – of crates of bottled ale. And I felt as Wordsworth did when he beheld a rainbow in the sky – my heart leaped up. 'Pass, thou noble beverage,' I cried. Not Goering and all his heroes, whose careful machine-gunning of children playing in fields, and whose equally careful avoidance of our Hurricanes and Spitfires raise our appreciation of the heroic Teuton soul to a new level, not these mighty men and all their engines of destruction, I said to myself, can prevent the prompt dispatch to all parts of London of a good regular supply of bottled ale.

So I had my tennis and rested a bit and then had to consider how to organise my evening. The point was, I was due in Whitehall at eleven-thirty to take part in a radio programme called *London After Dark*. My job was to be the final commentator, looking out from a window in Whitehall across to the Cenotaph and the great government buildings, describing what I saw and ending with a noble peroration of some sort or other, and taking thundering good care, I was warned, to end at just the right fraction of a second that would enable the opening chimes of Big Ben, high above my head, to be heard across the Atlantic. Well, this sounded rather rough to me, even if there wasn't going to be any interference with our plans. However, if they wanted me to do it then I must do it. But I had to be down there in Whitehall by eleven-thirty when the programme began, and if I stayed at home waiting for the appropriate time to set out and there happened to be an air raid just about then, I hadn't a dog's chance of getting down to Whitehall in time. I decided I'd better be somewhere in the neighbourhood, so I went to the theatre – to see a revue that was full of broad, low comedy – and the place was packed to the roof, and the people laughed so loud and long that even if there'd been an alarm I doubt if any of us would have heard it. (Last night, by the way, the alarm went during the performance, and as most of the audience couldn't leave the theatres, they were given extra shows afterwards, and in one or two places, I'm told, members of the audiences then took a hand and gave turns themselves.)

But to return to Saturday night. Once again, my timing was excellent, for I came out of the theatre, walked slowly along the dark, crowded streets and arrived at Whitehall just at the right time, and also as the alarm went. And there I was, for the next twenty-seven minutes, stuck in my large – I thought, much too large – open window in Whitehall listening for the arrival of the bombers, waiting for the tiny red light at my elbow that would give me the cue to begin, wondering what the blazes I was going to say, now that I didn't even know how much time I would have, or what was happening, except that that I'd still have to time it so that Big Ben came in comfortably. All I can hope is that it didn't sound too much like the rather desperate enterprise it seemed to me.

When the broadcast was over and the BBC expert who was looking after me was telephoning to know how we'd gone on, and we were lingering in that upstairs room, a whistling bomb which sounded as if a steamboat was arriving vertically came down, landing in the City, and the caretaker, who was an old sailor and appeared to think that this was like the good old times, took us down to the air-raid shelter below, a shelter that was most efficiently constructed but rather too cold for comfort; and there we were joined by one or two other people, including a large, smiling policeman who seemed to think, with the caretaker, that all this was rounding off the evening nicely; and we chatted of this and that for the next hour and a half, only interrupted by the sound of distant thudding and the noises made by fire engines in the neighbourhood. When the all-clear went at last, my own situation was anything but all clear because I was several long London miles from my own roof and bed, in which I was ready now to take a passionate interest; and several hundred thousand people in the centre of London appeared to be in the same predicament. After half an hour's wandering, I gave up the transport problem (which, by the way, has now been settled) and accepted an invitation to have a drink and sandwich and did not see my own house again until dawn was breaking.

In today's *News Chronicle*, Stanley Baron ends his daily diary with this paragraph:

Five hours in a suburban air-raid shelter, bombs falling before the warning and after the all-clear, and silence in between, four violently rapid excursions from bed, a filthy morning temper. Then this from a demolition squad man, cheerfully sweeping out glass from a cavern of eddying dust: 'Morning guvnor! 'itler's 'ousemaid, me!'

That's what the people are like here. In their prevailing good temper, their adaptability, their humour and courage, they're glorious, and their virtue shines like a great light in the darkness of this vast idiocy.

3 September 1940

First Anniversary of the War

Today we've been at war for a whole year. Let us, then, look back. It's like looking back from some high peak on a whole range of mountains we've crossed. We see grim precipices and black gulfs and also, here and there, some shining summits that we have conquered and passed. Let us note some of the outstanding features of this vast, wild landscape of war. And we must not only stare and wonder but we must also think, for though we can easily spend too much time merely staring and wondering at this war, we can hardly spend too much time really thinking about it.

We'll begin with the worst event: the sudden unexpected defeat and final capitulation of France. This is, to my mind, the most terrible event of the war so far, the one which haunts my imagination like some strange menacing dream. Over and over I have to remind myself of the grim facts, to tell myself firmly that on the other side of the narrow straits of Dover a German army is in possession of the familiar friendly cliffs, that the Nazis are swaggering round Paris, that enormous French guns are being used to bombard our coasts. It is all nearly as incredible as it is horrible. It is this fall of France, this sudden disintegration under a few days' hammer strokes of a country that was thought to be an impregnable fortress, that should be kept in mind and carefully analysed by anyone who wishes to understand this war. France is this war's great object lesson. Her lightning defeat represents the supreme triumph of the Nazi method – and that method is to apply the maximum possible force, used without scruple or mercy, to an antagonist that has already been weakened from within by every device of the Nazi propaganda system. Make no mistake about that. France was only defeated in the field after she had already been defeated in the bureaux and salons of Paris. Hitler could afford to throw in his last airplane, his last tank, because he knew the brave men still opposing his armies had been betrayed. His four columns – his planes, tanks, artillery, infantry – may have served him well, but he knew even before he set them in action that his Fifth Column had already served him better still, and that France was doomed. We cannot afford to forget France, what happened to her and why it happened to her, for a single day.

Now let us turn back from the black gulfs to some of the shining peaks. The most important event for us was the triumphantly successful embarkation of the BEF and other forces from Dunkirk. This last-minute snatch of a whole army whose entire capture was undoubtedly part of the general plan was immensely important, not only because it robbed Hitler of a victory he had promised himself and the whole world but also because it demonstrated in the usual desperate, dark hour that Britain still possessed the power of rapid and brilliant improvisation, a national quality that serves us as German method and organisation serve them. After a procession of disheartening events, Dunkirk, with its audacity, its almost impudent unexpectedness, came like a flourish of trumpets. It was as if Drake and Nelson had returned to waken the islanders from their sleep.

Then even more important has been the success, right from the very hour of the invasion of the Low Countries to this present moment, of the Royal Air Force, which I am positive will be recognised, if it is not already recognised, as one of the greatest fighting forces in the history of the world, one of those groups of heroes who capture the imagination of man for ever. These young men, whether they go roaring over half Western Europe every night to find an exact target or come flashing out of the blue these mornings in their Spitfires and Hurricanes to deal out terror and destruction to the clumsy armadas of the Nazis, combine superb skill with audacity after a fashion that we thought had left this world. You have to go back to the Elizabethan sailors to find their equals. They are of the great race. They are living in some splendid saga that we on the ground can hardly begin to understand. I find it as difficult to praise these magnificent young men adequately as I do to think of their exploits at all without deep emotion. These youngsters who go laughing and singing and charging about in their little cars with their girlfriends, who are as modest as they are gallant, who are clean, clear-cut and chivalrous, are saving the civilised world, and the best form our gratitude can take is a determination that the world they save shall be worthy of such devotion, skill and heroism.

So much, then, for the fighting side of it all. Now let's turn to the political. Perhaps the most significant event in political Europe during this last year was Mr. Churchill's offer to complete union with France. Because this offer was made, no doubt after other appeals had been ignored, at the last minute of a dark hour, and more dramatic news immediately followed it, the significance of this offer has not, I think, been sufficiently widely appreciated. What is extremely important is the fact that this offer of complete federation should have been made at all. It marks the emergence of a new world in international politics.

I feel too that the presence here in Britain of the great governments of the conquered countries, along with their great legions of soldiers, seamen, airmen, is a fact whose significance has been under-estimated rather than over-estimated and that this astonishing, if still rather confused, series of alliances must play its part in breaking down the old Europe. The Nazis are busy breaking down the old European system by imposing the same dread tyranny everywhere, but the free men who still defy them are equally busy, by the exercise not of tyranny but of mutual trust and co-operation, paving the way for a Europe that is no longer a cockpit of belligerent sovereign states.

And now we come to the grandest peak of all, to the fact that has given me personally more hope for the future not only of this war but for the world after the war than any other fact – and that is the way in which the ordinary folk of this island have emerged as the real challengers of Nazism. When the real blitzkrieg began and the Nazis sprang like a tiger, then the British people, instead of losing heart, rose at once in spirit to meet the challenger. They came out of a sleep with which some of us had reproached them before this war began. They cried, 'Give us some men to lead us,' and at once began to get the men, and these men told them to stop dreaming, to take their coats off and make a real fight of it, and, roaring with enthusiasm, the people waded in and began to show that democracy, when it's a real democracy and not a sham one, is just about as effete and decadent an antagonist as a wounded rhinoceros.

They were told to go to it and they went to it, with the result that during these summer months they achieved the greatest short-term war effort known to history, doing in a few months, as free men, what it took the Nazis with their vast population of serfs years to do. The output of planes and munitions went soaring. The people responded triumphantly to every demand made upon them and begged for more and greater demands. They worked till they reeled at the benches. Men and women who'd never worked hard with their hands in their lives demanded to be trained to do their share. Recruiting for every service went up by leaps and bounds. From all the great Commonwealth of English-speaking nations, from the ends of the earth, came young men for the fighting services, came instant offers of help. As the Nazi propaganda machine screamed its bestial threats, the spirits of these people rose and rose, and they demanded to defend this island to the last ditch. Then, from feeling that they were living in a beleaguered fortress, they rose to the conviction that, right in the vast threatening face of the enemy, they were now living in the world's great base of freedom, from which would finally emerge the triumphant armies of liberty. With the coming of the ceaseless air attacks, which are still raging, these people found themselves in the very front line and neither flinched nor whined, but cried again, 'All right, come on! Let's see what you can do!'

Unless it is understood that this is something more than an heroic war effort, we under-estimate its profound significance. What one must understand is that as soon as it was realised that this was indeed a people's war, immediately then vast new funds of courage, energy, power were suddenly tapped, to begin working miracles. And why? Because the people were awake at last, and such springs of courage, energy, power exist in the people. In other words, here was democracy – not, as the dictators had hoped, tottering on its last legs, but coming roaring to life again, within sight once more of another great revolution of the human spirit. What the dictators had sneered at and found it easy to defeat was not the real democracy but a shaky ruin of a sham old democracy that had long lost its old ardour, courage and vision. But when these dictators hit hard enough and the ruin began falling, their hammer blows suddenly rang against steel, and that steel was the will of the people, who will not only defend what they have but will not rest again until they find their way to a nobler quality of life.

This, then, is my faith now: not only that Nazism will be finally defeated, as I believe that it will be so that it will remain nothing but an evil memory and a lasting warning, but that already a new world order is being created out of the very stress and strain of this conflict, that men everywhere can take hope, for the new democracy is on the march. At last the British people are awake again, to astonish the world with their endurance, courage and goodwill – a great people ready not only to meet any challenge but also to shape a new destiny for themselves and to help other peoples along the road to security, freedom and the good life.

And that is what one man has learned from this first year of war.

10 September 1940

The Colossal Panorama of a Defiant City

In one of our newspapers this morning, there is a cable dispatch from their New York correspondent which begins: 'Front pages of newspapers here are black with headlines describing death and destruction in London and lurid with descriptions of threats coming from Germany.'

They are doing it, of course, because they feel it's good journalism – 'London now a hell on earth', that's one of the great stories of the century. Well, it may be good journalism, but nevertheless it's just playing the Nazi game. It's all part of the war of nerves. They've been screaming at us for some time now, without much result. And don't make any mistake: it's the people who are screaming what they're going to do, the people who have to magnify the stupid destruction of workmen's houses and tenements into a great military victory, whose nerves are failing them. We've only got to stick it – and sooner or later this gang of neurotic butchers will be on the run.

So much for that.

Well, what's it like in this so-called hell on earth? To begin with, it's a long way from being a hell on earth yet, except of course in certain widely separated places at certain moments. I'm here and I ought to know. Also, I know what hells on earth are – I've seen them. The Somme, Verdun, Vimy Ridge, Passchendaele – those were all hells on earth where tens of thousands of magnificent young men were withered away in a morning. We haven't got anywhere near that yet. These recent big raids, indiscriminate, vindictive and fundamentally stupid, like the plunging and lashings about of an enormous tormented beast robbed of its prey, have caught the world's imagination, and the fact that they have done this is itself a tribute to the might and majesty of London itself:

> *The resort and mart of all the earth*
>
> *Chequered with all complexions of mankind.*

Or, as a poet cried in the Middle Ages, when nobody had heard of Berlin: 'London, thou flower of cities all!'

I am not myself a Londoner, though I have lived here on and off for twenty years, but during these last few days I've been proud to feel myself a Londoner. I should think even these young Nazi airmen, who are notoriously not very sensitive types, must have been troubled by a feeling of awe as they caught glimpses far below them of the ancient, mighty capital city whose contributions, by way of government and law, arts and sciences, to the world civilisation have been incalculably vast. Time after time during these last few days, I have gone up to high places, my own roof and other roofs, at dusk, during the night and at dawn, to stare at the colossal panorama of the defiant city. This morning, for example, at daybreak, I climbed to my own roof, which is very high up on top of London's steepest hill, and stared about me, in the chill sweet dawn, feeling most deeply moved. There, lead-coloured in that sunless early glimmer, was every familiar monument, not one landmark of the city missing, all there – as if standing to attention at reveille as we used to do in the trenches at this hour – but far away, dramatic in their sharp vermilion and orange, were curling tongues of fire. I had gone up before, fairly early in the night, but then had only seen a distant glow or two of fire, like minor wounds on the colossal body of the city, which was raying out its searchlights and keeping the horizon pulsating with flashes of gunfire.

On Sunday night it was much more spectacular, when I went up very high in central London and watched the fires that for hours had cast a rosy glow over half the sky and turned the upper storeys of those whitish London terraces a bright pink. From where I watched, the greatest of the fires was just behind St Paul's, which was carefully silhouetted in dead black against the red glare of the flames and the orange pink of the smoke. It stood there like a symbol, with its unbroken dome and towering cross, of an enduring civilisation of reason and Christian earth as against a red menacing glare of unreason, destruction and savagery. You get the same significant contrast when you listen to and compare the voices and speeches of Winston Churchill and Adolf Hitler; one a gallant, reasonable man, seriously weighing evidence and considering chances, and the other a screaming, raving neurotic, hardly knowing what he's saying but mad with violence and hate. In the other half of the sky, where the blue night still held sway, the searchlights made rapidly changing patterns, now coming together sharply and now swinging in wide arcs, trying to locate the tiny objects that were droning round and round before dropping, quite indiscriminately, their cargoes of destruction and death.

It was much later – it was daylight, in fact – when I started on my way home, mingling with the crowds, some of whom, like me, were going home after their night's work, and others emerging to begin their day's work. Transport is still difficult after these long raids, and this is probably our chief ground problem right now, but I've no doubt whatever that soon ways and means will be found to speed it up. After various bouts of walking and waiting, I managed to get a bus or two to help me on my way. The people were all wonderfully patient and good. They were tired, of course, but in no way fearful or cast down or even fretful. We passed near – and had to slow up – by a scene of most fantastic destruction, where an exceptionally heavy bomb must have fallen during the night, for not only were several houses completely wrecked but immediately next door to this wreckage a large London bus had been half flattened out and hurled against the side of a building, clean up in the air, for now one end of it was resting against the second storey. Just as if it had been a little piece of tin that you picked up and hurled against a wall with such force that it stuck there. Fortunately, this bus had been completely empty at the time. Well, we all had a good look, in my bus, at this spectacle, but in spite of the long hours of danger and waiting and weariness, nobody was at all overcome; there were merely murmurs of indignation.

The elaborate ARP services, which were rather sneered at for some time, have proved themselves invaluable and heroic during these nights, not only because they are extremely well organised but also because the quality of service given by the men and women acting as air-raid wardens, as firefighters and as members of emergency squads has been really magnificent, something that could not be bought with money, that springs out of a deep devotion and love of this great city and its people. If the intention of the Nazis in this use of indiscriminate bombing, in which bombs of the heaviest calibre have been dropped anywhere and everywhere, is to terrorise the people of London then they are wasting men, machines and high explosives. So long as our people think they can hit back – and we're going to hit back harder and harder – Goering will never bomb them into suing for terms even if he sends over, night after night, every machine he's got.

In the meantime, of course, he sets some of us pretty little problems. I have no outside air-raid shelter, so we go down into the basement, and I've had one of the rooms down there reinforced and shored up with heavy timber. It won't stand a direct hit, of course – a direct hit with a bomb from any size and it's goodbye – but we're hoping that if a bomb comes near and brings down the upper parts of the house, this reinforced basement will be strong enough to withstand the sudden weight of debris. I was buried alive and had to be dug out in the last war, and it'll be odd if it happens to me all over again in this war – and at home in my own house, too!

What a lot of lunacy it is, isn't it? Add one part sheer wickedness to about a hundred parts downright stupidity and mental laziness and suddenly you find yourself spending your time in the basement wondering if some young idiot 12,000 feet above you is going to press a button and perhaps blot you out, and all for the sake of the greater glory of an ex-paper-hanging Austrian police spy who probably isn't right in his head.

But I was talking of the problems we have got solved now. For example, I have to be in London blitzkrieg or no blitzkrieg to do my work – such as broadcasting, though that's not all I do by a long chalk. And because I'm in London, my wife, who is otherwise a very sensible woman, thinks that she ought to be in London. And my secretary, who has a cottage in the country to which she could go, thinks that she ought to stay in London. And so it goes on. With the result that I find myself surrounded by women, who actually are all much calmer than I am, but that doesn't prevent my feeling that I'm responsible for their being here, and if anything did happen to one of them, I know I'd feel guilty about it.

Then again, it's all so complicated. Last night, they all rushed to put on trousers – these air raids are simply being used as an excuse by Englishwomen to put on trousers – and down they come, bringing mattresses and pillows to the shelter room in the basement, with the result that they filled it – and anyway I felt that I was intruding in this very feminine atmosphere – so I put a mattress in a kind of little cubbyhole under the stairs and got down there, and though it was fairly stuffy and smelt of mice and camphor and I could hear a lot of sinister bumps and bangs and the house gave an occasional little shiver – as well it might, poor old house – I somehow managed to obtain several hours' sleep. At the same old time in the morning, the letters were there, the newspapers were there, my breakfast was there, and we were all there, carrying on.

They are saying in London today that this is the critical fortnight, and that the Nazis, stung by the obvious failure of their previous threats and boasts, are about to make a major move, attempting invasion. That's one interpretation, though I would have thought that another was that this aerial blitzkrieg has been put on as a kind of noisy cover while one set of plans is scrapped to make way for another set of plans. I don't know. What I do know is that the latest high Nazi view – which is that this blitz will result in the resignation of the present government here – is just about the silliest put forward yet, and that the expression of such wildly nonsensical notions coupled with this wildly indiscriminate bombing suggests that the Nazi leaders are much worried men.

24 September 1940

Going North

I am going north for a week or two, back to my native Yorkshire. I'm not getting out of London because there are too many bombs for me, though I have had my adventures with them, and so contrived my existence last week that for five days I never succeeded in getting my clothes off and reaching the inside of a bed. If I thought the bombing of London would be intensified, I would stay on, but my own feeling is – and so far events have borne me out – that the bombing is decreasing in weight and violence. Therefore, as it does not seem likely that there will be anything new to report about the London scene during the next week or two, I thought I would take this opportunity of doing what I've wanted to do for the last two months: that is, to go up north, to that other and quite different half of England, to get some idea of what is happening there and how the people, who are responsible, of course, for most of our heavy industries, are taking it all.

It would be a surprise to the Nazi airmen we have captured recently to learn that I propose to go north, for it appears they have been told – and solemnly believe – that industrial northern England is completely under Nazi domination. This is merely one of the new German fairy tales with which these young men are now being lulled into a false security. They have been told that hundreds of thousands of German troops have invaded England and Ireland, and that the whole of Scotland has been captured by troops landed from Norway. The royal family and the government, they are told, are now besieged in London, and only this south-east corner of England is still in British hands. In addition, some of them believe that the whole of the British fleet has been sunk, that Portland is almost a German naval base, and that even in London great riots and demonstrations in favour of peace are taking place day and night. The end, according to this new fairy tale, is in sight. The starving British people are waiting to welcome the victorious Nazis. So they are, but in another sense. The British people, of course, aren't starving and the Nazis equally aren't victorious. But that our people are waiting to welcome the Nazis whenever they arrive is true enough. They will receive such a welcome as they've never had before, and it will be all the more surprising because they are being fed with such lying dope as this.

I must repeat that the Nazis, for people who have just had a series of lightning conquests, are now behaving in a strangely suspicious manner. What is the point of telling their people – even the very men called upon to fight – all this ridiculous nonsense? It is not merely a matter of touching up the facts, but of persuading their fighting men to believe the most monstrous lies, all calculated to persuade them that the war is won except for some small effort that they have to make during the next day or two. I can see the point of trying to persuade your opponent that all is over with him – which is the trick the Nazis worked with some success in France and Belgium – but to persuade your own fighting men that all is nearly over, when you know that at any moment they may be called upon to begin a long and weary campaign, suggests that these men have lost heart and need the most fantastic restorative.

It is true that these young Nazi pilots we capture, who discover to their astonishment that Britain is not starving, is armed to the teeth, and is ready, if necessary, to fight for years, cannot return to tell their comrades the truth, cannot spread their sudden disillusionment. And yet I would have thought that juggling with lies of these gigantic dimensions is like playing with an enormous boomerang which at any moment may return and knock you flat. A government that exhibited such an obvious contempt for my intelligence would soon lose my allegiance, for I would feel that it had not only been misleading me but downright insulting me.

And here are an air force and an army which in a few weeks completely over-ran half Western Europe and yet now, only a month or two later, it has to be fed with the soothing syrup of such colossal lies. Why? What has happened to these soldiers and airmen? And what has happened to the civilian population behind them? And, more important still, what has happened to the Nazi leaders that they take the risk of all their people being so horribly disillusioned and they themselves made to look like fools? Even Goebbels himself would find it hard to conjure a Britain almost at the mercy of invading Nazi forces back into a Britain that is completely untouched and has never seen a Nazi invader. Does it mean that the Nazis are changing their plans and making use of any nonsense as a cover for that change, or does it mean that now they feel committed to an attempt at invasion?

If so, the question of transport must be giving them a headache. One of our military experts has been working out the problem for them. He estimates that to transport a mechanised force of 100,000 men with the minimum of heavy equipment, a nice little armada of 1,300 to 1,500 large flat-bottomed barges would be required. This number would be necessary merely to convey the 100,000 men and their equipment across the sea, but of course it is only the beginning of the problem, for they would have to be supplied regularly with ammunition and supplies. To assemble 1,300 or 1,500 of such boats or barges, then to move them across the sea at a speed of probably not more than eight knots, in the face of our Air Force and the most powerful navy in the world, will be quite a task, even if wind and weather be favourable; and even then, if by some miracle of organisation this part of the greater task is accomplished without a loss of more than half the vessels and the men and equipment they carry, they will have still to be landed bang in the face of an army that has been waiting for them – and how! – ever since Dunkirk. Again, our expert estimates that for a seven days' mobile campaign, even this force of 100,000 men would require for its tanks and other vehicles something like 2,750,000 gallons of petrol, all of which will have to be transported across the sea. And all this for a force of only 100,000 men; that is, for five mechanised divisions with corps and army troops. But in order to over-run Poland, which had most of its Air Force put out of action in the first twenty-four hours, it took no less than thirty-seven infantry divisions, five motorised divisions, five armoured divisions, four light mechanised divisions and many tank regiments. To bring even a fraction of such a force across the sea would demand the most gigantic armada of vessels. Yet obviously anything less than such force and at least such an equipment would stand no chance whatever against our own heavily mechanised armies, all specially trained by this time to repel invaders on ground now familiar to them and quite unfamiliar to the attacking forces.

Well, they may try it, for they are nothing if not gamblers. But I am going north, for I feel that there is nothing more at the moment I can report about life in London under the air raids. I have paid my tribute to the grand resolution and courage of the great city of my adoption and all its folk, especially the women and girls – not only the mothers and housewives but the hundreds of thousands of nurses, secretaries, clerks, shop girls, waitresses who've turned up morning after morning, still trim and smiling, if a little weary, and who've defied Goering and all his Air Force. I can say nothing new, so I feel it is time I went back to my own folk in the north to see what life is like up there among the mills and the moors. Don't imagine that they haven't had their share of the bombing. They have not had the continued determined attack on their morale that the Londoners have had, but they've heard the bombers droning and the bombs thudding and roaring and stared at the ruins next morning.

Meanwhile, it will at least be interesting to see how the air-raid life is being lived in other, smaller cities, where it has not yet developed into a kind of grim routine, as it has now in London. The change up north will be less dramatic, for life is much grimmer up there, among the tall chimneys and the grey stone walls, at any time, and you might say that industry has been waging a kind of blitzkrieg up there for generations. Actually, I suppose that from the point of view of our war effort I am going from the less important to the more important region, for though London is the capital of our wide Commonwealth, the seat of government, the centre of all our financial interests, it is, after all, not the place where the machinery and the materials of war are made. Moreover, both industrial Yorkshire and Lancashire have groups of towns – and you can't tell where one ends and the next begins – that together make up centres of population as great as London itself. In fact, Britain could still wage this war if London had become uninhabitable, which it is, of course, far from being at the moment, except for the faint-hearted. But Britain without the industrial north, where the factories go on endlessly, would be in a sorry state. And the north is, as most of you probably know, almost a different country, with quite a different outlook from London and the south.

It always has its point of view. What that point of view is at the moment, I don't know, but with any luck I soon will, and you shall hear what it is – in the genuine accent of the region. Aye, you will that an' all. Goodnight.

27 September 1940

Bradford

Good evening. Here I am, as I promised in my last talk, back in my own native Yorkshire – and it is still Yorkshire. I'll tell you what I mean. The hotel I'm staying in is a gigantic brand-new affair, with hidden lights, air conditioning and a general appearance of being an hotel in a Hollywood film. Such an hotel would have been unthinkable in the Yorkshire of my boyhood. Wild horses couldn't have dragged my father to have a meal in such a vast palace of flaunting luxury. But though the hotels may have changed, the people haven't. I telephoned from my room this morning to have breakfast sent in. 'I'd like some breakfast sent to my room,' I began. The voice of the floor waitress cried, in deep disgust, 'What! Another!' I learned afterwards that there had been a phenomenal demand for breakfasts in rooms, hence that cry from the heart.

No, the people haven't changed at all. They are still and at one and the same time the grumpiest and rudest and yet in essence the staunchest and kindest people in the world. If they like you, they will work their fingers to the bone for you, and if necessary go and die for you, but what they find it really hard to do is to find a smile for you, and a little compliment. I'm like that myself – at least so far as the unsatisfactory part of it is concerned – and so I know exactly how they feel. But these are grand people to have with you in a war. Really, they've always been in a war. First, a war against the stubborn moors and fells. Then, after the industrial revolution, a war against the terribly long hours and grim conditions in the factories, then against vast trade slumps and depressions. I'll be surprised if they can't take a war against Hitler in their stride.

Now, yesterday, as I promised you, I went back to my native town to see what had happened to it during a recent, sudden, quite unexpected air raid. Although I really left this town for good at the beginning of the last war, when I joined the Army twenty-six years ago, and so have spent far more of my life out of it than in it, yet because my childhood and boyhood were lived there, it still seems my own town, you know, more real than other towns. Every street, every building, is solidly there, because they were fixed in my mind during childhood. Therefore, as I anticipated, it was far more of a shock to see a few damaged buildings in this town than it had been to see the much greater damage in London. The raiders appear to have dropped a few high-explosive bombs and then some incendiaries, with the result that the larger buildings were burnt out rather than blown apart. In the centre of the town, quite close together, part of a market, a large drapery store and a large old chapel had been destroyed or partly gutted. These ruins, blackened inside but with odd pillars and bits of wall still standing, looked quite extraordinary to me. I just couldn't believe in them. Actually, they looked far less ignoble and obscene than the now-familiar sight of bombed buildings, with their pitiful broken rafters and horrid mess of debris. These had rather an ancient Roman look about them. There was a tiny suggestion of Pompeii or Herculaneum about these Yorkshire ruins. But to see them there, in that place, was strangely shocking, and I think made a far deeper impression on me than all the bombing I had seen for weeks and weeks in London.

This northern raid, though it had caused considerable damage to property, and had taken place at an hour when people were still about, had been surprisingly light in casualties, there being only one fatal injury. It was really almost negligible stuff when compared with the heavy bombings in London. Yet because it somehow brought two entirely different worlds together – the safe and shining world of my childhood and this insecure and lunatic world of today – and mixed them up, it caught and held my imagination. I was appalled by the sheer stupidity of it. Nothing that by the wildest stretch of Goebbels's imagination could be called a military objective had been touched. These Nazi airmen had flown hundreds and hundreds of miles in order to destroy a draper's shop, part of a market, an old chapel and so on. Nothing that made the least difference to our war effort. Nothing that couldn't be soon replaced, except of course the old walls of the chapel. Even already the draper's have taken other premises, the market is open and I've no doubt that the congregation of the old chapel has found hospitality, if an inferior brand of sermon, at other places of worship. And then too the pie shop was there, in full swing.

But I must explain about the pie shop. Now, ever since I could remember, there had been, just at the back of this draper's and this old chapel, a small eating house that specialised in meat-and-potato pies. I remember it well because there had always been in the window, to tempt the appetite of the passer-by, an extra-large, a giant or jumbo, meat-and-potato pie, with a magnificent brown, crisp, neatly wrinkled, succulent-looking crust, out of which there came, at any hour when the shop was doing business, a fine rich appetising steam. That steaming giant pie was to my boyish mind – and indeed to my adult mind, for we never forget these things – as much an essential part of my native city as the town hall and its chimes. Now, I had heard that this shop and its famous steaming pie had been destroyed in the raid, and so when I went to see what happened yesterday, I had made up my mind that I would stand in the ruins of that shop – catching perhaps a last faint dying aroma of the great pie, a last lingering whiff of that strange steam – and would compose some kind of lament or elegy. And so, no sooner had I taken a general view of the black twisted ruins than I made for the pie shop. And what did I find? It hadn't vanished. It was there, open and doing business. True, it was showing scars, and instead of a window it had been neatly boarded up. But there was an opening in the middle of this painted wood. And what did I see through this opening? I saw the great pie, as brown, crisp, succulent as ever, and steaming away like mad. Every puff and jet of that steam defied Hitler, Goering and the whole dastardly gang of them. It was glorious.

Now, the owner himself – a tall, elderly man with one of those folded-in Yorkshire faces, and 'character' written all over him – was standing just inside the open doorway. So, in my delight in this magnificent resurrection of the pie, I addressed him, asking him what happened. He replied very shortly, and indeed grumpily, that the shop had had its front blown out but was now open, as we could see, and that the famous pie hadn't been damaged at all because it was his habit, when closing the shop, to remove this noble trademark to a place of safety. As he said this, I could feel his hand on my back and a distinct sensation of being gently but firmly pushed into the street. I'll confess that this unfriendly, this suspicious and hostile reception by the owner of the pie rather grieved me, but I thought that the man was getting on in years and must have had a worrying time and might be excused a touch of incivility. So I walked a little further along and turned down a side street to have a closer look at the ruins, at this Pompeii in the heart of Yorkshire.

I had not been there more than a minute or two when I was clapped on the shoulder. There was the pieman again, but this time wearing his coat and not wearing his apron, and extending a hand and beaming all over his long face. It seems that his wife recognised my voice – I'm not telling this for my own glory, though I must say it's one of the most handsome compliments I ever received – and so, after doing a quick change with his apron and coat, he came round after me. He didn't admit as much, but I think that he had imagined that I was some trade rival, anxious to discover, after years of unsuccessful Fifth Column work, the secret of the famous steaming pie. For now the pieman, all smiles and friendship and confidence, admitted what I in my turn had suspected ever since the age of fourteen: namely, that that succulent giant pie, forever jetting forth its fragrant steam, was not a real pie at all but an astonishing imitation. 'Aye,' said the pieman proudly, 'it's a secret, that pie is – an' a rare lot 'ud like to know how it's done. I've had it five an' forty year, that same pie, an' luckily I'd put it away in a good safe place, same as usual. An' so, soon as we got started again – an' we wasn't long, I can tell you – I got the pie out again and there it is, same as ever. There's only one thing,' he added, rather wistfully. 'That hole I left in the centre o' the boarding on the window to see the pie through – aye, well it's not quite big enough. Well, I'm right glad to 'ave a word with you.'

So we parted, and I went off to have a chat with the Lord Mayor in his parlour in our Gothic town hall. I'd known him years and years ago, when I was a youngster still in my middle teens and wrote an article every week about everything for a Labour weekly called *The Pioneer*. He was then a young man just back from Ruskin College, Oxford. Now he's white-haired and I turn the scale at nearly 200 pounds. Time – as they say – marches on. After he had genially dismissed a row of shy little schoolgirls who were presenting contributions to his Spitfire fund, we had a talk about our city, its trade – which is still excellent – and the morale of its folk, which is as high as he could desire. And I'm sure he was right. The main streets were filled with women shopping, and there seemed plenty of money about. Theatres, films, everything in full swing, though closing rather earlier than they used to do. In spite of the picturesque ruins further along, you felt that the war had hardly stretched the surface of life there yet. No really serious effort had had to be made yet to cope with it. And this, mind you, is the industrial north, where the bulk of the real work is done, where the tall factories go on endlessly, where most of England's great wealth was produced.

The women, as usual, suggested more pugnacity than the men. As I waited for the bus to take me away, a newspaper seller came up to two working women and cried, 'All the latest. Berlin bombed for four hours.' 'Aye,' said one of the women, 'and I wished they'd bombed it for forty hours.' No Fifth Column stuff among these people, and I fancy that as victims of an invasion based on panic tactics, they'd prove pretty hopeless. There used to be a lot of Germans in this city, and at least one of them who spent his early life here returned some years ago to Germany and rose to a fairly high rank in the Nazi Party. I'd like to read his report on the prospects of penetration by propaganda and panic in Yorkshire. If he told the truth, it wouldn't make very cheerful reading for his superiors. Well, there it was, my day in the old home town, and I'm not going to apologise to you because it hasn't been concerned with vast strategical plans or horrors on a large scale, but only with an old pieman and his pie, because my object always is to make you see and feel the war as we see and feel it here, bridging the great gap between us, and it's only by mentioning the little things – and the little people – I feel, that I can make it live for you. I hope you agree. Goodnight.

1 and 2 October 1940

Leeds

When I arrived in Leeds the other day, I saw from my hotel window that they were busy taking down the flags and banners and gay posters from the space round the statue of the Black Prince, for they had just finished their War Weapons Week, the first of its kind in the country. In a week, they had raised over three and a half million pounds in loans, many of them free of interest, to the government. This seemed to me a fine effort for a city of about half a million inhabitants. But one of the permanent citizens, who had been directing it, contradicted me at once. By the way, I'll bet if I'd said it had been a poor effort, he would equally have contradicted me. For this, I'm afraid, is our habit in the north of England. 'Oh, it's not,' he said, 'they haven't started yet. Wait till a few more bombs fall, and then they'll begin getting their hands down into their pockets. We'll have ten million before we've finished with the job.'

This mutual effort, by the way, was under the chairmanship of a big industrialist, Mr. Kenneth Fraser, who has many friends in America to whom he sends a regular letter describing what we are feeling about the war in the north. Here's an extract from the last letter.

After saying that the promised invasion had not materialised, and that we were sorry because we were looking forward to killing a lot of Germans here, he goes on:

> *From the preceding, it will be thought we have become very bloodthirsty. We have, and will continue in this mood until the war is over and we and our neighbours on the Continent are able to pursue our several ways*

according to our own ideas of liberty and civilisation. We haven't always been in this mood, but as the murderous plans of Hitler and his gang have unfolded on the Continent, we have passed from our usual philosophic state of mind until today we have only one object in mind, and that is to win the war at any cost.

Well, that's what the industrial north thinks, and they always know their own minds. Actually, up here, the war has hardly scratched the surface of their lives yet – a fact of some importance considering how deeply these people are engaged in essential war industries. Theatres, cinemas, dance halls are in full swing still, though everything tends to close earlier. I heard a great noise the other night coming from a tavern called the Black Lion, round the corner here, and looked in to discover a large room crammed with soldiers, airmen and their girlfriends, led by an astonishingly sedate-looking little woman thumping a piano, and a mournful man blowing a saxophone, all roaring out 'Roll Out the Barrel'. And a vaudeville show I looked in on last night was very much in full swing. And during the day, women everywhere shopping, and streams of cars about. It all seemed quite gay after London. Not that they aren't hard at work in this region. In fact, yesterday, having rashly agreed to do some local sight-seeing, I was worn out by being shown how hard people are at work round here.

Among the places I visited was a gigantic metal works in the neighbourhood where tubes of every possible size were being manufactured out of various alloys. Miles and miles of shining tubing appeared to be arising like magi. Great machines took hold of glowing long bars of metal, and by some mysterious process punched out into tubes. Best of all were the beautiful new alloys now used in the production of aircraft, as strong as the finest steel, and yet fantastically light so that you could with ease pick up an armful of them. These will go into our new fighters and bombers. Thousands of women and girls are employed in this factory as well as men, to do the lighter work, and it seemed queer and rather touching to notice in that grim, masculine atmosphere of din and smoke and hot metal two young girls in overalls – only their bright curls distinguishing them at a glance from young men, sauntering along together with their little fingers locked as if keeping even in that masculine inferno of noise, heat and fierce effort some secret little thread of feminine sympathy.

Another enormous factory in sharp contrast to the metal works was engaged in what is one of the staple trades of Leeds, the manufacture of clothing; partly uniforms, of course, but also still a great deal of civilian suits. This was a colossal beehive of a place where you looked down long vistas everywhere until your eyes ached and your mind reeled. Eleven thousand men, women and girls were at work in this one factory. The firm has several other factories elsewhere, and the canteen where I had tea – and a thundering good tea too – provides 8,000 meals at once. The medical and welfare department was almost the size of a young hospital. This business was started in 1900 when the owner of it borrowed a hundred pounds from a relative to open a small tailor's shop. Now it is worth over eight million pounds. It was once this cheap tailoring trade – a notorious sweating trade – but there is no sweating except among the middle-aged women working in the canteen kitchen in this gigantic factory, which is the owner's hobby and pride as well as his livelihood. This owner, by the way, is a Jew, Sir Montague Burton, and I hope he gazes in satisfaction at the hundreds of thousands of khaki battle dresses which is now the service uniform of the British fighting soldier, and fine tough stuff it is made of too. That good chief has magnificently organised and humanely planned his factory to clothe the men who will eventually smash the people who are trying to outlaw this intelligent and industrious race. And let me add this, that in the last war I was in the trenches with a lot of men of the Jewish race from Leeds here, and they were grand soldiers. Some of them won high honours and decorations, and a complete answer to the familiar lying charge that the Jew wants other people to do his fighting for him.

This afternoon, I noticed a lot of activity further along the corridor in my hotel. I went to investigate and found that a well-known wholesale London firm of dressmakers was having a show in one of the end rooms. So I went in and found the room lined with women's winter coats and fur coats – hundreds of them – and various buyers, male and female, from big local shops examining the stock. I was astonished to learn that instead of the trade in fur coats having vanished, it was doing quite nicely, thank you! – not, of course, with the Russian sable and mink departments, but in the cheaper lines. Trade, it seemed, was much better than it was a year ago in the first month of the war, though the fact that very soon the purchase tax will be imposed and this is the last chance to obtain things at the old prices may have something to do with it.

But undoubtedly, here in the north, money is circulating briskly, and indeed, I must confess that in my hotel, where last night I was charged six and threepence for a whisky and soda and a few tongue sandwiches, it is expected to circulate rather more briskly than I quite enjoy. But these charges in this hotel, I must explain, don't point to any abnormality due to war conditions. On the contrary, they show that this kind of hotel, which fancies itself as a deluxe hotel, still finds itself almost in a normal pre-war world where it can afford to demand such rates. When the war has its effect, it will be to reduce, and not increase, such charges, which couldn't be made unless people were obviously making money.

If all this suggests a certain detachment from the war, I should be giving you a totally wrong impression, and here I will return to the letter I quoted from earlier – the circular letter that Mr. Fraser sends out. He ends it by saying:

> *The war-like spirit is very high. For instance, my colleague in business has all his three sons in the Army, two of these having left reserved occupations. There is a regular fight going on all the time on the part of the older men to get into some kind of active war work; old fighting men of sixty years of age and thereabouts all seem to have the idea there must be an opening for them in the fighting forces.*

Nothing detached about these Leeds folk, clearly. I notice that the chief topic of letters to the press round here is the question of reprisals for the Nazis' indiscriminate bombing. Every day there has been a whole column of letters on this subject. Very bloodthirsty gentlemen quote the Old Testament: 'Now go and smite Amalek and utterly destroy all that they have and spare them not.' Two readers at the other extreme retort that they cannot 'reconcile the mass murder of women and children with the preservation of decency', and that we must not put Nazi ideas into the heads of our own airmen. It is perhaps significant that the correspondents who announce that they know Germany and the Germans well seem to be all in favour of reprisals on the ground that the Germans tend to be Huns who, as the Americans say, 'can dish it out but can't take it'.

There is a good deal of approval of what might be called the limited reprisal. Here, in one letter, is a pungent statement of the case.

> *Sir, how much longer do we intend to tolerate the inhuman atrocities perpetrated by those German brutes? Could we not, through neutral channels, inform Hitler that unless he stops the sinking of children's ships, bombing of innocent civilians, churches and hospitals, we will select certain German cities and blow them out of existence?*

It seems to me a mournful comment on the moral courage of the world that it should have known for years now exactly how the Germans would behave when they began their much-advertised social war and, knowing this, didn't make one vast protest and then turn its face away from the people who were already coldly planning to do such foul things. It is possible that the Nazis would have been indifferent to the condemnation and scorn of the whole civilised world, but the point is that because they were powerful, had money to spend, trade to offer, they were never even shown that wholesale condemnation and scorn, and now it is too late. The tiger is loose, and all we can do is to point our guns. What it amounts to can be shown in what seems to me a singularly moving passage from a letter I have just received from my friend and philosopher W. A. Sinclair, who has been visiting the East End during the bad raids. He says:

> *A very heavy bomb has fallen on a tightly packed building. It was a direct hit and about half the building had disintegrated into heaps of iron and stonework surrounding a thirty-yard crater. Out of this vast mass of bricks, rafters, girders and rubble were projected two*

hands – dead – a man's hand holding a woman's. They were old hands, and on the woman's there was a thin and worn wedding ring. Perhaps he hadn't been a very good husband. He may sometimes have treated her badly for all we know, or can know, but that sight moved me after I had ceased to be moved by the sight of the shattered bodies of little children, and by all the mass of present and impending human suffering among which I had been going about that night. That is what is going on simply because a gang of German outlaws are crazy for power, and because the world lacks moral courage and would not speak in one strong, sure voice.

6 and 7 October 1940

Travel

Good evening. During the last two weeks I have been doing some travelling, in order to obtain new material for my talks to you. So I think that tonight I will give you a picture – as truthful and frank as I can make it – of what it is like travelling in England at the present time. I have used both the railways and the road on my travels. We'll begin with the railways.

Here, conditions vary a great deal. For example, on one or two slow cross-country train journeys, I have been very late indeed, not so much because of air raids but rather because of normal wartime circumstances, such as the demands of the military and the fact that the railways, being short-handed, tend to hold up their slow trains longer than usual while luggage, milk cans, parcels etc. are being unloaded at the small stations. On the other hand, many of the long-distance trains and expresses are running almost to time. Thus my train from London to Leeds, an enormous train, was only about thirty-five minutes late, and this was only because there was an air raid just after we left London and so the train had to slow down for the first part of its journey and so lost half an hour. The trains are mostly very crowded, of course, just as they were in the last war, but this is chiefly because enormous numbers of men in the services are always on the move, and loaded as they are with kit, they seem, poor fellows, to take up twice as much room as ordinary passengers. But except temporarily in places that have just been heavily bombed, there is no real dislocation of rail traffic. The kind of inconvenience you meet with is only what you might expect in peacetime during a holiday period. Nobody's going to pretend it's enjoyable travelling by train now, but I can say honestly – and I speak as a man who detests waiting about and slow crowded journeys – I've always found it rather better than I expected it to be. By the way, I don't know if anybody has already told you how splendid the behaviour of our railwaymen has been, but even if they have, there's no harm in mentioning it again. Some of these drivers and stokers and shunters who've carried on through raid after raid have been real heroes.

Travelling by road, of course, is much easier – at least, by day – than it is normally in this over-crowded island. At night, during the black-out and with only dim side-lights allowed, it's no joke at all, and is to be avoided at all costs, for you have to crawl along – though everywhere at night you hear the Army and Air Force lorries thundering through towns at what sounds like an incredibly high speed – and then again, unless you know your route very well, you can easily lose yourself. Remember, there is now not a single signpost or any other identification mark of the kind left in this country. The Germans once announced that that didn't matter to them because they'd plenty of good maps of this country, to which I can only retort that so have we and that this is our own country and even then we get lost. The other night I was travelling with a BBC recording van, and although the driver was a very experienced traveller, it was a dark wet night and we imagined we were in one town when all the time we were actually in another, fifty miles away. But the real trouble about road travel is, of course, the severe rationing of petrol – gasoline to some of you – to the civilian. I don't think there's any shortage of petrol in the country, for the Army and Air Force seem to splash it about as if it were mere water and must use a fantastic amount – at least so it seems to us civilians, wondering how best to use our poor little ration of this vital juice. Between ourselves, I think it would be no bad thing if the Army and Air

Force used a little less and the civilian was allowed a little more.

Soldiers are everywhere. No matter where you go, there they are, with all their extraordinary camouflaged vehicles of every kind. People can't get used to the idea that the whole country is crammed with troops, and have a naïve habit of assuming that their particular district has more than any other, not realising that almost every district is the same, swarming with khaki-clad men, noisy with armoured cars, bristling with guns. And all of them ready and eager for action. How in the name of Von Moltke the German General Staff ever imagined that even if they could land half a million men and their equipment, which would in itself be a terrific feat, these same half-million would ever set about conquering this country, with several million angry armed men ready to fight for every inch of ground, is a mystery to me. Unless, of course, which is what I suspect, they imagined that they could work some of the tricks they worked in France all over again – Fifth Column, wild rumours, panic, stampedes of refugees – which they certainly won't. They'll have to fight here, for every yard of ground, and won't succeed by performing conjuring tricks.

It is the presence of this enormous and rapidly growing army, the like of which we have never seen before in this island, that complicates travelling, for the military have commandeered so many buildings everywhere, including hotels; though with hotels they were forestalled – and a little too thoroughly for my taste – by the civil servants, who at the beginning of the war requisitioned hotels right and left. My great grumble is that they had a nasty habit of singling out those hotels where I remembered having some decent food and a reasonable standard of comfort – and you all know what our hotels tend to be like (no wonder we're considered a tough and hardy race!) – and using them not as hotels but as office buildings. Certainly the main problem of the traveller now is not transport but accommodation, for with at least half the hotels taken over by the military or the civil authorities, and with boarding houses and lodging houses either used as billets for evacuees or filled, in the safer areas, with resident guests, the traveller has to take what he can find, and often is lucky if he can find anything. This is especially true of the places that were inland resorts before the war, and of all those pleasanter areas far removed from the industrial centres and therefore reasonably free of raids. I have only caught a glimpse of one or two of them but can quite believe that they are all packed to the roof. My own job, of course, takes me to the large industrial cities, and here I have always been able to find a decent room in one of the larger hotels, though of course I have had to pay handsomely for it – out of my own pocket too, alas! – for I still go about as a private person, which means I can say what I like, and not as a government employee with an official expense sheet.

Now, what about food? I need hardly tell most of you, for you probably know I am a comfortably sized man – though the overseas listener who wrote to say she would like to fling her arms round my fat neck was, I think, carried away from accuracy by her enthusiasm – but, I repeat, I need hardly tell most of you that I am not a man who is indifferent to his food. I'm definitely not one of those insufferable people who say they hardly know what they're eating. I know what I'm eating – except when I've made a bad mistake in the restaurant – and if I don't like what I'm eating, other people soon know about it too. So, what about food these days? Well, I'm not going to pretend that I enjoy food as much as I used to do, but that's chiefly because I'm neither living at home nor eating at the same excellent restaurants. I can't honestly say, however, that the quality of food I found on my recent travels seemed worse than usual. There might have been rather less choice of dishes than there used to be in peacetime. It is possible too that there's rather less quantity than there used to be, but then there used to be too much – I'm speaking now of the rather more expensive provincial hotels, where people seemed to sit about eating all day. But there's certainly always been as much as I wanted, and generally rather more than I wanted. And though I believe housewives in the big provincial towns have to restrict their choice of some foods – especially meat – so that this week there will be a lot of beef, and next week hardly anything but mutton, and so forth – all the provision shops I saw seemed to be crammed with good eatable stuff, and, unlike the last war, there is little sign yet of any shortage of such luxury foods as chocolate, of which the British people are inordinately fond. There can be no doubt that the Ministry of Food, under the command of that super-shopkeeper Lord Woolton, has done an exceedingly good job of work. Incidentally, though we are all provided with ration cards, which we are supposed to take with us wherever we go, I have never yet taken mine on my travels and could not say at this moment where it is.

And if there is no shortage of food, there is certainly no shortage of drink and tobacco. I don't mean by that that we're all getting drunk and giving ourselves smokers' heart, but there is a tendency, very understandable, I think, for people to get together during these strange grim times and try to be convivial. And as the government duties on drink and tobacco are now colossal, we may be said to be making a good contribution towards our war effort even during our hours of relaxation. Some other forms of relaxation are, of course, very difficult now. Theatres and cinemas are still open everywhere, however, though most of them close very early in order that their patrons shall not be badly held up if there should be a raid on the way home. I paid a call, the other day, on the largest bookseller in the north of England, fully expecting him to declare that business in books had ceased to exist. But, on the contrary, he told me that business was not at all bad, was in fact quite brisk, and what I saw while I was there confirmed this statement, for people were going in and out all the time and books being briskly sold. The chief trouble, he said, were inevitable delays in transport, which meant that a great many orders could not be fulfilled at once. Then again, a Sunday afternoon orchestral concert in a northern industrial town, which I attended because I had to make a short speech, filled the largest motion picture theatre in the city and must have been attended by over 2,000 people. There will necessarily have to be some re-organisation of recreation and entertainment if the raids continue during the darker months, but I have great hopes that this can be done on a large scale, for the people themselves refuse to settle down to a grey monotony of wartime life, are determined wherever possible to have a bit of fun – bless them! – and to keep going as normally as possible.

And now, finally, for the air raids and their damage. I have seen a good deal of this damage, and have also been in some more raids in various parts of the country, but what I have not seen anywhere is any evidence whatever of any large-scale devastation of our essential industries. Please take my word for this. Time after time I would see factory after factory whose work was vital to us that had never yet heard the sound of a bomb, and the sight of a damaged aerodrome or munitions works or war factory was a complete rarity. On the other hand, time after time I would see signs of air-raid damage in some residential suburb, a chapel torn in half, a few workmen's cottages destroyed, a shop or two blown apart. Which proves that this blitzkrieg so far has failed on both counts, not having held up our war production and having completely failed to break the civilian morale. And now I must plan further journeys for you. Goodnight.

10 and 11 October 1940

Manchester

I am talking to you tonight from Lancashire, and from that part of Lancashire that is the home of the cotton trade. This is a trade, as most of you know, that has seen some very dramatic changes of fortune. After the last war it swung upward on a colossal and highly dangerous boom, became the centre of wild speculation, its shares being manipulated by people who wouldn't have known a bale of cotton if they'd ever seen one – with the inevitable result that when the slump came, the whole gigantic bubble burst. Meanwhile, much of the Eastern trade vanished, and on this Eastern trade whole towns in Lancashire depended. India, with an unlimited supply of labour, began to manufacture her own cotton goods. And Japan, of course, came into the picture. They came to Lancashire. They learned how to card, spin and weave cotton in technical schools here, at the expense of the Lancashire taxpayer, whose livelihood they soon began to take away, when they went back to turn out vast quantities of inferior cotton goods at cheap prices. I would ask my listeners to consider, before they buy such goods, whether they are anxious to make an offering to Japan's war chest, for that is really what such purchases amount to.

I was brought up in a part of England that manufactures woollen cloth, and so I know, roughly, how the trick is done with wool. But until yesterday I could never imagine how the trick is done with cotton, how these short, dry, fluffy threads of vegetable fibre are somehow spun and woven into all manner of strong, enduring fabrics, from the heaviest, toughest canvas – like some I saw being manufactured for naval hammocks and gun covers – to the finest little pocket handkerchiefs. But yesterday I was given a day's education in the textile trade. I was marched through what seemed miles of sheds, all of them trembling and roaring from the multitude of whirling bales, and there I saw the cotton being cleaned, then carded, then drawn – to make the threads in the slivers more even – then put on roving frames, then put through ring spinning, then wound from hanks to bobbins, then engaged in intricacies of warps and wefts, with looms that had women looking after them and other looms that appeared to work away, at full speed, entirely on their own. I could make a good shot at describing many of these processes as they were described, with Lancashire thoroughness, to me, but I am a merciful man and will refrain.

What is important is that at the end of these processes, and out of all these extraordinary long noisy sheds, slightly misty at times because of the tiny pieces of cotton in the air, there came the most astonishing variety of materials. It was like a gigantic conjuring trick, like a large-scale version of one of those magic hats out of which the conjurer produces a rabbit, a dozen eggs, masses of paper flowers, a string of flags. Take the government orders alone. They were a kind of comment, in cotton, on the extent, scope, variety of our vast war effort. There were the heavy canvases for hammocks, gun coverings and various kinds of equipment. There was shimmering fabric that would afterwards find its way into our balloon barrage. There was strange stuff that after fantastic treatment would become part of war planes. There was light khaki drill for our armies in the desert. There was a delightful fine blue shirting for the lads in the Royal Air Force. There was an equally delightful fine khaki shirting for the girls of the Auxiliary Territorial services, who serve as cooks, waitresses, clerks etc., with the Army at home. There was stuff for camouflage purposes.

So it went on, until one's mind reeled, and one remembered, with a shudder, how much the war is costing us. In order to help to pay that cost, we must export as much as we can, so that these factories, no matter how great the various government orders, must still continue producing their most successful lines of peacetime merchandise, so that the world can still buy British goods of the highest quality. And may I add that there could hardly be an easier and more practical way of showing sympathy for our cause, of giving some expression to the world-wide admiration of the really magnificent courage and endurance of our ordinary folk, than to insist that at least some proportion of your purchases should consist of the goods we are trying to export to you. We are still, as Napoleon described us, a nation of shopkeepers, but please remember that in that shop we still keep there are more things than goods to sell and cash registers and ledgers: there is defiance to all tyranny, there is love of liberty, there is hope for all struggling mankind. So I do not hesitate to appeal to you to pay a visit now and again to our shop. The wares it sells are still as good as ever.

I went from top to bottom, down about eight enormous floors, in a great Manchester cotton goods warehouse, where this fluffy white stuff that comes in bales along the Ship Canal from the ends of the earth now appeared as a bewildering assortment of materials – velveteens and tapestries for the furnishing trade, flannelettes for the nurseries, sheets and blankets and bedspreads, shirting and pyjama fabrics for men's wear, all those black and coloured linings that tailors sew into our coats and that we hardly ever notice, lingerie and dress wear – and here I watched the designers working out new and amusing ideas, and thought what an amusing job they had of it – every possible kind of handkerchief, every kind of light drill material for tropical suits, gaberdine for rain coats, heavy rubberised cloths for various industrial purposes, and so on and so forth. I was even initiated into the mystery of corset cloths, which were pink and brocaded and very feminine and seemed to have nothing whatever to do with the sturdy Manchester business men who had them spread out on the counter before me. And I will whisper a secret to you. So great are the government orders that it is doubtful if it will be possible to manufacture anything like the usual quantity of these corset cloths, so that if, in a year's time, middle-aged ladies in this island appear to have a – shall we say – more majestic outline than they formerly had, this will not be because they have been over-eating but because – well, there may possibly be a temporary shortage of corset cloths in this island as everything must go overseas. Which shows you, if you didn't know it already, how interdependent we all are, how the world is really one vast organisation. It is our tragedy that we still refuse to recognise this fact, and so suffer accordingly.

These Lancashire cotton factories are now working at such full pressure that they need all the work people – chiefly women and girls for the spinning frames and looms – that they can find. Many of them live twenty or thirty miles away from the factories and are brought to work and then taken home again in buses provided by the firms that employ them. I was talking yesterday morning to a pretty little girl of about eighteen who came and went from her work in this rather lordly fashion, very different from the hurried run to the mill, just after dawn, in clogs and shawl, of the factory girls I remember from my boyhood. I asked this girl, idly, where she had spent most of her life, and was astonished when she replied, 'New York.' It seemed that up to five years ago she had lived in America, and then her parents had returned to Lancashire – a very unusual move, this, I must confess – and now here she was. She didn't hesitate to add that after the war she was all for returning to the United States, and I don't know that I blame her, for working girls of her type still have a much better time overseas than they do here, though some of us hope – and indeed are determined – to change that, as well as a good many other things.

Another young woman I spoke to was older and indeed was married, though I suppose she must have been still in her early twenties. Her husband was a house painter and decorator, and they have a baby of eleven months who is cared for during the working days by his grandmother, who, I have no doubt, is now busy thoroughly spoiling him. This young woman had just stopped work – for it was the midday break – and was settling down, between her machines, to eat the lunch she had brought with her and also to indulge her feminine imagination in the raptures of a paper-backed novel called *Sands of Love*, which had a brightly coloured cover, showing some impossibly handsome characters against a desert background, characters who no doubt were wearing some of the fine white drill made in that very factory. She was very happy with her job, which probably earned as much as her husband's work, with the thought of that magnificent baby, and now with her lunch and the staggering passions of *Sands of Love*. Yet just round the corner were the air-raid shelters, concrete tunnels beneath the ground, where at any moment she might have to take refuge from the bombs. And indeed, not very far away, for I passed them going and coming away from this factory, were signs of a recent raid, a wrecked tavern and several ruined little houses, the usual indications of how carefully Goering's air force has been trained in its military objectives. Some of these work people have been bombed clean out of their houses, but they stoutly refuse to leave the neighbourhood, not because of their work, for they would still have that, but because of some deep feeling of local attachment. And so they spend their nights in air-raid shelters nearby, and make use of the houses of relatives in the district for meals and other purposes.

If this seems fantastic to you, I can only add that I am more or less living the same kind of life myself, for though I started this war the proud owner of two beautiful old houses, one in the country and one in London, now I have the use of neither, for the government requisitioned the one in the country, and the one in London, which recently had many of its windows blown out, has only a small air-raid shelter in the basement and into this we put an evacuated family, and naturally I can't turn them out on my recent occasional visits back to London, so really I haven't a place of my own at the moment, and – so to speak – live in a suitcase – and a very expensive life it is too, let me tell you, worse than the most extravagant form of housekeeping – with the family scattered across the country.

Fortunately, I am not a person with strong attachment to a locality. I am used to wandering about, and rather like it. But a great many of our working folk have this extraordinary strong attachment to the neighbourhood where they have spent most of their lives, and this has created one of our most difficult temporary problems, for such people, though they have been bombed over and over again, simply refuse to be evacuated to safer areas, and cling like cats – and that's a good simile – because I've often noticed cats haunting the ruins of houses that they still consider their homes – to the neighbourhood of their choice, where every stick and stone is familiar and friends are abundant. But though this creates a difficult problem for our Ministry of Health, who want to get such people away, I think it helps to explain why the German Air Force, which is nothing but a vast terror weapon invented by pitiless bullies, has for the first time failed, striking a rock, the rock of British character. And the Lancashire folk, who have always been – in Churchill's phrase – 'grim and gay', have character enough and to spare. Goodnight.

18 and 19 October 1940

Blackpool

They were quite right when they said I must not leave Lancashire without paying a visit to Blackpool. Now, some of you who are listening probably know Blackpool better than I do, but for the benefit of some of the others, I'd better explain that Blackpool, which is situated on a flat, bleak part of the Lancashire coast, is the most popular seaside resort in this country. It has been known to deal with half a million visitors in a day. It's the English equivalent of Coney Island. There is absolutely no natural beauty whatever in Blackpool and its immediate neighbourhood, so the town has always concentrated on providing its visitors with the maximum amount of amusement, which includes, at the height of the season, a gigantic fun fair, three piers, a famous circus, many different vaudeville shows, dancing on a vast scale under the well-known tower and at the Winter Gardens, music of all kinds, and all manner of genial nonsense. Blackpool is the favourite holiday town of the North Country working people, though it's by no means confined to them.

I've known it all my life. The last time I was here was during the Munich crisis, when I came here because I was trying out a new comedy. It was Illuminations Week in Blackpool, I remember, and we did enormous business at the theatre, but I also remember that I hated it all – I hated the illuminations, I hated the town, and above all I hated the Munich settlement. But what a difference then and now! That week the promenade for miles was nothing but an endless glitter of lights, the very street cars flashing and glowing with coloured lighting. Now, the whole length of that promenade – and I believe there's about eight miles of it – is in darkness. On the other hand, the spirit of the place is anything but subdued. War or no war, Blackpool is Blackpool still, I'm delighted to say.

It may have lost most of its usual holiday-makers, but in their place it has new – and more interesting – types of guests, for the boarding house accommodation of this giant among seaside towns has been put to good use. It is now, in fact, the very oddest mixture. For example, it has many civil servants still here, though nothing like as many as it had. I have a feeling that the civil service, which is not inclined to be hearty and democratic, and Blackpool, which is very hearty and democratic, don't make a perfect match. The Blackpool landladies, who are lavish with their food but not with their bedroom and sitting-room space, couldn't understand why these haughty people from London wanted so much room to themselves, and suspected this exclusiveness.

Much more popular guests are the many lads in the Royal Air Force who swarm into the town whenever they can get enough leave – and a fine time they have of it too. To begin with, the Blackpool caterers and landladies take a pride – at once professional and Lancashire – in keeping a generous table. Then they're in what is probably the healthiest town in England, swinging along a promenade swept by bracing sea breezes. Then everything possible is done to make them welcome. Then the town provides them with innumerable clubs and canteens, and in addition allows all these men of the services admission into all the theatres, vaudeville shows, dance halls etc. at half price. For a few pennies, a man can have a long gorgeous evening's amusement. Good lord! – if I'd been stationed here as an Army recruit, twenty-six years ago, I'd have thought I'd been sent to Paradise.

But not all the airmen here in Blackpool are British, for Blackpool attracts large numbers of visitors also from among men of the Allied Air Forces who are now in this country. They also are welcome, all of them, but the special favourites seem to be the Poles, who in their turn obviously regard Blackpool as their special favourite. Many of these men reached this country after incredible adventures in Poland and then in France. I couldn't help thinking, while I was talking to some Polish officers yesterday, how widely incongruous and unexpected all this was – that Blackpool of all places should now have as visitors men from Warsaw and Krakow, from the shores of the Baltic and the banks of the Vistula! They are a fine lot of men, those Poles, as gallant and dashing in the air as they are when they are amusing themselves on the ground. And that is saying a good deal, because there can be no doubt that, to the delight of the visiting comedians, who now find a whole series of jokes ready-made for them, these Polish airmen, members of an ardent and amorous nation, have played havoc among the more susceptible young women of Blackpool, who have undertaken the rather dangerous task of teaching them English with great enthusiasm. Last night, I looked in at one crowded vaudeville show, where one of London's favourite comedians, Bud Flanagan, was appearing. Bud announced to his partner that he proposed to pop off and pick up a nice girl. His partner said that no girl in her senses would want to have anything to do with him. 'Ah, but you see,' said Bud, a grin lighting up his mournfully droll face, as he showed us what he'd been hiding behind his back, 'I'm all right. I've got a Polish cap.' And there was a tremendous roar from the packed house. That shows the sort of welcome the gallant Poles have from this large-hearted Blackpool.

Then, in addition to these visitors of the fighting services, there are thousands of evacuated women and children here. This does not leave much room for ordinary visitors, who come in search of bracing winds and quiet nights, but there are as many as can be accommodated, and it is now hard work finding a bed in Blackpool.

I gather too that a great many vaudeville people now make Blackpool their headquarters. As well they might, for it seems at the present moment to be Britain's number one entertainment town. Last night, the manager of the town's amusements took me with him on a quick conducted tour of them, and I found one star after another playing to the crowded houses.

At one theatre we visited, the Grand, one of New York's favourite comediennes, Beatrice Lilley, was delighting a huge audience with her sly and perfectly timed drolleries. I had a word with Miss Lilley afterwards, and asked her why she – who, by the way, was paying her first visit to Blackpool – had stayed on in England when she must have had many tempting offers from New York and Hollywood. And I liked her reply: 'Well, one just couldn't leave, could one? I wouldn't like to be anywhere else now, though I love America.' And that, you'll agree is the spirit.

Then we went on to a huge vaudeville theatre, the Palace, to see the final item – the comedians – in a variety show, and I must confess that although the comedians were very good, it was the great audience, balcony upon balcony, that I watched from my box. They were all roaring with laughter, but I wasn't. To tell you the truth, I felt strangely and deeply moved, partly because the sight of such an audience has been so rare lately, and reminded me of happier times – after all, I'm a bit of a showman myself, you know – but also because there is a kind of innocence about a great crowd enjoying itself, a suggestion of a universal childlike quality in us all, and suddenly to discover this again, embedded in the horrors and miseries of this war, seemed to me very moving. One of the comedians gave a wonderful impersonation of an oldish Lancashire women gossiping to her neighbour over the garden wall, and during this gossip he kept pretending to be annoyed with some children, and in one of his sudden shouts to them cried, 'Now put that shrapnel down,' which brought a roar from the audience. And I thought how strangely our lives had been shaped that we could find it funny that our children should be playing with shrapnel. Death comes roaring from the skies at night, and then in the morning the children are playing with what remains of the recent menace.

Curiously enough, this same comedian, whom I ran into later, had with him a bit of shrapnel – though 'casing' would be a more accurate term for it – that had penetrated the roof of his car and hit him on the shoulder only a few nights ago, outside another city. All these entertainers are working desperately hard, not merely in their particular shows, but also travelling at all manner of hours to charity concerts or entertainments for the fighting men. The two-star comics of the evening, Flanagan and Allen, told me that in a week or two they are taking a fortnight off from their tour to return to London specially to amuse the folk in the air-raid shelters. And that, you'll admit, is the right spirit too.

I found when I received my bill at the hotel this morning that Blackpool's boast that it did not allow war profiteering was no idle one, for although the demand for rooms at this particular hotel is so great that I'm sure I would never have found a bed in it if I hadn't been doing a semi-official job in connection with the town and strings hadn't been pulled, yet there had been no attempt to make capital out of this situation. My bill was no more than it would have been at any time, very reasonable indeed. I wish I could say as much about all parts of the country – but certainly in Blackpool they are trying not to take advantage of the war, and to give the visitor a square deal. But then Blackpool is a hearty democratic resort – none of your snobbish nonsense about being 'exclusive' there – that has always catered chiefly for the working folk, who were dancing in the great ballrooms of the Tower and Winter Gardens long before dance palaces sprang up everywhere, and so it is taking care to behave in a sensible, hearty, hospitable, democratic fashion.

My only complaint – and this is not the town's fault, but rather its misfortune – is that so much of the town's accommodation has been taken over that not enough is left for the general public, many of whom could do with a week of its bracing air, long wide promenades and huge amusement palaces. In fact, I could do with a week or two of them myself, but no such luck. Still, it was good to catch a glimpse of such an old friend. Which reminds me that on Sunday I want to talk to my friend Harvey Mott, newspaperman of Phoenix, Arizona. And will somebody tell him, please? Goodnight.

20 and 21 October 1940

Our War Is Yours

As I promised at the end of my talk on Thursday, tonight I am talking to my friend Harvey Mott, editor of the *Arizona Republic*, of Phoenix, Arizona. But though it's his talk, of course you can all listen in. Well now, Mr. Mott, I'll explain how I came to get on to you. Sophie Burden – you know, Jack's wife out at Remuda Ranch – recently wrote a fine long letter to my wife, telling her all that had been happening at the ranch, and in this letter she enclosed a newspaper cutting, which my wife sent on to me. It was your column 'An Arizona Bookshelf', and in it you wrote about the interview I gave you, out at Jack's ranch, five years ago, and how I was now doing these short-wave broadcasts to America, and how right I'd been in what I'd said five years ago – and by thunder, I was, wasn't I? I was surprised to see how right I'd been – and how everybody ought to listen to me.

Now, I've had the luck lately to have had a good many bouquets thrown at me – and some things that weren't bouquets too, of course – but nothing that's come my way lately has pleased me as much as this column of yours, this bouquet of desert flowers, straight from Phoenix, Arizona. And that's the truth. As I read your column, the 6,000 miles between us dwindled to nothing, and I was back again in the desert, with the clear blue of your sky above me, the fantastic ranges of amethyst and lilac mountains along the horizon, and the diamond light of the south-west twinkling in my eyes. Don't think I haven't missed coming back this past winter.

And as for my family, well, you remember what they thought about Arizona. Some kind correspondent sent me a copy, the other week, of the last *Arizona Highway*, with some grand photographs of many desert roads we knew, and I happened to be visiting the children at school just then, and we all looked at these photographs as if we could have eaten them. But of course we've got to be here. I might have sent the children out. Jack and Sophie up at the ranch have implored us to send them out – as many of our American friends have done – but we felt it would be difficult to split up the family, and also, if there was no big general evacuation scheme, we didn't feel that our own children should leave the country.

I believe if you were here, you'd feel as we do. In fact, if you were here, you'd feel about everything more or less as we do. And I believe you'd behave as we do. You know, there really isn't an awful lot of difference between us. You'd call yourself, I imagine, a fairly typical American, and a lot of people call me a fairly typical Englishman. Well, we got on all right, didn't we, when we used to have our talks out at Jack Burden's ranch, just yarning away with plenty of tobacco about and perhaps a drink or two in front us? Nothing I said in that interview five years ago gave you a very terrible shock, did it? You didn't feel that here was a man who looked at life from an altogether different point of view from your own? Of course you didn't. And I believe that you and I represent our two publics pretty well. It's taken this terrific tragedy – for however necessary this war is to fight to the end, it must remain a tragedy – to show us how fundamentally alike we are, not in the show our respective governments make but in the attitudes and behaviour of our two peoples. So I feel at this moment – and I'd still have felt it if I hadn't read your grand column – that there isn't a twist and turn of this war that you people, 6,000 miles away in Arizona, aren't following with your minds and hearts. And that's fine. That's as it should be. If you were in the same tough spot, I hope – and believe – we'd be doing the same thing.

Well, you know how things are here. We've just done something to the Nazis that they thought nobody could do to them, and that is to put them back a little bit further than where they started from, and to write FINIS in large letters across their plan. You'll admit, I know, because you're a fair man, that most of you over there didn't believe that this would happen – and indeed some of you, last June and July, began to think that all was over with us; and it was very much part of my job to point out that one factor not understood by the German General Staff had hardly come into play yet – and that was the character of the ordinary British people. I knew the faults of my own people – I ought to, I've attacked them often enough – but I also knew that until events had shredded away their customary apathy and laziness, these people hadn't yet shown themselves to the world. As Chesterton sang in his poem 'The Secret People':

For we are the people of England; who never have spoken yet
Smile at us, pay us, pass us. But do not quite forget.

Now, this poem by a great democrat can be quoted at this hour because during the last few months a great change has come over this country. When Nazi Germany, contemptuous of all rules of warfare, swept away the neutrality of the small

Western European states, a neutrality that we had respected to our own peril, and over-ran them with dive-bombers, tanks and guns, blasting all opposition out of the way, something even more important was happening in Britain. The people were being really brought into the war. Suddenly the government was immensely enlarged in its representation. Men like Ernest Bevin were given key positions. A great new source of power and energy was tapped.

It is typical of the stupidity that lies only a little way beneath the superficial cleverness of the Nazis that they never realised what was happening, and that their propaganda, which is rapidly becoming less and less effective, went on hammering away at the same old points, never noticing that the Britain they were trying to undermine was a quite different Britain. I want you to take my word for this, and I think I'm as much in touch with ordinary public opinion as any man. This is a *new* Britain. The people have awakened and are showing themselves now in their true colours. Do you remember some articles I wrote, months and months before the war began – they were quoted in the *Reader's Digest*, so you may have seen them – called *Wake Up, Britain*? Well, it's happened. The people are awake.

You might say, 'There's nothing surprising about that, seeing that you've had all Goering's air force blitzkrieging you.' But the awakening came before that. It had happened by the time that the Nazi propaganda machine began screaming its threats at us, telling us what was going to happen to us when the invasion had succeeded. These threats, of course, as I could have told them, only helped the awakening. The people said, 'All right, come on then. Let's see what you can do.' Then the immense air attack began. You know all about that, how the Nazi air force tried to destroy our fighter defence, and lamentably failed, only losing an immense number of machines and trained men.

Then, with typical German stupidity – for I maintain that, fundamentally, these Germans are stupid – they decided that they could achieve their aim by bombing London on a huge and quite indiscriminate scale. We've taken, of course, a lot of punishment, and nobody is going to pretend that life in London just now is as pleasant as it is in Phoenix, Arizona. But unless this incessant wild bombardment of villas, flats, churches, hospitals, shops, theatres succeeded in completely breaking down the morale of the people, it was clearly a waste of time and trouble and valuable ammunition, for if you are busy bombing civilians and their dwelling houses and amusement places, you cannot at the same time be equally busy bombing important military objectives. The result was that although our civilians, especially the citizens of London, have gone through a trying time – and I'd be the last to under-estimate the demands it made upon their courage and endurance – our war effort remained unchecked, and our plans to carry this air war into Germany and make the Nazis rue the day they ever thought of bombing have been going forward, a fact that the Nazis have secretly acknowledged, if we may judge from their hasty change of plans, their hurried conferences, the confusion that can be seen in their propaganda.

And at the same time, repeating their old mistake, they decide that American opinion does not matter, that American help cannot possibly be in time, and so do everything calculated to enlist your sympathies on our side. I needn't tell you, for you've had all the news, what a wonderful stand these ordinary folk of London have made, but as you are a newspaperman I'd like to tell you what a grand job our newspapermen have done throughout this blitzkrieg, keeping going all the time so that every morning there on our tables were the morning papers and every noon there were the early editions of the evening papers on the streets. I was delighted to see that a tribute has just been paid to our newspapermen by your own trade journal, the *Editor and Publisher*, which says: 'The high courage and fine spirit shown by London newspaper workers in their determination to exercise and maintain a free press deserves and receives the highest admiration of every American newspaperman.' And when the whole story comes to be told, the same tribute of admiration will have to be paid to our radio people here, who have carried on, never missing a minute in all the various complicated programmes – and remember, we broadcast here in no less than twenty-three different languages – whatever may be happening here.

So there it is. Goering played his ace, and it was trumped. I'm not going to talk to you about the present strategical position, or to show you how our own blockade continues whereas the attempted German blockade of this country never could come into being, or how we are now building up both here and overseas a vast air force that will end by wrecking the whole vast German war machine. You hear enough about all that. I think my job is to tell you the things I have special knowledge of myself, and those are the things that our ordinary folk here feel and think. I don't pretend to be a strategist or a war expert, but I do know our public here, and I can speak about them with knowledge and confidence. And what I say is this – that what the majority of our people are determined to do is not only to put an end once and for all to this Nazi and Fascist menace, which is simply the equivalent in international affairs of the gangsterism and racketeering that some of your cities have known, but also to show the world that democracy is not a form of government that has been tried here, there and everywhere and that has failed, but a gigantic creative force that needs another great release and is about to have it. We were told for years and years that democracy was hopeless and that we people who still clung to that peculiar outmoded form of government were obviously decadent and effete. You don't hear much of that talk now, for even the Germans are compelled to admit that the people of this island are about as tough as they come, and they are now pretending that they never said anything else and that any successful attack upon us will be a long, tough job. Now, apart from the fact that in the long run our security is yours, there is this: that both your people and mine believe that the twin problems of liberty and security can be solved through democracy, which is not ending its course but just beginning, and that the successful defiance of this huge challenge to all the values we live by will result in both our peoples marching forward to greater triumphs, not of conquest but of full, happy living. And I wish we could drink to it. Goodnight.

22 October 1940

The Spirit of Britain

You might call this talk 'The Two Faces'. The story begins early yesterday morning. I spoke to you – from London – at two-thirty in the morning, and a most unpleasant hour it is to talk to anybody. I slept badly after that, and by six o'clock was thoroughly awake. So I shaved and dressed, took a hot drink and then went out. It was light, but only just, and the beginning of a raw misty morning. The night's raiders had been gone for some time. It was all clear, but as yet with nothing very clear about it. I went wandering round the West End, for I had been away for a week or two and wanted to see what damage had been done since. Already, the men who sell newspapers were at their posts – and I think I can call them 'posts' in the military fashion, because this area is not unlike a battlefield. And please note that never once, throughout this blitzkrieg, have the newspapers failed us. They've always been there, every morning.

There was a cheerful light coming from the milk bars, where people were ordering early breakfasts or warming up with a cup of hot coffee. A few people – chiefly, I noticed, young couples, with the girls always in trousers – came yawning out of shelters, with rugs or blankets over their arms. The men looked a bit greenish in the cold morning light, and the faces of the girls – bless them! – yes, I'm sentimental about our girls, now that I've seen how they can take all this – I say, the faces of the girls had that small crumpled look which follows a night of uneasy dozing. But they were all cheerful, and mostly chattering away. What a love story somebody could write of these air-raid days and nights! Who will give us the Romeo and Juliet of the blitzkrieg?

Already, the buses were taking their loads of early workers to warehouses and offices. The ARP people – wardens, firemen and the rest – were going home. The policemen were all in their places at crossings, as massive and imperturbable as ever. As a cold light came filtering through the mists of autumnal dawn, I walked down one familiar street after another, looking at the fabric of buildings at each side as one might look at the face of a friend stricken and ravaged by disease. At one moment, passing a section that had been left untouched, I would wonder at seeing almost no signs of the city's ordeal. At another moment I would stare in horror and dismay at the wreckage, at buildings – though they might be only shops or restaurants – famous for generations that were now heaps of rubble or burnt-out blackened shells.

Perhaps because I have worked so often in the theatre, I

found the theatres most pathetic witnesses to this new madness that has been launched on the world. One theatre I knew well and liked – for a play of my own had run successfully there – had had a direct hit, and you can – as I did – stare through the front entrance, over the great heaps of mournful debris, into what is left of the auditorium, still catching a glimpse among all that wreck and ruin of the plush and gilt that had known so many happy evenings.

Perhaps even more moving was a corner of Soho that had been very badly knocked about, with little restaurants and cafés and shops selling foreign produce all obliterated or buried under great heaps of charred rubbish. You all know something about Soho, which has long been London's chief foreign and bohemian quarter. It is not a region I have seen a great deal of during these last years, but there was a time when I spent many of my evenings there, for it has been for several generations now the favourite haunt, for inexpensive dining and wining, of the young writers, artists, musicians, actors, journalists, who haven't much money to spend and have sweethearts or young wives to take out to dinner – perhaps celebrating some long-looked-for success – so that there are few of us who haven't a thousand tantalising happy memories of this quarter; who don't remember those mysterious five-course dinners at half a crown that we used to grapple with there; and the bottles of wine, of strange vintages, that we used to send out for and then get gay on, though I think the gaiety came bubbling out of youthful hearts and not out of those dubious bottles. And side by side with the little French, Italian and Swiss restaurants were the shops that offered you things to eat and drink and smoke that reminded you of the occasional holidays you'd had abroad; and when you'd made a bit more money, and could afford to launch out a little, then perhaps you'd decide to give a party or two and would visit one of these shops to buy exotic eatables and drinkables to give a cosmopolitan air to your entertainment.

Well, of course, most of those restaurants, cafés and shops are still there, but I did strike one corner of the quarter where they weren't there, where there were only fragments of walls, heaps of rubble, broken beams, all the obscene debris that comes out of an air raid, and I think I felt as moved by this spectacle as any I had seen in this war, if only because this corner of Soho had been so unoffending, so easy and gay in its own cosmopolitan fashion, and awakened so many memories of my early life in London. The melancholy sight seemed almost symbolic of what these madmen – for madmen they are, in their insane lust for power, their cruelty, their lack of all those qualities that enable men to live harmoniously together – had let loose on this suffering world, bringing ruin and destruction, desolation and death, on innocent hard-working pleasant folk that they had never seen, smashing through with their red-hot steel and explosives into a tiny distant world of harmless gaiety.

This mood lasted throughout my exploration of the battered West End, where nothing that has been hit – not one of the shops, the blocks of flats, the churches, the theatres and restaurants – can by the wildest stretch of imagination be considered a military target. All just terror bombing. So many louts, almost as crazy as their masters, sent high into the air with a cargo of explosives, to destroy and to murder just as they pleased, with the object of destroying not so much the body of London as its soul – that gay and defiant quality of the spirit that these bullies and cruelty-mongers can't understand. And the soul of London, which is a great and ancient city, the home of noble poets and famous lovers of liberty, remains indestructible, because it *is* a soul, a spirit shining through the scarred body.

A chill early Monday morning, especially to a man who has been working late and is short of sleep, is no time to indulge in mere whimsical fancifulness, so I think it was more than that which stirred my imagination into seeing this battered fabric of buildings as a kind of familiar well-loved old face, now scarred and ravaged but with its eyes bright with courage and unconquerable defiance, and I felt that I wanted to take that face gently between my hands and kiss the worn forehead.

So much for one face, which will never be forgotten while men love liberty and hate tyranny in this world. But there is another face, here in Britain, and it is not another face of suffering and defiance, but a huge iron face of calm determination, and on that face is written the doom of Hitler, Mussolini and all the screaming, roaring, chest-thumping rabble that follow their blood-stained banners. And I saw that face all yesterday, after I had left London, taking the train up here to Scotland, and running through 400 miles of our countryside. Along this route, which passes through one great industrial region after another, you see no trace of bombing. Goering's airmen have been too busy destroying shops and restaurants and blocks of flats and London churches and hospitals to devote much time to these districts. But they are devoting their time to *him*, and written in their smoke is the order for the extinction of him and his air force. For what do you see as the train reels off mile after mile? You catch one glimpse after another of Britain's industrial might; you see factory after factory after factory, workshop following workshop, all untouched, all working at full pressure, turning out still bigger bombing planes, still faster fighters, more and more quick-firing guns, big guns, tanks, munitions. And behind all this vast activity is a cold anger, which if I were a German and knew anything of the British people would keep me sweating at night. 'Beware the fury of a patient man,' said the poet. The British are a patient people. No other Europeans have their easy patience. They will stand, as few other people will, insult after insult, injury after injury, but once you have set your foot behind the mark of that patience – look out! – for their coats will come off like lightning, and then they will sail into you and fight and fight like bull-terriers.

We didn't want all this destruction from the air. Threatened by its evil lunacy, we made every possible effort to avoid it, so many efforts indeed that the whisper went round that we weren't the people we had been once, that we were rich and old and weary and so many easy-living cowards. So the Germans, who understand nothing and learn nothing and might as well be daydreaming on another planet, piled up the bombing planes, bragged and boasted and screamed louder than ever and made up their mind to be the world's gunmen and racketeers. In one morning, at Rotterdam, the city of their harmless and friendly neighbours the Dutch, they killed over 30,000 people by the foulest dive-bombing raids imaginable. Now, it seems, it is London's turn. But now, believe me, they have passed the mark of our patience, and from this time on, it is their turn, and it will not be long before they will wish, as many of them do already, that destruction from the air had never been heard of. They shall have such a dose of their medicine that they will be cured for ever. It is coming to them, and for all their boasts and screams and threats and swagger, they know in their hearts that it is coming to them, and that they can't stop it. The scarred face with the light in its eyes has looked at the vast iron face of industrial Britain, and that face has nodded and pronounced sentence on the destroyers and murderers. We know that we can take it. They know now that we can take it. But can they take it? Because – by thunder! – it's coming to them.

And now I want to read you a quotation, which by an odd chance I discovered among the hundred and one letters and papers I had to read in the train yesterday. Listen to this:

> *It is a gloomy moment in history. Not for many years – not in the lifetime of most men who read this – has there been so much grave and deep apprehension; never has the future seemed so incalculable as at this time. In France, the political cauldron seethes and bubbles with uncertainty; Russia hangs, as usual, like a cloud, dark and silent, upon the horizon of Europe; while all the energies, resources and influences of the British Empire are sorely tried, and are yet to be tried more sorely ... It is a solemn moment, and no man can feel an indifference (which, happily, no man pretends to feel) in the issues of events ... In time of peril we have nothing but manhood, strong in its faith in God, to rely upon, and whoever shows himself truly a God-fearing man now, by helping wherever and however he can, will be blessed and beloved as a great light in darkness...*

Well, that sounds timely and topical enough and might have been written this morning. But, oddly enough, it wasn't, but appeared in *Harper's Weekly* in this month of October in the year 1857. Which just shows you, doesn't it? Goodnight.

24 and 25 October 1940

Glasgow

And so to Glasgow, where I am at this moment. Glasgow is by no means the handsomest city in Scotland – it cannot compare with the really beautiful Edinburgh – but it's my favourite. I like the great sprawling smoky place. I like it because it is full of energy and industry and life and devilment, crammed with rich racy character and no genteel nonsense about it. The importance of this city to the country, to the whole British Commonwealth of Nations, indeed, to the cause of democracy in this world, can't be exaggerated. Go down one of those long – and, to be truthful, rather ugly – roads to the west of the city, and gradually you begin to hear a certain sound. It's as if something was throbbing in the air. It takes you some time to realise what this noise is, and then you remember that you are now on the banks of the Clyde. What you are hearing is the sound of the riveting in the ship-building yards of the Clyde, and they might be so many nails going into the coffins of the Nazi leaders. For ours is a Commonwealth based primarily on sea power, and the chief basis of that sea power are the ships built along here on the Clyde.

And don't imagine that the all-pervading sound of the riveting has lessened in wartime. On the contrary, it's louder and faster than ever, for more and more ships are being built here, and a huge army of skilled men are at work in these yards. There are, of course, miles and miles of them, and I couldn't begin to take you on even the shortest tour of them. Perhaps the most famous is John Brown's. I know this great yard; I went there to describe the launching of the *Queen Mary* – when it rained so hard that I ruined my only top hat and morning coat – and I remember that what fascinated me then was not the royal pageantry, impressive as it was, but the enthusiasm of the ship-building men themselves, the craftsmen, who recognised this great vessel to be a masterpiece. One of the chief difficulties was concerned with the colossal chains that had to take the strain as the vast hull went into the water, and I remember that as these chains paid out perfectly, without a single hitch, the men below raised a separate cheer for their foreman, who had fixed this difficult job. Yes, they're tough down there; they're always ready for an argument, and if you want to turn the argument into a fight, they are ready for that too; they drink not whisky *or* beer but whisky *and* beer – a 'pip and a pint', they call it; and they have a passion for association football, about which they'll argue day and night; and they haven't a glimmer of respect for grand personages of any kind; but they're real craftsmen, who respect the job they're doing and set about it manfully, with the result that there are Clyde-built steamers still being pounded by the seven seas after forty years' hard wear, and there isn't anybody in the world who knows about shipping who hasn't heard, and always with respect, about Clydebank.

The last time I was in John Brown's shipyard was just over a year ago, in the early months of the war, when I did a long tour of the country for the press, and then I saw them putting the finishing touches to the *Queen Elizabeth*, which looked an even better job than the *Queen Mary*. I remember that it was then that I tried my hand at automatic rivets, which looked easy enough until I came to do it. The number of different kinds of craftsmen, ranging from fellows dealing with vast deck plates to men fitting in the tiniest turbine blades, like safety razor blades, was astonishing, but the final impression I had was like my first: a sense of huge and furious energy, as if Titans were at work. And, I repeat, there are miles and miles of it, with the air throbbing with the sound of the riveters smashing home their white-hot bolts of metal to defy the worst gales, and though this colossal din makes conversation difficult – I never understood a single word my last guide said, what with all this tumult and his strange Glasgow accent, so that scores of good Scots pawky jokes must have been wasted that morning – it's a very comforting sort of din, for while it lasts you know that this seaborne Commonwealth of ours will never be defeated. The U-boats may sink ships, but more ships than they can ever sink are rapidly coming into existence along this great riverbank.

No wonder that Glasgow thinks well of itself. It does a grand job in the great style. And I hadn't been two hours in the city before I ran into its first citizen, Pat Dollan, the Lord Provost – the Scots equivalent of our Lord Mayor. I was delighted, for I had met Pat Dollan before and knew him to be a man after my own heart. To begin with, he's a man of the people, this Lord Provost of the second city of the empire. He understands them, and they understand him. Everybody recognises that shock of prematurely white hair, that small but robust and energetic figure, that fiery eye and quick tongue. He keeps his fingers on the pulse of the whole city and is as quick to defend what he knows to be good about it as he is to attack any abuses.

As a matter of fact, I must say that if I wanted to start throwing my weight about, I wouldn't choose Glasgow as the city to do it in, for if you want to be tough then they can be very tough in Glasgow; it's a tough city. But it's also a city of strange contradictions. One thinks of it as being one of the new industrial cities, and yet of course it's very old, with a very ancient university indeed. It's easy to see it as a place that cares for nothing but work, whisky and football. Yet it's long had a notable school of painting of its own and has an excellent arts club. In August, when the London Philharmonic Orchestra completely broke with all musical genteel convention by setting out on a tour of the big provincial vaudeville theatres, they opened their tour in Glasgow and were an instantaneous and smashing success, many people going over and over again to hear them. Which proves, by the way, an old contention of mine that if you give the great mass of people the best stuff, in an atmosphere that is congenial to the people, they will readily appreciate it. But the atmosphere must be right, and too often the atmosphere in which serious music is performed seems to the people too forbidding in its mixture of gloom, pompousness, diamonds and boiled shirts.

But Glasgow is anything but a boiled-shirt town, though I imagine it could afford to buy all the diamonds it wanted, for there must be a great deal of money about here. The folk in these parts, who don't conform to the familiar Scots puritanical pattern, seem to have a passion for entertainment of all kinds. There are five or six theatres and vaudeville shows open and doing fine business, including a big touring production of Ivor Novello's Drury Lane musical show *The Dancing Years*, which Ivor Novello wrote, composed and plays the lead himself. He has just been telling me how the large audiences here in Glasgow sit so rapt that the players imagine for a time that there is hardly anybody there, and then the audience suddenly bursts into a great roar of approval and enthusiasm. This is probably the only really big spectacular show on the road, and Novello tells me that people are often strongly moved just because they feel that this is perhaps the last *big* theatre stuff they will see for a long time. 'I don't know why I cried so much,' one middle-aged woman said to him. 'It's because you felt you were saying goodbye to something,' Novello told her.

As for motion picture theatres in Glasgow, they seem to be innumerable, and include in their company the largest film theatre in Britain, holding between four and five thousand persons. I haven't been inside it, and I don't intend to go. I do enough for you people as it is without spending my time inside giant picture theatres.

Then Glasgow, among its many oddities, has the only restaurant in Britain where you tell the management what you owe them and then pay them that. In short, they trust you. And apparently it works very well, though not all the customers acknowledge everything they owe at the time, but many of them, it seems, are conscience-stricken afterwards, so that the restaurant is always receiving money through the post. Some unkind southerners would say that a Scots city was the last place in which to try an experiment of this sort, but I think they would be wrong. There are two sets of people in this island about whom it is common to make jokes on the subject of their meanness. They are the Scots and the Yorkshire folk. You know the kind of jokes – when the Scotsman opened his purse, a moth flew out, but when the Yorkshireman opened his purse, the moth inside was dead – all that stuff. Now, my theory about these jokes is this: that these jokes are made about the Scots and Yorkshire folk not because they really *are* mean but because they so obviously aren't, so that it's safe to taunt them. Whereas about some other people in this island it simply wouldn't do to hint at meanness because it comes too near home. For the real breadth and warmth of hospitality, give me Scotland or Yorkshire. I admit that in both places people are usually careful about money and like to get their money's worth, but this trait seems to me a virtue and not a fault. The fellows who splash money about without caring what value they're getting for it are either fools or men who've never had to set about earning some money but have been born into some artificial little world where bundles of pound notes miraculously appear when you need them. This careless splashing about of money is, of course, part of the aristocratic tradition, and neither in industrial Yorkshire nor in industrial Scotland does the aristocratic tradition mean very much.

Not long ago, here in Glasgow, they had a Yorkshire battalion, and I'm proud to announce that the Yorkshire lads were a great success, displaying, under a deceptively quiet exterior, great cunning in the matter of finding attractive dancing partners. There was a film show one night, with some pictures of the Expeditionary Force, in which nothing but Scots troops could be seen. 'There y'are,' jeered a Scot to one of the Yorkshire lads, 'all Scots. What were you Yorkshiremen doing?' The retort came like lightning: 'We wor fighting the Germans while you got your photos taken.' And now, having given Yorkshire the victory, I can say goodnight.

26 and 27 November 1940

Evacuees

In order to be fairly quiet to do some work, and also in order to see something of my family, I have lately spent a week or so in the country, not far from the Welsh border. Here, my wife is very busy – and when I say 'busy' I mean hard at it from morning till night – trying to find empty country houses and to convert such houses into hostels for women, small children and babies who have come from badly bombed areas. We feel that it is better to take houses, furnish them simply but properly, and put in a staff of trained helpers, in order to shelter these evacuees with young children and babies, than it is to billet them in private houses, for it is easier to ensure that they are properly looked after, living a communal life of this kind, than it is when they are in private houses, and naturally they themselves prefer it, because women do not like to feel that some other woman has had them and their children pushed on to her. Moreover, even with all the goodwill in the world, it is not easy for all these women – hostesses and guests – to hit it off together at once. The reasons are clear. Most of the wives and mothers who are evacuated into the country are women who have spent all their lives in the poorer quarters of the large cities; they are nothing if not townsfolk. They are used to the bustle and chatter of amusements of the crowded streets; they are entirely unaccustomed to the quiet and solitude of country life, and at first they do not understand country ways and manners and country folk. On the other hand, the women in the villages who have to take these wives and mothers from the cities into their cottages cannot help feeling at first that they have been invaded by strange creatures who make the most impossible demands and will never settle down peaceably, whose habits are suspicious, to say the least of it, whose influence may be to nobody's good. All this is easily understood by anybody with a little knowledge of human nature.

Unfortunately, the first hurried great evacuation of women and children that took place at the beginning of this war was organised without much reference to any knowledge of human nature. There was no attempt to bridge the gap between the city-dwellers who suddenly arrived and the country folk who suddenly had to receive them into their homes. Hundreds of what we might call evacuation liaison officers should have been appointed, to explain these two different classes of folk to each other, to smooth out differences between them, to put an end to all the initial bewilderment and the succeeding resentments. For the result was often tragic. The evacuated wives and mothers complained that the country folk were often hard and unsympathetic, and that life among them was not worth living. The country women, on their side, complained that these people from the slums and dock areas were lazy, dirty and ungrateful. I call this result 'tragic' in many instances because what happened is that thousands of these evacuated women and children returned to their former homes, refused all appeals to go away again, and in the end found themselves still in those dangerous areas when the bombing began in earnest. Because of this lack of understanding, a great many lives were lost that never should have been lost.

Another thing that was not taken into account at first by the government and its officials was that the poorer folk in this country are not used, as the more well-to-do parents are, to seeing their children go away. This is the usual thing among the more comfortable sections of our society, in which parents almost automatically send their children away to boarding schools. It was difficult for such people – and nearly all senior officials belong to this class themselves – to understand that working-class parents, when danger threatened their children, would not necessarily be eager to send them away. They forgot the difference in the point of view. To these working-class folk, or at least to many of them, the mere talk of danger meant that the family must stick together, all under one roof, and what seemed to any official a merely prudent and sensible arrangement, this dispersal of the children, seemed to these other parents a strange and sinister proceedings, to be avoided at almost any cost.

Here, by the way, I want to interpolate a protest. A listener in Chicago has sent me a newspaper cutting in which the writer, Howard Vincent O'Brien, quotes a reference of mine to 'humble working men' as proof that Britain – including, I take it, myself – is no democracy and really has, I quote his words, 'a feudal outlook'. Britain, he goes on to say, has 'humble working men', and the United States hasn't. Now, in the first place, if I used such a term as 'humble working men' at all – and it certainly isn't one that would come readily to my lips – it must have had some special reference, now lost to me. Secondly, as I am nothing if not a very ardent democrat, with a pretty good long record of outspoken criticism of anything anti-democratic, there could hardly be a worse example of British feudalism than myself, who come of working-class stock. Thirdly, though American life is more equalitarian than British, as I myself have pointed out quite frequently, it is a fact that workers in Britain are in many respects much less 'humble' than the same sort of folk in the United States, for many of them belong to highly organised and powerful trade unions, which would not for a moment tolerate the sort of treatment often handed out to American workers. But all this is by the way.

Let us return to this problem of evacuation. The first great exodus, at the beginning of the war, was undoubtedly not very successful, partly because of the mutual misunderstanding I have already mentioned, and also, of course, because there was no bombing and therefore no danger to be avoided, and so the game did not seem worth the candle. During the last three months, we have had the second great exodus, this time under the immediate threat of danger, and though of course very large numbers of women and children have been settled in small towns and country districts, it would be absurd to pretend that the problem of evacuation has been successfully solved. One of our chief troubles is the shortage of empty country houses that could be turned into hostels for women and small children. There are several reasons for this shortage, but the chief one, I think, is that now we have an enormous army in this country and the War Department has requisitioned thousands of suitable buildings for its own use. In some towns the troops seem to occupy every available inch of covered space. And wherever you go, there they are. This is, you must understand, something quite new in our history. We are not used to having enormous standing armies. Even in the last war, when we raised a tremendous army, most of the men at any time were with the various expeditionary forces overseas. But now most of our soldiers are still here, and their presence everywhere naturally increases the congestion.

Once you are out of the invasion and bombed areas, which have been considerably thinned out, you do get a feeling of congestion, and the market towns seem packed with folk; all hotels are full, and even in remote villages it would be difficult to find a vacant room or empty bed. This partial migration has of course made various services, transport and communication more difficult to run successfully than they used to be. A market town that has two or three times as many people in it as it had before the war, but with no more wholesale and retail traders serving it than it had before the war, is obviously liable to be often in temporary difficulties, and this applies particularly to certain kinds of foodstuffs, which may be unobtainable in these towns not because there are no supplies of them in the country but because the local distributing service may be slow in coping with the demand. Thus – I speak from my own experience – one town may run clean out of biscuits, another out of chocolate, another out of dried fruits. This is of course a nuisance, and housewives get annoyed, but it must not be mistaken for a real food shortage. Of that I have seen no genuine sign yet, though it would be idle to pretend we are as well off as we were a year ago; but so far we are certainly better off than we were during the last two years of the previous war.

No, our most serious shortage at the moment is of good buildings with an adequate water supply and drainage system that could be used to house evacuees in the comparatively safe areas. I would regard this – and not, as many people think, a better provision of strong shelters – as being our chief home problem during this period. In itself, this scattering and mixing up of the population seems to me a good thing, for unlike people in the new countries we here in Britain are apt to stay too long in our own particular social ruts and to forget how other sections of the population are living. It will do us no harm, even if there is a bit of quarrelling on the way, to go from the city into the village, or from the country into the town. Our chief fault as a people is a certain smug complacent stupidity, due not so much to a real lack of intelligence – most English have rather more brains than would at first appear, a fact that always teases and puzzles the Germans, who can never decide whether we are stupid oafs or clever fiends – but due rather to a tradition of lazy-mindedness. If this war shakes us out of that complacent stupidity, as it rapidly is doing with all except the incorrigible, it will have done us far more good than harm.

I have had very good special evidence recently about this mental shake-up that our people are experiencing. Two or three weeks ago, I suddenly brought to an end the series of short Sunday night radio talks, known as *Postscripts*, that I had done on our home programme for the past five months. The result was that I had an avalanche of letters, the reading of which has occupied most of my spare time during the past two weeks. These letters were from listeners of almost every age, type and background and represented a very good cross-section of our public. Short of an elaborate survey on the Gallup model, this mass of correspondence was as good a clue to the public mind as you could want, and they had one advantage over even a survey and that was that most of them were written at some length, the writer expressing his or her opinions in an easy friendly style, and were not mere answers to questions, as a survey demands. Well, what came out of these letters? First, I think, a very general determination to see this war through, because of a now deep-seated dislike and distrust of the whole Nazi and Fascist racket. Secondly, an almost complete absence of jingo sentiments, fervent nationalism, 'Rule Britannia', and an obvious dislike of being appealed to along those old-fashioned lines. Thirdly, a very strong desire to use this war not merely as a means of disposing of Hitler and all that he stands for but also as an attempt to attack the root causes of this catastrophe, to make this a better country, to try to make this world a nobler planet.

Let me impress upon you all that this feeling is much stronger here than our official pronouncements would lead an outsider to imagine. Here, I think, and not for the first time, the majority of ordinary folk who think at all are more advanced than many of their political leaders. Hundreds of thousands of them are beginning to reflect and discuss who never reflected and discussed before. This morning I received from a well-known London bookshop an invitation to attend 'a bridge-opening ceremony and party'. The bridge is one that has been laid across a large bomb crater just outside the shop. Well, this war may be like that – a bridge across a crater and, waiting at the far side, like the bookshop, all men's ideas and aspirations and compassion and poetry. Goodnight.

4 December 1940

Propaganda

Tonight I want to discuss with you as openly and frankly as I can this question of British propaganda. Isolationists in the United States are very fond of referring to huge, highly organised propaganda by ourselves, and of repeating such statements as Senator Burton's that the British have the greatest propaganda organisation.

You'd gather from these references that the Nazis, who've actually spent more time, trouble and money on propaganda in a month than we've done in any given year, are mere children at the sinister game compared with ourselves. It's their sheer clumsiness that brings these Nazi propagandists into the open, whereas we subtle British keep our gigantic organisation under cover; therefore we're really the dangerous people, working day and night to bewilder the poor American citizen. Men with strange accents, wearing monocles and spats, are probably spending millions in Whitehall on this gigantic propaganda machine of ours. And so on and so forth.

Now, this makes me laugh, but not very heartily – bitterly, perhaps, rather than heartily. The joke, such as it is, is this: that so far from being assisted by this gigantic machinery of propaganda, I've had so little assistance, so little official interest in what I was doing, that lately I've threatened to resign from doing these talks altogether. It is, I assure you most earnestly, with the very greatest difficulty that our government can be persuaded to give propaganda even a moment's serious consideration. They don't understand its value and will simply not be bothered with it.

The propaganda of this country, instead of being highly organised, lavishly prepared and distributed, both subtle and energetic, is simply terrible. I've written one newspaper article after another pointing this out, and so have many of my colleagues.

Now, I've some right to speak with authority on this matter, and I defy any Isolationist to contradict this, for since last June I've probably broadcast more talks overseas than any other person. If there is such a thing as a British propagandist then I'm one, for month after month I've stayed up until all hours doing these talks, and if there is a big propaganda machine then I'm certainly one of the people who ought to know all about that machine and ought to be in charge of a few pulleys and cogwheels myself. But my complaint – and it's been repeated and echoed by everybody who has tried to state our case to the world – is that not only is there no such elaborate machinery but that the whole business of propaganda is most shamefully undervalued and neglected by our government, and any American Isolationist who knows all about a gigantic British propaganda organisation either inside or outside this country will do me a great service by putting me in touch with it. As it is, those of us whose task it is to state the British case do so with little official encouragement and with many obstacles to overcome. I suppose the kind of man who believes that American citizens are being victimised by a huge and elaborate campaign of spell-binding and truth-faking by the British authorities also believes that a broadcaster like myself is paid immense sums by officials who tell me exactly what to say.

Well, I'll explain exactly what my own position is. I'm employed privately, talk by talk, by the British Broadcasting Corporation. Occasionally it is suggested that I might like to deal with a certain subject, but it's up to me whether I adopt the suggestion, and how I treat the subject is entirely my own affair. No important official, no official of any kind, has ever seen me and told me that I ought to talk in a certain way about a certain subject, and if he did I should ask him who the blazes he thought I was, and who he thought he was.

As for immense sums of money, I think I can truthfully say that this is about the worst-paid job I've had for the last ten years, for each one of these talks is at least half as long again as the kind of newspaper article I write, and I've not only to write it out but also to travel to a studio and then to deliver the talk over the air, and for all that I receive just a quarter of the amount I receive for a weekly newspaper article.

No, there's no money in this job; there's no official prestige, no public advancement, no honour and glory on their way. Why, then, do I do it? I'm a free agent, nobody's threatened me with conscription if I refuse to do it – in fact, nobody in any position of authority cares two pence whether I do the job or not, or for that matter whether anybody does it. But why, then, do I keep at it? For it's extremely tiring work, week after week, month after month. I keep at it because in the first place I have many friends overseas with whom I like to feel that I'm in touch. In addition, there are hundreds of thousands of good folk who are at least acquaintances, though we've not met, because they've read my books or seen my plays. I feel it's a privilege, during a time when it's hard to offer them any more books and plays, to be able to talk to them in an easy, friendly fashion about how things are going here, as good as being able to write 100,000 letters at once. Thirdly, I have my own 'slant' on this war, and it happens that my point of view coincides with that of most of the people who listen to our overseas talks, so that I feel that here is an excellent audience. Now, what that slant or point of view is ought to be pretty obvious by this time. It is that this war must be fought for the democratic idea: it's either for that or it's nonsense. And I don't think it's nonsense.

Moreover, it happens that so far in this conflict the real heroes and heroines, the outstanding characters of the war, are the ordinary British people. Those of you who have been listening to these talks all along will remember that quite early in them I promised solemnly that when the real challenge came, the character of the ordinary folk's hero would stand up like a rock. Well, that's happened, as nobody can deny, which only confirms me in my opinion that it's the people who are taking it in this war, and so before we have done, this will be the people's war – by which I mean not merely that they'll go on taking it and be patted on the head but they'll show the world that democracy in this hemisphere isn't dead but is about to take on a new and more glorious life.

This brings me naturally to a now-familiar criticism of Britain that is made by those people in the United States who want any excuse to keep their heads in the sand. This criticism is that Britain is no longer a democracy, that democracy is dead here, so that any talk of our fighting for democracy is just so much humbug.

Now, I'm a very good person to answer this charge, and for this reason: that before this war, I was saying, and had been saying it in one form or another for several years, that democracy was dying in this country. I said it because for one thing I disliked the government of that period, and for another thing that the indifference of most of our people to the antics of this bad government seemed to me to suggest that we were no longer a politically minded, public-spirited, truly democratic people. It's all there in print, though I won't take this opportunity of advertising my goods by telling you exactly where it is. The point is that these critics of Britain are only saying now what some of us were saying two or three years ago. But now we're at war, fighting – and let's make no bones about that – for our very existence as a self-governing, free people. Are we still less of a democracy now? Have we arrived, for all our tall talk, at a kind of disguised Fascism?

I'll deal as honestly as possible with this searching question. First, I'll say all that can be said in favour of this view. Thus it's true that the powers of the government, the executive powers, have been immensely enlarged at the expense of some ancient liberties; things can be done that couldn't have been done two years ago and that would have been regarded with horror thirty or fifty years ago. In theory, many of the traditional liberties and rights of the British citizen have vanished. Let so much be freely admitted. Then again, it's true to say that there are persons who wouldn't greatly mind a thinly disguised Fascism who are still occupying places of power and influence. There's been no great direct attack upon privilege; most of the faults of our system still remain. And I will admit this much: that if our Parliament, our press, our people were all indifferent, showing much the same spirit – or, to be more accurate, lack of spirit – that they were doing during the years just before the war, I'd regard this state of affairs with considerable dismay. Indeed, I'd be wondering now what we were all in for and how soon I could smuggle my family and myself to a freer air.

But let's look at it from the other side of the picture. In the first place, with a few minor exceptions, these increased powers of the government were themselves the result of a popular demand. The people, through Parliament and the press, said in effect, 'More government, please.' And, ironically enough, a familiar grumble – I've made it myself more than once – is that the government doesn't make enough use of its enlarged powers, that it ought to be riding us harder and not pretending so often that things are still normal, when we all know that really they're wildly abnormal and should be treated as such.

Secondly, what about Parliament and the press? If these are sinking into silence and oblivion then some sort of Fascism is arriving, but if they're still lively and outspoken then democracy hasn't been defeated. Now, this Parliament, although in my opinion it was elected far too long ago, 1935, to represent truly our opinion today, has shown itself not at all unworthy of its old tradition, for it's by no means a company of 'Yes-men' but hasn't hesitated to be critical and outspoken, the members often voicing the discontents of the people who elected them. And the press has been still more critical, lively and outspoken. Though working under all manner of disadvantages – with less paper, less advertising and all the difficulties created by the raids and faulty communications and transport, nevertheless the press seems to me ten times more alive than it was before the war. With one or two exceptions, it's much more sharply democratic in tone than it used to be, much more like the sort of newspapers that most of you read. Anything less like the government-controlled press of a Fascist country can hardly be imagined; and any suggestion, sometimes made by a harassed official who has been subjected to fierce attack, that the press should be curbed has been instantly and vigorously resented.

Last, but most important of all, we come to the spirit of the people themselves – everything really hangs on this. If democracy is decaying for them then our democracy is doomed, but if their spirit is more democratic then sooner or later the government will be more democratic – you may bet your last penny on that. And I have no hesitation whatever in declaring that the spirit of the British people is more truly and sharply democratic than it's been for at least a generation – perhaps than it's ever been before – and that these people who are 'taking it' know what they are taking it for, and that in the end they will have their way.

So please don't talk of Britain and forget the British people. They are Britain. You'll see! Goodnight.

11 December 1940

Hitler's Plans

What is going to happen during the next few months? Reduced to its simplest possible terms, I believe the conflict will be between Adolf Hitler and two plain men: the average British citizen and the average American citizen. In short, the bout is the Fuhrer versus the ordinary English-speaking citizen.

This may sound surprising to some of you, in the light of recent events, especially the startling moves in the Eastern Mediterranean and in Africa, and though I don't want to under-estimate the importance of these active theatres of war where the fundamental weakness of Italy is being exposed, it would be a mistake to regard them as the centre of the combat. The main issue must be decided elsewhere; that is where these two plain men – the British and the American citizen – come in.

In order to have a clear view of the whole situation, we must take a look at Germany's strategy. Since his terrific and startling successes in June, when France collapsed and Germany took control of the whole Western seaboard of the European continent, Hitler's strategy has had to be constantly changed because one plan after another has failed. It's very important we should realise this fact, and it's sheer common sense, and not wishful thinking, to dwell upon it. In France, Hitler's secret weapon, which I agree with this morning's *Manchester Guardian* editorial in thinking is his Fifth Column organisation, succeeded in the Low Countries and in France. But when he turned his attention to Britain and announced that our utter defeat was only a matter of a few weeks, possibly he overlooked the fact that here his secret weapon wouldn't help him. Such tiny Fifth Column elements as existed in this country were put in places from which it would take a successful invading army to rescue them. However, if his Fifth Column tactics would no longer work, there were still the heavily armoured divisions, which had a weighty momentum when once set in motion that would pulverise our defending army, who still lacked adequate heavy equipment; hence the boast, which I believe at the time was sincerely meant and not merely propaganda talk, of triumphal entries into London and the dictation of peace terms before the summer was over. But though he now controlled the Channel ports on his side, the narrow strip of water was still there. Armoured divisions can't come roaring across the sea as they did along the straight, flat roads of Flanders. So the armadas of barges and other transports were assembled at what we now call the invasion ports. Meanwhile, the German Air Force had to destroy our fighter defence, so there followed the mass attacks of August, which resulted in enormous losses to the Germans in good machines and highly skilled pilots but didn't succeed in destroying our defence.

Two plans have now miscarried. First, the British people have refused to be stampeded by the loud threats of invasion terror; they have replied by redoubling their war effort and by forming a Home Guard of a million men. Secondly, the RAF have defeated Goering's attempt at mastery of the air. On the approach of mass formations of raiding planes, the terrible Hurricanes and Spitfires still came tearing down out of the sky, liberally dealing out destruction.

So, while still preparing the invasion, Hitler switched his plan again and the German Air Force concentrated on bombing London. This was, of course, in early September. It was an attack on civilian morale; it was hoped that under the weight of these vast nightly raids, the citizens of London would appeal to the government to stop the war. Well, we know what happened: the London citizen did nothing of the kind, so the third plan failed.

But, during this time, we were doing something more than merely taking it, though we took plenty; the RAF began roaring over to the invasion ports and turned the basins where the barges were assembling – often with troops already concealed in them – into blazing infernos. How many miserable German soldiers were caught in those terrible raids we shall probably never know until the end of the war, but there is no doubt that these heavy blows made immediate invasion impossible. So that, for the time being, was the end of that.

But let's give the Nazis their due: they are powerless and unwearying servants of their own evil star. They set aside no possibility of mischief. Now, here was Britain still unconquered, delivering heavier and heavier blows herself in return, and with her prestige throughout the world steadily rising because of her undaunted defiance. So the next move was a vast diplomatic one. Ribbentrop got busy again and this time was energetically assisted by Hitler, who, contrary to his usual custom, because – we may reasonably argue – he realised how serious the situation was, began moving about Europe himself. His plan was now to confront Britain, the United States and the world with a Europe united under his so-called New Order, which was to extend from the North Sea and the Baltic to the Black Sea and the Mediterranean. If we weren't terrified into submission by the sight of this solid front then he'd be able to make one of those vast pincer movements dear to German strategists – the largest yet conceived, a movement down to Gibraltar at one end of the Mediterranean, and another movement by way of the Danube and the Balkans at the other end of the Mediterranean. But this move, which looked at first as if it might succeed, began to show signs that were ominous for him. Not France, nor Spain, nor Russia, nor Bulgaria, fell completely into line. Turkey was unimpressed; Greece, suddenly attacked by Italy, not only defied Mussolini but began to take the offensive against his doubtful army.

Now, this is a war, as Hitler knows perhaps better than anybody else, of prestige. The bombs and armoured divisions are really there to deliver the final stroke at an enemy already weakened by doubt and conditions. The Greek campaign proved a bad business for the Axis, stiffening resistance everywhere to its arrogant demands. The fight is on in and around the Mediterranean, and no doubt it is from there that most of the hot news will come. But, make no mistake about this, Hitler knows only too well, here in this island is his great enemy; unless he breaks us here, then inevitably – sooner or later – we shall break him. Therefore, during the last few weeks, even while the plan on the diplomatic front was still in force, Hitler began what we might call the Second Battle of Britain, the first battle having been concluded with the virtual defeat of the Luftwaffe in September.

This second battle, though it may be less spectacular and make less exciting reading than the first, is really the more serious and searching of the two. It consists of a weighty and ruthless attack upon two fronts. The first is a tremendous counter-blockade far out to sea by U-boats and raiders. The second is a systematic and very heavy and cruel bombing of the ports, industrial towns and the civil population in general, with the three-fold object of reducing our imports of essential war materials and foodstuffs, of cutting down our rate of production and of terrorising civilians.

It's obvious, then, that in this battle the ordinary civilian, who must soon be called upon to consume less, to do more and to withstand very heavy raids, is bang in the front line. The main attack is really being directed against him; it's his will to resistance that is being assaulted. Hitler knows that he can depend, for some time yet – though not for too long a time, as already recent tactics show – on his own slave population; not because they are not weary of a war in which they stand to gain nothing, for even if their side wins it only means that the chains and shackles they wear will be even more securely riveted on them, but because he knows that they have no voice whatever in his policy, that they must obey orders or face the secret police, the concentration camps, torture and death. Here, he knows, we have no such slave population; the tiny group of Members in the House of Commons are at liberty to rise and propose that peace should be negotiated as early as possible, and any citizen who wishes to support this small group is also at liberty to do so. This is a fight between disciplined slaves, under a few enthusiastic gangsters, and relatively free men. Therefore, if his main attack is upon the British citizen, whom he hopes to terrorise, to stun or weary, that's why I said that for the next few months it's Hitler versus the ordinary plain Briton.

But I mentioned a second plain citizen, belonging to the United States; where does he come in? Is Hitler considering him at all, this ordinary American citizen whom Hitler's never seen and doesn't really understand, far away in a land as strange to Hitler as a place in the moon? Are these men in offices downtown in New York, in the factories at Detroit and in California, on their farms in Iowa or Kansas, in the picture at all as Hitler and his gang see it? Undoubtedly, they are, as shown by the efforts of Goebbels and Himmler and their organisation to establish a network of Nazi sympathisers and necessary saboteurs throughout the United States. And this attack on the ordinary British system is also an attack on the ordinary American citizen, but of course in a different way. The American citizen hasn't to wait for bombs, to continue his work while the sirens are screaming their warning, cut down his scale of living. We can do all that here, and you may be sure we shall do it, but what the ordinary American citizen has to do is to share our faith and hope, to stand up and say with one voice, 'No, you can't do it, this cruel madness.' And there's a sign of that faith and hope, of that great democratic 'No', an attempt at defiance, to redouble every possible effort to help his fellow citizen over here, who shares the same decencies, kindnesses and values as he shares, with the same great language. So that this latest and grimmest plan of the mad Nazis, who are now very desperate indeed, will go the way of the others and bring back dreams from which we have all awakened. Goodnight.

17 and 18 December 1940

Disciplines of War

There has just arrived here a handsome-looking book called *Britain Speaks*. Yes, it is a selection from these talks of mine made by my American publishers, Harper's of New York. I've been glancing through it, half fascinated, half afraid. The reason for this attitude towards the book is that it consists of things I never intended to be publishing in cold print. It is almost as if somebody suddenly popped up with a book and said, 'Look, this is a selection made from your conversations during the last few months.' Wouldn't *you* be fascinated and half frightened in my place? Of course you would. Wondering what you'd been up to, and if you mightn't look a fool, now that so much of the stuff was there in black and white for anybody to take to pieces. After all, it's very late at night here when I do these talks, and a man might be excused for saying almost anything at such an hour. Except shouting that 'the lights are going out', like the man in my friend Hitchcock's film *Foreign Correspondent*, which should not be taken as a guide to radio conditions over here. But I've taken a risk of looking very silly, by allowing so many of these talks to be printed, if I *have* said many foolish things. Of course, I don't believe I have – if I did, you can bet your life I'd never have introduced the subject – and my glancing and dipping in have really chased away any genuine doubts.

I admit that I haven't gone in much for prophecy, unlike the military experts, who do nothing but prophesy, but take care, most of them, to prophesy every possible alternative, so that while they're always wrong, they're always right, too. But I notice that when I did come out with prophecy, I came out good and strong. For instance, answering the doubts of some American commentators early in July, I said there was no chance of an appeasement group taking charge and asking for terms. I also said, answering these same doubters, that the British people, whom I knew better than they did, could take everything that was coming to them, and would surprise Hitler. I also said what was by no means so obvious then, and I quote the exact words: 'In the air, both the British machines and personnel are definitely superior to the German.' I also said that although invasion was undoubtedly being planned, I did not believe it would be seriously attempted this summer or autumn. I also said – and this is the last – that the serial blitzkrieg on London would fail and would be seen to be a mistake. Well, that's not bad, you know, for a man who makes no pretence of being an expert.

And now, having established my reputation as a prophet, I am ready to risk losing it again by indulging in a little more prophecy. And let me add at once that what I say comes entirely from outside. I have no inside information. No Cabinet minister tells me his secrets. I have no spies in Downing Street. I do not even move – and I hope this is not too disappointing for you – in what are called 'well-informed circles'. And nobody has put me up to saying this. It's pure unadulterated prophecy. And I declare here and now my belief that very, very soon the whole war effort of this country will be geared up, compelled to take as big a jump again as it did in the early summer. I believe too that this gearing up of the war machine will bring about more social changes, all within a month or two, than we have known so far during the whole course of the war. This last statement is a pretty safe sort of prophecy, almost cheating as an example of the prophetic, because I know very well that we cannot possibly speed up the war machine any more *without* making big social changes. It is actually in great part the reluctance to make those changes, to interfere drastically with the whole social and economic structure of our society, that has, I think, prevented the government from throwing the whole machinery into a higher gear.

The position, as I see it, is this: in spite of prodigious efforts, on the one hand, and great economies, on the other hand, we are still producing too little and consuming too much. It is not that we are no longer making the effort we began to make after the collapse of France, when we found ourselves facing the full might of Germany and Italy, spread over half Europe. It is not that war weariness, indifference have crept in. It is that now we are beginning to feel the full effect of Germany's conquests, reaching from the North Cape to the Bay of Biscay, giving them submarine and air bases almost in every direction. Therefore, we must increase our effort, cutting down our scale of living and at the same time speeding up our rate of production of all the munitions of war. We are like a fighter who must now go into stricter training, getting rid of every ounce of superfluous flesh, turning himself into so much sheer bone and muscle.

Now, this can be done – and the more help we are given from outside, the more easily it can be done – but it cannot be done if we still try to interfere as little as possible with our social and economic structure. The point is, we cannot live in a fortress and pretend to run it on comfortable country mansion lines. People of every class will have to make still more sacrifices, and I think it is essential that they should be all *compelled to make them at the same time.* For example, it is more than likely that a great deal more compulsion will have to be applied to labour. Men will not be allowed to go and work where their fancy, or the lure of higher wages, takes them. They will have to go and work where their particular brand of labour is most urgently needed, just as a soldier has to go where he is sent, as one small unit in a campaign. You cannot run war industries on a basis of peacetime organisation. The factories are just as important now as the battalions or the squadrons. It is essential that there should be a factory front as carefully and thoroughly organised as any other front, and the men working in it cannot be allowed to do as they please, not because what they would choose to do would be dictated by any antagonism to our war effort, for labour as a whole staunchly supports this war – and in Coventry, I am told, the rate of production has actually gone up since the bad bombing it had – but because unless there is complete control of the whole labour front, there is waste, there is overlapping, there is delay, there are too many men here and not enough there, there are dangerous bottle-necks in our war production.

Now, will labour, which jealously guards the rights and privileges that it has struggled for years to obtain, oppose the loss of such rights and privileges, refuse to submit to such wholesale compulsion? I have no authority whatever for saying so – remember that from first to last, this is private guesswork – but I think that labour will offer determined opposition *unless –* and this is the point – unless further compulsion is also applied elsewhere. In short, other people must also lose their rights and privileges, if it can be shown that they are impeding our war effort. For example, if you can conscript youth for the Army, and labour for the factory front then there is no reason why you should not – and many good reasons why you *should* – also conscript property. This is to some extent already being done. In some parts of the country, the local authorities are telling owners of large country houses that they can no longer be allowed to occupy the whole of them with themselves and their domestic staff. We can no longer afford such luxuries as the sight of two elderly people occupying a house of perhaps twenty rooms, and being waited on exclusively by a staff of six or seven adult persons, probably including a chauffeur who could be doing a job of work for his country in a war factory. This whole style of life must go, and some of us do not greatly care if it goes never to return.

Now, our taxations are, of course, terrific. In direct taxation, the well-to-do are paying at least two thirds of their income, and then in addition there is severe indirect taxation, including this new purchase tax, which has increased the prices of many things, not necessarily sheer luxuries, by 20 or 30 per cent. But taxation is clearly proved to be not enough. Even when all these taxes are paid, some people have still enough left to keep on leading the kind of life that in a grim struggle for existence simply will not do. Such persons are like heavy useless passengers in a small leaky boat. I am speaking now of individuals and not of a whole class, for a great many men and women, especially the younger people, who before the war led this luxurious and parasitic sort of life, are now producing as much, in one way or the other, and consuming as little, as almost anybody in the country. Even with some of the elderly rich, it is not that they are being deliberately selfish by clinging to all the comforts and service to which they have been accustomed but that they have little imagination and it has not yet been brought sharply home to them that their old style of living is now no longer possible. In my very first talk to you, I observed:

> We've probably done more to make ourselves really
> fit and ready in the last three weeks than we did in
> the previous eight months. One reason for the delay is
> that you can't persuade a lot of the English that they
> don't live on a magic island. They believe, these nice,
> comfortable, stupid folk, that disasters and tragedies,

fire and slaughter, treachery and invasion, are things that happen over the sea, to those strange excitable beings called 'foreigners'.

Now, we shall have to make a second great attack on the same complacent mentality, in whatever section of our society it shows itself. Everybody will have to contribute something to this new gearing up, and the country as a whole is ready now to take its new orders, readier indeed than the government is to issue them. The reason for that is plain. The government knows that the people are not reluctant to make sacrifices – in many directions, voluntary effort in Britain is prodigious – but naturally it wishes to be as little totalitarian itself as possible. Behind this hesitation in issuing commands is a genuine dislike of letting go of old freedoms and privileges. And remember there is no Gestapo in all this, no spying and reporting and sudden arrests. No concentration camps and mysterious disappearances. We are still, war or no war, incomparably the freest people in any great state outside America. And if we surrender some of our freedom, we ask for it to be surrendered ourselves, ask that further commands should be laid upon us. And – a last thing to remember – please do not imagine from what I have said that we are not already, nearly every man and woman of us, making considerable sacrifices, in almost every department of life, for we are narrowing our existence to a finer and finer edge so that it shall be a sharp sword, with which to defend Christian civilisation from the gravest menace it has known since the Asiatic hordes, swarming like locusts over the great plains, were at last checked and halted, and life bloomed again. Goodnight.

24 and 25 December 1940

Christmas at War

I t's Christmas Eve. I don't feel like giving you the ordinary sort of talk, but I imagine that most of you won't want the ordinary sort of talk. A great many of you, as I know from your letters that have reached me from all over the world, have been listening to these talks of mine ever since I began them in early summer, which means that we've really spent quite a time sitting together, with you listening at your end and me talking at this end. (Yes, I know it's been very one-sided in the matter of talking and listening, this companionship of ours, but that just can't be helped, can it?) So I feel I've a right to assume that we're friends in a way, good friends too, for I know that I'm sincerely grateful to you for listening, and I know too that at least some of you are grateful to me for at least some of my talking. So I propose to treat you like friends. Those of you who live in places with cold evenings, pull your chairs nearer to the fire or the stove, and those who live in a warm climate please settle yourselves comfortably on the veranda or wherever you like to sit of an evening, and let's make this a cosy Christmas chat.

It's a queer time to be having a Christmas at all, of course. At first, one feels that it ought to be conveniently ignored, forgotten. The old phrases of greeting don't sound too well just now, do they? 'Peace on Earth' and all the rest of them. We ought apparently to be celebrating now not the birth of the mystical Son of God and Son of Man, of the baby who would afterwards show us the way to the Kingdom of Heaven, but the birth of the inventor of the bombing plane, the serial torpedo, the magnetic mine, the multiple anti-aircraft gun. For that's the kind of world this Christmas of 1940 has found its way into, a world seemingly bent upon huge senseless cruel self-destruction, a world infinitely far removed from the Kingdom of Heaven.

But was it a much better world 1,940 years ago or thereabouts? It had less elaborate method in its madness; and let us admit that there is something peculiarly shameful and sickening in the way in which we have prostituted our science and superb engineering skill, the way in which we have all bent all knowledge to this task of idiotic destruction. But that old world was not a good world. It was blood-stained, murderous, often diabolically cruel. Look at the marble faces of those admirably realistic Roman busts. What a sneering sense of cold-hearted power often stares out of them, at a world that was so frequently nothing but a vast extension of the blood-reeking circus arena. It was a world that worshipped power, often so unashamedly that half-mad emperors could pretend to be gods. It was to rescue men and women from bondage to this world that Christianity came into being. It refused to acknowledge the force and majesty of this power. It said there was something stronger than sharp words of command to iron legions of troops. It whispered to the sad heart and the bewildered soul of other loyalties. It announced that there was a way of escape from the desolating routine of the battlefield and the counting house, the circus and the saturnalia; there was a way out, and through it a man might find the Kingdom of Heaven. And in this faith, men died cruel deaths, and died happily. But before they died, they could be heard crying out strange words:

> *We know that we have passed from death into life, because we love the brethren. He that loveth not his brother, abideth in death. Whosoever hateth his brother is a murderer; and ye know that no murderer hath eternal life abiding in him. Hereby perceive we the love of God, because he laid down his life for us: and we ought to lay down our lives for the brethren ... No man hath seen God at any time. If we love one another, God dwelleth in us, and his love is perfected in us...*

Yes, strange words to be crying out in that old marble and iron empire of Rome. And I believe – and if I didn't believe it, I doubt if I should be talking to you here and now – that we are at war today, reluctantly at war, after trying every reasonable way out, not to advance one national flag against another, not to keep so much territory or trading rights for ourselves, not for power and glory, but to prevent the forced return of humanity to that world of the first Christmas, that world of drill and wild feasts and blood-stained shows, the world that had not yet heard of the Kingdom of Heaven.

These men we are fighting now are the enemies of Christendom. It is not that they are bad specimens of our civilisation; we may be that ourselves. But these Nazis are really outside our civilisation and deny all its values. They are the latest manifestation of the old enemy of Christendom – Goth, Vandal, Hun and Mongol. Their New Order is as old as Genghis Khan and Tamburlaine. It is the order of the cruel and raging heathen.

It is the order of the slave-driver and the torturer. For nearly 2,000 years men may have been bad Christians. But these men are not Christians at all. They understand nothing but fraud, force and cruelty. They delight in making war not only on other nations but on faith, hope and charity. To give in to them would be to say goodbye to all that Christmas, with its tender message of hope, its innocent joy, its grace of the spirit, has ever meant to us.

That is why we need not feel too ashamed to find ourselves at war again – yes, again, after so many wars – this Christmas. I do not mean by that that the war could not have been avoided. It could have been avoided perhaps if ten years ago all the nations had really co-operated, honestly and frankly co-operated, to discover why the whole world was beginning to feel the blizzard of scarcity economies, if the whole sad face of jealous national sovereignty had been abandoned, if men everywhere had refused to tolerate what they knew deep down to be evil. But failing all this, the war could not be avoided. And I believe most sincerely that we people here, whatever our mistakes of judgement may have been, came into this war, reluctantly, rather sadly, but with clear consciences. And nothing that people have said and done since seems to me to have spoilt that reluctant and solemn entry into war. I know as much about our faults as most men. I am nothing if not critical, so much so that it is a wonder that I am allowed to go on so long, speaking my mind. We have here our fair share of the stupidities, silliness, complacencies and timidities of our species. I claim for us no special virtues, unless it should be an easy temper and a dislike of cruelty. But I will say this – and I would not say it now on Christmas Eve, when I feel I am talking intimately to my friends, if I did not believe it to be scrupulously true – that the behaviour of the British people during this war, and especially during these last six months, has been of such a kind that any men who knew it would not hesitate to praise it even at this mystical festival of Christmas, that it has been worthy of folk who believe in their hearts they are defending Christendom itself.

You all know enough now, without my adding any more well-worn phrases, about the constant courage of so many – nearly all, in fact – of these people. You have heard over and over again how so many of them have endured weeks and sometimes months of raids without ever losing their smiling good temper, their occasional flashes of wit and high spirits. You know how little they have complained and whined, to the great astonishment of the Nazis, who apparently did not know that such fortitude could exist in a people. What I want to stress now is another characteristic, which makes the behaviour of these people so fit a subject for a talk on Christmas Eve. That is: the strange absence of hate among them for the enemy. I am not going to pretend that men and women here who have seen their children crushed to death or blown to pieces and their homes and all their possessions destroyed in a moment do not sometimes curse the hand that released the bomb and have not cried out, in their grief, what they would do if they could only get at the raiding airmen. So much is only to be expected. But it is exceptional rather than usual, even among the sufferers, and there is never enough of this feeling about at any one time to create one of those great hysterical waves of hatred that we sometimes noticed during the last war. One used to hear, especially among civilians, ten times more bloodthirsty hymn-of-hate sort of talk in the last war than one does in this. There is extraordinarily little of the 'you wait till we gets hold of 'em' line of talk. For one moment of that, there are a hundred moments of outspoken wondering about the chances of really making this a better world and never going through such hell again. Even Hitler – often referred to by the Cockneys and their like as 'li'l ol' 'Ittles' – gets very little cursing, though this does not mean that the stupid propaganda that Goebbels pours over the air is having any effect.

It is not entirely without significance that the commonest term now for the raiding Nazi planes is 'Jerry'. You hear it on every hand. 'I see Jerry was over again last night,' you hear them say. Or 'Jerry bin round your way much lately?', they'll ask. I think myself that this almost affectionate 'Jerry' is rather too good a nickname for the average Nazi flying man, who is apt to be a surly young brute. But there it is. No blind hatred at all. No hysterical screaming of threats at the enemy. Just a kind of rather good-humoured acceptance of what has to be gone through.

And please don't make the terrible mistake, which the Germans, who simply don't begin to understand us, have made before now, and think that this absence of hatred and this good humour are due to any *lack* of real character, a sort of devitalised apathy. They are not, as you would soon find out among these people. There's real character and enough to spare among them all. No, this attitude comes, in my opinion, from a real honest-to-God goodness in these people. May I repeat what I said to you before these people had been as severely tested as they have since? I said then:

> *There is a faith in our people that in spite of our many mistakes and our numerous imperfections, we are fighting so that the good life – not just our attempts at it, but yours, everybody's – should continue in this world ... and for people who feel this deeply, there are invisible sources of help and power, great unseen stocks of courage and initiative.*

I believed that in the high summer, and I believe it yet in dark winter. And now, on behalf of us all on this side of the Atlantic, I wish all of you who listen the compliments of the season – the old wish, a Merry Christmas! And God bless us all, every one!

26 January 1941

Cigars from America

Good evening. I'm addressing this talk to my friends Cass Caulfield and Eugene Saxton of Harper & Brothers, the publishers, of New York City – but of course all the rest of you can listen in. My dear Cass and my dear Gene, your noble Christmas present has arrived. I was told it would be late. What I wasn't told was that when it did come it would be a box of magnificent cigars. Romeo and Juliet – enormous fellows. Big enough for Winston Churchill. I thought I had said goodbye to such superb luxuries for the duration of the war – but no – bless your kind hearts. Thanks to you I can still occasionally smoke like an emperor. One or two of the cigars were a bit knocked about, but that was only to be expected, for at a time when huge factories, ships, rows of houses are being blown up and blasted, what chance have cigars – those most delicate works of art – of escaping without a bruise? But no real harm has been done. I smoked one the other night, down in the country, and it was much admired by all our evacuated mothers whom I was helping to entertain by organising round games. Talk about a new order! As far as we're concerned, it's begun already.

The life you remember us leading and into which we were always so delighted to welcome you both has completely vanished. It's all quite different. The social revolution has happened. The new age has already dawned. For example, we can no longer use either of the two houses you remember. All our furniture, or as much of it as we have been able to collect and transport – is now being used in a large country house that is one of the hostels for evacuated women and small children that my wife is running for the Ministry of Health. When I am not in London or travelling about, I come down to this hostel, occupy a room and pay for my board and lodging. I also help to serve the food at mealtimes. We all live communally, and I have exactly the same food – and good sensible stuff it is too. I say the dining room looks like a female lumber camp with its three tables crowded with nurses, helpers, mothers – all females, of course. Unless a husband should visit us, I'm the only male. You should see me dishing out the soup or pudding among this terrifically, and often embarrassingly, female mob. Suppose one night it suddenly struck them that all this vast idiocy of war which has taken them so far away from their ordinary life and threatened their children is all due to the pride and stupidity of the male. They could tear me to pieces in two minutes. I must say, however, that so far they have been all amiability.

And what is more surprising is that so far too they seem to get along very well with each other, and that's surprising not only because they're women all cooped up under one roof but also because their backgrounds are very different, for they not only come from places as far away as the East End of London and Liverpool and Manchester but also from widely different social backgrounds, ranging from intensely respectable suburbs to the dockside slums. And it's grand to see how quickly the poorer women, many of whom have had a terrible rough life, pick up health and confidence and better looks. As for the babies and small children – and the house seems to be packed with them – they respond like lightning to the country air, the good food and sensible handling, and you can fairly see them budding and blooming, many of them the prettiest little creatures you could even imagine. Our future citizens; war or no war, they are not making a bad start in life here in the country, and by heaven we'll see to it that they inherit a better world than we did, or we'll perish in the attempt.

And – Cass, Gene, everybody – that's not mere rhetorical stuff I'm talking either. We've just got to go on and on – getting rid of Hitler and their gang first, but not stopping after that, not leaning back, but carrying on the fight for the ordinary decent man and woman everywhere to a full and satisfying life – no more interference by gangsters and brigands and crooks and thwarted, twisted minds who hate human happiness. We've got to fight them whenever and wherever they appear and to go on fighting them if they weary us until we drop in our tracks. 'We all dwell in one country, oh stranger, the world; one chaos brought all mortals to birth.' So it gives me pleasure to add that this small but not ignoble experience in compassionate planning and child welfare, the creation of these hostels, would not have been possible, for their initial cost is much higher than our official allowances provide for, if money from the United States had not found its way to us, and once again I thank you for all that unfailing generosity.

I need hardly tell you that I myself am not down in the country very often, for much of the time these days I seem to be travelling about on various jobs, a man living out of a suitcase, spending whole days – far too many of them – in railway trains, accepting a bed here, a shakedown there, sometimes passing surprisingly peaceful nights, at other times listening to the barking of guns, the menacing drone of the bombers, the shuddering crash of explosions, like a man suddenly hurled into battle in his dressing gown and slippers.

I don't often meet old friends – and this separation is one of the hardships of this war – but on the other hand I am forever making new friends. You remember the old saying 'More people know Tom Fool than Tom Fool knows'. That applies here, for people feel that there is no harm in in talking freely to a man they consider something of a public character, whose face or voice they recognise, with the pleasant result that I am never long among strangers, but share a meal or a pipe or a gossip with all manner of folk, and not only pass hundreds of hours that might have been lost in tedium or aimless brooding but also constantly learn what people here are thinking and feeling. So when I tell you at any time what I believe the British people have in mind, you may assume that I know as well as the next man – and better than a great many – what I am talking about.

Not that I'm always right, of course. For example, about four or five months ago I took the line that unless our government handled our people with more imagination, by the time we reached the middle of winter, public morale here would show a steep decline. I believed this because I know the British people, who are temperamentally able to cope with any sudden crisis, are apt to become bored and sullen if they have to submit to many restrictions and do not feel in any immediate danger. But though imagination on the part of the government has certainly been lacking, I have not yet noticed the sudden drop in morale that I prophesied. This may be due to the fact that the winter has not been as dull and gloomy so far as one might have reasonably expected. There has been, for example, the new challenges of the big incendiary raids, which, if successful, are terribly destructive to property. Again there have been our triumphs in Libya, which are not only of immense strategical significance but are also clear proof that we on our side are capable of absolutely first-class modern staff work.

But whatever the reasons may be, it is a fact that that our morale is high and so far the public mind shows no signs of apathy and war weariness. Indeed, our two most serious weaknesses are faults of the government and not of the people, many of whom are not too anxious to be rid of these weaknesses. The first of them is the official reluctance, based on typical British conservatism, to put the whole country and everybody in it on a total war footing, making the most complete use of every man and woman and every scrap of wealth, machinery and property. Too many people are still living, or at least half living, in the pre-war world. There are still too many idle and expensive passengers in our crowded little open boats. These people may belong to many different classes and it does not follow that because they are making little or no contribution to our war effort, the fault is theirs. Not a few of them would be glad to receive their commands, to make their contribution, and to be relieved of tasks and commitments that belong essentially to the pre-war world. There are difficulties, of course. We do not wish to become totalitarian ourselves. But if we can preserve the free critical spirit of real democracy, and our government can remain sensitive to public opinion, then we can put the whole nation and everything we possess on a total war footing without becoming like the bad thing we are fighting.

The second most serious weakness is our official refusal to treat this war as a war of ideas, as a new kind of war entirely different to the last war. It is this refusal which makes our propaganda, which ought to be the strongest part of our war effort, at present the very weakest part of our war effort, almost a gap in our line of defence and attack. It is true enough that security against Hitlerism is a sufficient reason for fighting, for unless the power of the Nazis is completely destroyed, the world would still never know peace in our time. There is no coming to terms with any of these people, who know in their hearts that they are outlaws who can never be fitted into a secure world order. Thus they must win everything or lose everything, which fact alone makes this a very different war from the last or from the wars of the nineteenth century. But a great many of us here feel that that this mere anti-Hitlerism is not enough, is negative and too narrow. Millions and millions of Europeans, including many Germans themselves, all of them now living under the terror of the Gestapo, must be roused to fight not merely against something but for something. They need to be given new hope, faith and courage.

It is no use asking them to risk everything in order to return to the world before the war, because most of them hated the world before the war. They need to feel that the whole bad set of conditions which produced slumps and terrible unemployment and poverty, national jealousies and refusals to co-operate and finally produced the dictators with their huge armies and secret police and torture chambers must be swept away once and for all; that the common man everywhere can come out of the shadows again; that their children will once again live amply and nobly. For such a cause, men will risk everything and gladly die. I realise ours is such a cause – and you know that there is nothing I am saying now that I was not saying several years before the war – and it seems to me, as it does to many of us, a monstrous weakness that we do not produce a simple programme going beyond the mere destruction of Hitlerism and proclaim it day and night to the whole waiting world. We should nail our colours to the mast, and it should be neither our flag nor yours but the flag of all decent humanity. Goodnight, Cass. Goodnight, Gene. Goodnight to you all.

2 and 3 March 1941

Women at War

Good evening. This is a talk about women and this war, and it is topical because here plans are now rapidly going forward to bring a new army of women workers into our war industries. Young women are to be conscripted for this work just as young men have been conscripted for the fighting services. So, you may say, women are in the news. But that is not the only reason why I want to talk tonight about women and this war. I found myself talking about this subject only a day or two ago when I fulfilled a promise to give a short lunchtime address to the Society of Women Journalists in London. Their lunch – a modest affair of coffee and sandwiches – was held in what is left of the noble old Stationers Hall, one of the beautiful old City Halls that is now half a gaping ruin, with the actual hall itself, where I have made more than one speech and eaten more than one good dinner, a mass of charred rafters and damaged walls, all open to the sky. But in a room still whole, with the sound of the workmen's shovels in our ears – for the debris was still being cleared away – we met for this lunch. I told them then how glad and proud I was to be with them when they were animated by such an undaunted and resolute spirit, rightly refusing to abandon their meetings, keeping going in the old place, blitz or no blitz. And some of the things I said to them later I want to say to you tonight. But just as I began to put down some notes for this talk, my eye was caught by a letter among a pile that had just arrived, and as this letter seems to me very much to the point I am going to read some passages from it. The writer is a retired school teacher, a downright sensible woman from my own North Country, where we speak our minds. She says:

> *If women have any grit when this is all over – the women of the world, I mean – they will say, 'No, you men, you've largely been running this world for years and years and a nice old mess you've got it into. From now on it's going to be fifty–fifty, and all this war business is going to stop right here and now!' One realises that Nazism, Fascism, Iron Guardism, Gestapoism and all the other horrifics are purely masculine movements – in short, man at his worst. No one has yet, strange to say, tried to lay the blame on women. The first thing Hitler did when he came into power was to put down all the women's organisations which were beginning to function on social questions with good effect. A world-wide-known English businessman said to me a few years ago, 'If you women make up your minds to do anything there is nothing you could not accomplish.' And it seems to me now is the time to be up and doing. I have for forty-six years taught boys and girls in large departments, and have had both men and women over me, and for the last thirty years both men and women under me, and can quite dispassionately affirm that taking it by and large any one average woman is the equivalent of any two average men. Women are more conscientious, more social minded, have infinitely more moral courage to do and dare to say what they conceive to be right whether it is popular or not...*

So there! I don't know myself whether the average woman is so vastly superior to the average man, though she might well be, if only because the male sex shows a much greater variety than the female. There are more criminals, lunatics, suicides and generally hopeless types among men than there are among women, but at the other end of the scale there are more outstanding personalities, great inventive minds, geniuses, among men than there are among women. In short, we men tend more towards extremes than women do. But this is not a reason for but perhaps rather a reason *against* man's domination in the major affairs of life.

I have myself long been in favour of women playing a much greater part in our political life, and for the very sound reason that some of the essential feminine qualities seem to me the very qualities necessary – and now urgently necessary – for the proper guidance of our public life. To begin with, women tend to have a great deal of common sense, especially when it comes to dealing with matters of any importance. (They can be fantastic enough about trifles, of course, but then, I think, they're just giving themselves a holiday.) They have a better sense of reality than perhaps the majority of men, who often appear to be far more practical and realistic than they really are. Women usually have a sound notion of what is important and essential and what is not. Finally, although the best men – the poets, the seers, the prophets – have perhaps more wisdom and insight and wider sympathies than any woman, women in general have a better sense of spiritual values than the average man.

Now, I believe that a great deal of political and economic activity in any modern state is really nothing more than glorified, large-scale housekeeping. What is needed to solve its problems is not a super-brain or a mind of extraordinary insight but simply a mixture of patience, enthusiasm for the task, and sturdy common sense, and a great many women seem to me to have precisely that right mixture. They could, I believe, get some of the jobs done while men, clinging passionately to their ideas and enjoying their own cleverness and rhetoric, were still merely arguing about it. And although I think it is true to say that in small matters women are apt to prove themselves singularly unco-operative, displaying all the petty vices of individualism and egoism, I believe that in affairs of real importance, which every woman would recognise to be of supreme importance just because they affected the welfare of millions of human beings, women would soon show themselves to be more truly co-operative than men are apt to be, if only because they would recognise that the thing to be done was more urgent than their own ideas about it or their own prestige. I may be wrong, but that is what I sincerely feel.

It is true that often in political life and public affairs, the women who have been able to find positions of some responsibility seem out of place and anything but at ease. But that, in my opinion, is because the atmosphere of public affairs and political life is still so obviously masculine, so that it is like seeing a woman in a man's club. But this world is not a man's club. It is a place where men and women equally have to share the adventure of living, where what is a tragedy for the men becomes equally a tragedy – indeed, perhaps far more of a tragedy – for the women. This war, for example, is certainly not of woman's making, but on the whole I think the price that women are paying for it is greater than what we men are paying. For there is something in this atmosphere of huge destructiveness that has a certain sneaking appeal to something in the masculine nature, whereas it is entirely abhorrent to the feminine mind, a sheer unmitigated horror. These amazing machines and instruments of destruction that masculine ingenuity has evolved are not without interest and attraction to the average man, whereas to the average woman, who sees everything she holds dear threatened by them, they bring nothing but thoughts of mutilation and death.

Though he may hate war, the average man, even in these days, often finds some compensations in the new life he is compelled to live in wartime: movement and change and adventure and a new comradeship, with perhaps some chance of distinguishing himself and proving his worth. But most of these compensations do not exist for the average woman, and it is upon her that all the restrictions of life during total war press more heavily. It is she who must cope with rising prices and dwindling rations, who must bring up the children, who must wait, one black night after another, for news of a husband or a son. And, as I told you months ago, what roused my admiration to the highest pitch, during the Battle of Britain, throughout the days and nights of indiscriminate terror bombing, were the conduct and the bearing of the women and girls of London and other bombed cities. Not only did they stand up to all the raids, but they contrived through it all to keep up their own feminine standards of appearance and behaviour, to be at once charming and compassionate. It was almost as if the brutal Goering had hurled all his iron and steel at so many feminine fripperies, impudent little hats, shoes, handbags – and yet had been defeated.

And these women and girls of ours are obeying a very profound instinct when they summon up all their resources of endurance, enterprise, inventiveness, to defy the Nazis, and their sisters throughout the world should be on their side. For if the modern world has shown itself to be over-masculine in its atmosphere and values, it is certain that in Nazism and Fascism we have this one-sided masculinity developed to the point of idiocy. These are men who would create a world in which it would hardly be possible for a true woman of sense and personality to breathe properly. No sooner had they achieved power, these Nazis and Fascists, than they gave the whole crazy game away. Women were ordered back to the kitchen. Women were told that it was their task to amuse the tired warrior, if he happened to be that kind of tired warrior, and to breed more soldiers for the state.

Just as women themselves disappeared from public life, so feminine values vanished from this world of loutish, swaggering hobble-de-hoys. All the things that women care for began to wither. The family was broken up, and children set to spy on their parents. Realism and humour were practically banished. You could be beaten up merely for smiling in these vast mad houses. All the little graces of life began to disappear. While women were ordered not to spend their time and money on making themselves look attractive, the curious males who gave these orders spent more and more time and money devising for themselves and putting on the most fantastic glittering uniforms.

Perverted sadistic impulses, resulting in the most abominable cruelty, all of a kind quite foreign to the true feminine nature, were allowed to run riot. Murder became part of state policy. And all the time while these huge unwieldy ships of state were being relentlessly driven towards the whirlpools of war and destruction, the voice of Woman, apostle of realism and common sense and sane values in living, was not allowed to be raised.

How the women in these dictator countries, where the men, unchecked, were obviously going mad, ever allowed themselves to be deceived, or if not deceived then silenced, is still to me a mystery. But what is clear is that any world dominated by Hitler and his Nazis is not a world in which Woman can find her true place. Nothing fifty–fifty about these Nazis. There are certain types of loutish or mentally twisted males who might have found their own grim kind of fun in such a world, but it meant nothing less than permanent slavery for womanhood. Thus we fight for something more even than the democratic idea. We fight for a sensible, fifty–fifty world – and I do not pretend that it has arrived yet, but I do believe it is on its way – a world in which both feminine and masculine values are recognised, in which womanhood is something more than a passport to cleaning, cooking and breeding, in which at every step a man takes on his great adventure he can find by his side, guiding as often as she is following his lead, his eternal comrade – Woman. Goodnight, ladies – and gentlemen!

9 and 10 March 1941

The White Cliffs

Good evening. You will be interested to learn that Mrs. Alice Duer Miller's long poem 'The White Cliffs', which has been so successful on your side, is just being published here, and a few days ago I received a copy from the publishers. I can understand its wide appeal now that I have read it. To begin with, it's extremely ingenious, being a number of very varied short poems that together make a long poem; and the manner is so contrived that the writer can pass easily from ordinary speech, even slang, to that heightened speech that a long poem sometimes demands. But at the same time that it's ingenious, I believe it is also passionately sincere, not something got out to catch the public eye at an appropriate moment but the expression of a living faith. What Mrs. Miller *says* she has felt about England, that, I believe, she truly has felt. We are very grateful.

This is a poem that must have made many friends for England – and when I say 'England' I mean 'England' and not Britain, because the poem's not about Britain, it's about England – and if anything that I am going on to say should sound ungrateful and unchivalrous, let me apologise in advance and say that nothing of the kind was intended. What follows is *not* an adverse criticism of Mrs. Miller's excellent poem, which does what it set out to do perfectly. The concluding lines are now deservedly famous:

> *I am American bred,*
> *I have seen much to hate – much to forgive,*
> *But in a world where England is finished and dead,*
> *I do not wish to live.*

That could not be better said, and I have no doubt whatever that the superb emotional impact of this conclusion has made the poem itself a notable ally in the cause of democracy. We are very grateful to Mrs. Miller. But my own difficulty is this – that the England described in this poem is not *my* England, is only a tiny part of the real England, and, to be candid, is that part of England and English life that has been described too often. I don't blame Mrs. Miller for describing it, because I take it that this is the England she herself knew, as well as her heroine in the poem. You remember:

> *A light blue carpet on the stair*
> *And tall young footmen everywhere,*
> *Tall young men with English faces*
> *Standing rigidly in their places,*
> *Rows and rows of them stiff and staid*
> *In powder and breeches and bright, old braid…*

and then the portraits on the walls, of generals and admirals and lord-lieutenants of shires, and then 'the family place in Devon', and the young man's mother, the Lady Jean, and the panelled upper galleries, a world of parties in Mayfair, Oxford and Cambridge, and life in remote large country houses. Now, of course all this existed right up to the outbreak of this war – and there is something like it, a fairly robust spectre of it, still existing – and I'm not pretending for a moment that it is unreal. What I am saying is that it should no longer be taken as being representative and that for a long time we have heard far too much about it. This is the England that the novelists are so fond of. It is the England that the films are always showing us. The old hall, the hunt breakfast, the villagers touching their caps, the hunt ball, the family portraits, all the old bag of tricks. But this isn't the England that's fighting this war. This Christmas-card-Hollywood England couldn't fight this war in a couple of days. This is a war of machines and of the men who make and drive those machines. They don't make sixteen-inch guns or Hurricanes and Spitfires down at the old family place in Devon. And most of the young men who are manning those guns and are flying those Hurricanes and Spitfires have never seen the old family place in Devon either, and wouldn't know what to do with themselves if they found themselves surrounded by 'tall young footmen everywhere'.

It is industrial England that is fighting this war, just as it was industrial England, those scores of gloomy towns half buried in thick smoke, with their long dreary streets of little houses all alike, and their rather short, bandy-legged folk, usually with bad teeth, who aren't much to look at but happen to be among the most highly skilled and trustworthy workmen in the world, who produced most of the wealth that enabled this other fancy little England to have its fun and games. And it is this other big England that is having to take it in this war. The bombs fall on Coventry, Sheffield, Birmingham, Manchester, not on the old family place in Devon.

Don't mistake me here. The people from the old family place can take it too all right. They're very tough and as brave as lions, those old family English, and perhaps the best fellows in the world to have as officers in a war, so long as it's character rather than brains you need. But the fact remains that the England that stands up and sets its teeth and suffers with a wry grin is the smoky industrial England, the England of those long streets of dreary little houses, which you see, in some parts, flattened out by the bombing. That's the England that is taking it, and, believe me, that is the England that is going to dish it out, because beneath that smoke there is work going on that will soon make Goering and Company wish the idea of bombing planes had never been thought of. These decent little folk didn't want to be plunged into this horror; they were willing to make sacrifices to avoid war; but if it's a question of being tough or knuckling under to these Nazi bullies then these people will set their faces and just show the Germans how tough they can be when thoroughly roused.

Now, it's very natural that to most people from overseas, this hard-working, manufacturing, coal-mining, textile-making, ship-building England is not the one that appeals to them first. What you enjoy seeing most over here is the traditional old England that has found its way into so many books and pictures. Often you can't help seeing England in terms of quaint villages and charming old country mansions, of the ancient colleges in Oxford and Cambridge, of fashionable functions in Mayfair; of all that is venerable and traditional. There is much here that we should like to preserve, whatever happens to us in the future. I for one do not believe in rooting out and destroying everything that reminds us of the past, just as I equally don't believe in wearing the past like a millstone round our necks.

But I do suggest that it is deceptive – and sometimes even rather dangerous – to regard this storybook traditional England as the real England, the country that is now at the very heart and centre of all active resistance to Nazism. It is deceptive because obviously such a Christmas-card-Hollywood sort of place, all charm and antiquity and rigid conservatism, could never challenge, with any hope of success, the up-to-the-minute armed might of Nazism. It would have about as much chance as a duchess taking on ten gunmen. It is dangerous because people unsympathetic to our cause, and searching for any excuse to avoid troubling themselves, can retort that if we are fighting for democracy then there doesn't seem much democracy in this England to fight about. And this, of course, would be not untrue. But the other England, the big hard-working England, really *is* democratic, and is becoming more so every day, and it is in this truly democratic industrial England, which never saw a row of footmen in its life and doesn't want to, that you find the hard centre, the very core, of this triumphant resistance of Nazism. It is actually this fact that baffles German propaganda, which adopts all manner of devices, some of them comic, to try to get at the industrial workers, without any real success. And this is the England that some of us love, not because it's quaint, because it isn't, not because it's charming, because it isn't, not because it's old, because some of it is comparatively recent, but because it contains the ordinary decent English, who take a whole lot of rousing but once they are roused simply won't give in to anybody. These are the people, as I've said before, that Hitler doesn't know. How should he? The only ones he's ever seen were some in uniform during the last war, and certainly he had anything but contempt for them.

After the fall of France, the Nazis announced that the war was all over, bar the shouting. They expected in all seriousness that Britain would pack up. Now, why did they expect that? Because in the same circumstances, with everything against them, they themselves would have packed up. There can be no doubt whatever that that was the reason for their mistake, and it gives us a valuable clue to their real nature. Once everything goes against them, they'll begin to panic and then suddenly will collapse altogether. They're all success worshippers, swaggering and aggressive when all goes well but lacking real inner confidence, which accounts, of course, for the swagger and boasting and bullying, which in their turn explain why these fellows are so disliked everywhere. The further they travel from home, the more they bluff and swagger and bully, and the more enemies they make, piling up grievances that will fall on them one day like a toppling mountain. And I say that these ordinary English, who live in the smoky towns or in the rather dreary suburbs, are just the opposite. They're very reluctant to start anything. They don't want any trouble. But once they're shaken out of their sleep, they'll go on until they drop.

These people are now emerging from the second winter of this war. The spring flowers are coming out, the days are rapidly getting longer, the winter is quickly vanishing. And half a dozen doleful prophecies of six months ago are proved to have been wildly wrong. By this time, it was said, their morale would have taken a sharp decline. But it hasn't, it's up. The winter bombing, it was said, would make large-scale production, quick transport and even a reasonable standard of life impossible in many of the heavily blitzed industrial towns. Well, they've had the winter bombing, but production goes forward, transport is much better than it was, and the blitzed towns are looking after their citizens. I don't know how the fancy-picture-postcard, footmen-and-old-family-place England is going on – and, to tell you the truth, I don't much care – but I know that the other real big England has taken it well and is now preparing to dish it out even better. And I wish Mrs. Miller could write another long poem, as good as her 'White Cliffs' – she might call this one 'Dark Mills' – about this other England. And that suggestion I hope she'll accept in the spirit it was offered – not as a criticism but as a compliment and a tribute to a gifted friend of our country.

16 and 17 July 1941

Giving the V-Sign

Good evening! A lot has happened since I last talked to you. In the East, Nazi Germany is locked in a vast grip with Russia. In the West, Nazi Germany is being invaded and assaulted day and night by our RAF. All that, you know. But other things are happening too, and some of them are more important than you might think at first. For instance, this V sign. You've probably heard or read something about it already. We needed a simple sign of Allied defiance, of faith and hope, and we found it in the letter V. V is for 'victory', for *victoire* in French, *vreiheit* in Flemish and so on. And it's become the symbol of our cause. You remember in the trial in *Pickwick Papers*, when Sam Weller was called as a witness, he was asked how he spelt his name, and he replied, 'I never had occasion to spell it more than once or twice in my life, but I spells it with a V.' Whereupon a voice from the gallery, belonging to old Mr. Weller, exclaimed aloud, 'Quite right too, Samivel, quite right. Put it down a we, my lord, put it down a we.' And that's what is happening now all over Western Europe. We're spelling it with a V. In Belgium, France, Holland, Czechoslovakia, the letter V is found everywhere, painted on house-sides, chalked on walls, pencilled on packing cases. Towns have been fined by the worried Nazis for allowing these V inscriptions to remain on their walls. But there are more and more of them. Men passing each other raise two fingers and then separate them, thus making the V sign with their fingers. Then V happens to be the Roman numeral for five, so now anything to do with five becomes part of the signal of defiance and hope. Men working in the fields of these occupied countries now turn to the village clocks as they chime the hour of five.

Now, all this has been going on for some months, but recently there has been a new development. The V sign can be given in sound, simply by using the Morse code taps for V. This is three short taps followed by a long. Like this – [taps]. So we have been telling our friends in the occupied countries to use this signal. If they have to knock, let them knock like this [knocks]. If they are in a café and wish to call the waiter, they must call him in this fashion: 'Waiter!' [taps] 'Hurry up!' [taps]. Don't make the mistake of thinking this is a little childish thing. It's supremely important. As I've said over and over again, this is not only a war of machines but also a war of morale, not only a war of planes but also of propaganda. It is a psychological war. Now, those four rhythmic taps, three shorts and a long, remind you of something, don't they? Yes, that's it – the opening theme of Beethoven's 5th Symphony, which was always described as Fate knocking on the door. Here it is:

[Opening bars of Beethoven's 5th.]

Yes, Fate knocking on the door. And our V sign of victory, our symbol of defiance, of faith and hope, of our belief that modern man cannot be enslaved and that the Nazis are doomed – yes, those are the knocks of Doom, and I hope that very soon all the Germans in all the occupied countries will hear them day and night. That is why this V signal is so important, for not only does it provide all anti-Nazi elements with a simple sign of their unity but also it suggests to the Nazis that their doom is on the way. Fate is knocking on the door. For, remember, the German is always haunted by this sense of doom. It is the German myth, forever ending in Siegfried's death and the twilight of the gods.

Let me quote to you what a brilliant young German, Sebastian Haffner, has written on this very point: 'The Germans', he says,

> *are easily encouraged and discouraged by irrational conceptions; and crazy heroism, with them, lies at only one remove from panic-dread. These elements in their character must be grasped if we are to influence them. Deep-rooted in all of them is the feeling that adventures such as the Nazis have contrived must sooner or later bring disaster in their train. The course of the mythical play – the sallying forth, triumph, turn of the tide, collapse – is preordained, but it has no time limit ... The reaction of the Germans will depend on their perceiving that the hour has struck. They are also brave as any other nation so long as they feel the wind of battle and victory behind them; but they yield helplessly to panic and dread when they notice that the tide has turned ... And how do they know when the hour has struck? They know it, once again, solely by the use of their imagination and senses, never by a hard-headed weighing and reckoning of their chances. A change in the atmosphere; a sudden and startling set-back or counter-blow; the feeling, above all, that the initiative has been irretrievably lost to the enemy – such things will make them forget, in their utter dismay, what power they have to defend themselves, just as before a consciousness of invincible strength enabled them to defy overwhelming odds. Had they found themselves in England's position after the French collapse last summer, the Germans would have capitulated in a swoon. Proof: the certainty with which they expected it of England.*

That is what a brilliant German says of the Germans. And now you see why, at a time when the German Army is locked in a death-grip with the Russians, when day and night our war planes go deeper and deeper into their territory, producing terrible havoc, when American aid assumes a shape ever more menacing to them, I think it important too that everywhere the V sign of Allied victory should be chalked on walls and that the

Nazi forces of occupation should constantly hear the three short taps and then the long, the sound of Fate knocking on the door. It means that these creatures of the tragic spirit begin to see the sky darken, and hear already from afar the horns of doom, ushering in the grim last act, the death of the hero, the twilight of the gods...

But we have to remember this: that although these people will surely crack and their whole crazy empire vanish like smoke, we can no more afford to lean back and wait than we could if we were in the house with a wounded tiger. In all previous wars, the leaders of the opposing forces have always felt that if the worst came to the worst, if defeat came, they could at least capitulate as gracefully as possible and then retire into obscurity, as the Kaiser did after the last war. But now we are dealing with men who are outlaws, who know that there is no easy retirement for them, who must fight on or perish. Therefore, while they retain any power, they will drive their people as people have never been driven before, will take the craziest risks, knowing very well it is neck or nothing, and won't allow the smallest scruple of human feeling to stand in their way. They'll use this vast terrible war machine of theirs without mercy, keeping nothing in reserve, hoping as always to overwhelm us while we are still unready. Therefore, though the doom is coming, that doom has still to be of our contriving. Instead of leaning back, now is the very moment when we must increase the tempo, ringing the wounded screaming lashing beast round with steel.

And that, if you'll allow me to say so, is where all of you come in. Just as much as we on our side do, now's the time to pile it up and pile it on, plane after plane, tank after tank, ship after ship. They asked for it; they wanted the game played this way; so let them have it, until suddenly, the old Teutonic fury gone, the door shaking under the thundering knocks of Fate, they realise that they have been betrayed again by that tragic weakness within, and throw down their weapons and cry once more for mercy.

Some of you may say: 'But there isn't much we can do. We're a long way off. We can't chalk up V signs under their noses – we wish we could – or make that fateful tapping. Where do we come in?' I'll tell you where you come in. And it's one reason – quite apart from the great friendliness you've always shown me – why I'm glad to be back talking to you. Because, from now on, you come in all over the place. You're all of you terribly important, although you may be thousands and thousands of miles away from the battlefields. I'll explain why, and here I want you to follow me carefully. The Nazis can't win, unless of course we all lie down and let them win. But the old Europe's finished. When you take Hitler's New Order away – and it's going to be taken away all right – there'll be a kind of political and economic and social vacuum. I don't mean by that that the old states won't reappear. Of course they will. The people of those countries expect it, and we've guaranteed it. But you can't put back Europe to what it was. Nobody even wants it to be where it was, except Hitler and Mussolini and their friends. There has to be a new Europe. But inevitably the whole continent will be suffering from a terrible exhaustion, spiritual and mental as well as physical. They'll be like men who've been imprisoned for years in some narrow dungeon and then suddenly find the walls have been knocked down and that the daylight's streaming in. Such people at first won't know what to do. No matter how much they may have liked their old life, before Hitler came along and turned it into slavery, they won't find it possible to get back into that old life. So they'll want help. Yes, of course, some of it will be obvious physical help, foodstuffs, machinery and the like. But more than that, they'll want the help, the goodwill, the faith and hope, the inspiration, of people who have been outside the prison walls all the time and so have not felt that all civilisation was going to pieces. And that is where all of you come in. From the Dominions of the British Commonwealth, from the United States, from the great English-speaking democracies, this help, this faith and hope, this inspiration can come.

We're not going to pretend we've settled all our problems. If you think we have then you ought to know by this time that I for one profoundly disagree with you. We've a lot to learn, and, by thunder, we've a lot to do. *But* – and this is the point – we're living neither in a vast prison, which is all that Hitler's New Order is, except of course for Hitler and the gang, nor in a huge disintegrating society, a weary muddle, a kind of vacuum, which is what most of Europe will be after Hitler's prison has been knocked down. With all our faults, we are at least living in a society that has the capacity for decent growth and sensible development, that has not made it impossible for men of intelligence and goodwill to solve their problems; a society that is, except for the usual untenable sections, beginning to see how many errors it has made. And so it is to us that men will turn, and above all, I believe, to you, in the new democracies overseas, who can even yet sit down in security and think how best to serve this shattered old world. Men, women, children in noble old cities now under Nazi domination are risking much just to make that sign of V for Victory. It's up to us on this side to endure everything to make that victory certain. And it's up to you on your side to make sure that the victory is complete, so that not only Hitler has gone but also the world that could produce a Hitler has gone for ever too. We can be the surgeons, performing the operation, but you must be the physicians, curing the world of its disease of stupidity, greed, fear and violence.

13 and 14 August 1941

Take Down the Railings

The other morning, turning unexpectedly into a famous square in the West End of London, I noticed that there was something different about it. For some time I couldn't make out what this difference was. All I knew was that this large square suddenly appeared to have a charm that I didn't remember it having before. The sunlight was twinkling through the leaves of the lime trees. There was an enchanting little green dusk in the shadow of the trees. Where there was no shadow, there were patches of bright gold on the grass. I caught sight of a flash or two of colour from the dresses of women and children. A little bubble of laughter came from one of these miniature glades, which, if you forgot the tall buildings all around the square and kept your gaze fixed on the trees and grass in the centre, might almost have been a tiny corner of that Forest of Arden, where the banished duke and his companions, as we know, for ever 'fleet the time carelessly, as they did in the golden world'. Staring a little harder across the grass and through the green dusk under the trees, I noticed in the very centre an absurd but charming little nonsense building which might have been a toy pagoda. This sight of this too – and I never remembered seeing it before – gave me great pleasure.

And then I asked myself why I was enjoying the sight of this square so much, and what had made the difference. I knew that something must have happened. And then I saw what it was. *The railings had been taken down.* Yes, that was it. For the first time I was seeing the central garden of this square as it really was, with nothing between me and the friendly trees and grass. Before, there had always been the railings, a sort of rusty iron stockade. Now they had gone. They had been placed there originally as a symbol of the grandeur and exclusiveness of the people who lived in that square. They had been there to prevent strange children from playing on the grass and courting couples from strolling, whispering and kissing in the shadow of the trees. Now, I am one of those sensible healthy souls who like to see the great river of life rolling along unchecked, and in the very middle and deepest waterway of that great river of life are children wishing to play and lovers wanting to kiss. That, whether you like it or not, is life as lived on this planet, and if you don't like it then leave us and try to find your way to some other planet.

Grandeur and exclusiveness seem pretty poor things when compared with this rich current of existence. As a matter of fact, they are pretty poor things when compared with almost anything. People who have real merit are content to let that merit speak for them, and do not need to strut behind any symbols of grandeur and exclusiveness. They don't, in fact, need railings. This square is far better off now that its railings are gone. Not only does it look far more charming but now it is far more use to everybody. It is alive now, whereas before, all secure behind its railings, it was half dead. Of course, now that anybody can wander beneath the trees, and children can run screaming from seat to seat, the grass will not wear as well as it did before, when it was all railed off, and probably some enthusiastic young lover will carve initials and a heart on one of the trees, and perhaps some nasty urchin will scrawl rude words on the little pagoda. There will, in short, be far more wear and tear, but that is the price – and a very reasonable price too – you pay for being alive. If you prefer to have less wear and tear, you can keep yourself half dead until you are really dead, and you shouldn't have long to wait, and nobody will mind very much if you haven't to wait at all.

It must be about a year and a half ago that I wrote a little article pointing out that this war gave us a fine chance of getting rid of our railings. They could be used as scrap metal. Let them be pulled up, I urged, collected and taken back to the foundries. We can put them to good uses in this war for our freedom and civilisation, and in the meantime our freedom and civilisation will look a lot better without them. There must, I said, be more iron railings in this country than in any three countries anywhere. Our grandfathers must have had a passion for them. They planted them everywhere, as if there was some curious virtue in these ugly thickets of iron. London, I pointed out, is almost a jungle of railings. The parks have miles of railings round them. The little gardens in the squares were severely railed in, as if there were tigers lurking in their bushes. All the older private houses bristle with railings, just as if at one time the owners imagined there were Red Indians about and thought some kind of stockade was necessary. It's the same in our larger provincial towns. As soon as our grandfathers felt prosperous, up went the railings. They felt they had to begin hedging themselves in and hedging other people out with these rows of iron spears. Some of these railings, of course, may do something to protect valuable property against thieves, but most of them are not really there for that purpose. They are really there for grandeur and exclusiveness. They indicate to most of our fellow citizens that they are only moving about on sufferance. 'Hey you! – don't you see those railings?' It is not without significance that the only time during these last hundred years that a London crowd really lost its temper, it proceeded at once to tear out the railings in Hyde Park.

You may imagine that these railings are both a product and symbol of the old aristocratic England, but there, I think, you would be wrong. The England of Elizabeth, for example, needed no railings. Differences in rank and station then were so obvious, to be seen at a glance, that no railings were needed, even if their manufacture in those days had been possible on any scale. I think these iron thickets and stockades arrived with the industrial revolution, when of course they could be manufactured conveniently and cheaply, but when too they suddenly became necessary. For now differences in rank and station were no longer so obvious. The fundamental difference was to be discovered best in bank balances, though if these were substantial enough they usually led to some outward elevation in rank, wealthy manufacturers and the like being transformed into peers of the realm, and leaving the grimy towns where they had made their money for distant large estates, where, secure behind railings, they could pretend hardly to have heard of coal-mining or cotton-spinning. And the top-hatted and black-coated rich employer looked hardly different from top-hatted and black-coated clerks in his offices. It was the railings – the railings round the country estate, the railings round the town houses, the railings round the gardens in the city square – that began to make most difference.

And if you were not careful, you tended not only to rail the mob out but also to rail yourself in. Your children could play in the railed-off garden in the city square, because you as a resident had a key for the locked gate and this key you handed over to your children's nurse, while you thanked Heaven that you could procure for your children this security and exclusiveness; but I think that often your children had a very poor time of it in that exclusiveness and security, and listened with envy to the shouts and laughter of the urchins who had been so neatly railed out. And often behind the other railings, round the country estates or the great town houses, there were wistful faces, frequently belonging to young women who could feel the tide of life murmuring and stirring within them, and who began to wonder whether it would not be better to risk some wear and tear but *live*, instead of being cooped up and railed off and feeling only half alive. So it wasn't only the people on the outside who sometimes cursed the railings. There were in fact more amusing things happening, more colour, comradeship and fun, more *life*, on the outside than inside, as you may gather from that great satirist of the railed-in, our immortal Dickens.

Now, in one sense the railings have been disappearing for some time. They were going, in this symbolic sense, even before the last war. And that war did much to hasten their departure. Even physically it did, I imagine, for it stopped their being painted and cared for and made them rustier than ever. Nevertheless, it didn't entirely get rid of them in any sense. And during the twenty years between wars, somehow the railings stayed, and even at times began to look a more formidable barrier than they had done before. And then this war arrived, and we discovered, just before it was too late, that we must fight for the very existence of our Christian civilisation, for, make no mistake about it, that is precisely what we're fighting for – not simply for Britain, for our Commonwealth of free nations, for the independence and integrity of France, Belgium, Holland and all the rest – but for the soul of Man, which is more terribly menaced now than it has been for a thousand years. For there is a force now let loose in the world, a force of which Nazism is simply the immediate political expression, that aims at the destruction of the civilised individual consciousness, of the very soul of Western Man. And now because we have to fight as never before, because we need everything we can lay our hands on for the weapons of this battle, the railings are being pulled up at last. Yes, the actual material railings are disappearing, to be transformed, we hope, into the swords and shields of man's free spirit.

And with them is vanishing too all that they stood for, the nonsensical grandeur and exclusiveness, the sense of privilege, the divisions of society that set poor men and rich men into two camps. Now that the railings are going, we shall seem in truth more like the democracy of free men and women for which we are fighting. Not everybody will like that democracy, just as not everybody likes to see the gardens in the London squares open to any wandering band of children or strolling lovers. There will, I repeat, be more wear and tear. Certain haughty notions of grandeur and exclusiveness will receive many a rude shock. There may be more noise about, more argument, more obvious conflict of opinion, more loud laughter, more cheerful vulgarity. But there will also be more *life*. We can see at last – and that means any of us who can use our eyes – the sunlight twinkling through the leaves of the lime trees, the enchanting little green dusk in the shadow of the foliage, the patches of bright gold on the grass, the birds flickering across from branch to branch, the flash of white and coloured dresses; and we can hear the laughter of children and catch the endless whispering of lovers. And all because the railings have gone – and gone, I believe, for ever. Goodnight.

4 and 5 September 1941

Three Years of War

Good evening. Just because we've now entered the third year of this war, I've been trying to work out a kind of balance sheet, and doing it as honestly as I possibly could. In a short talk you can't do more than indicate some of the main items on the debit and the credit side, and no doubt many of you will disagree with what I consider to be these main items. But my rough notion of a balance sheet may help some of you to work out one of your own, and in any event we ought to be able to clear our ideas.

Let's begin with a very big item on the debit side: Nazi Germany's war material. Now, I always thought, right up to the fall of France, that there was a large element of bluff in Hitler's war machine. I imagined that all the goods were always being put into the front window. After all, the Nazis were notorious bluffers. But whatever the real size of the machine may have been at the beginning of the war, there can be no doubt whatever that by the end of the first year, Hitler's armaments – in planes, tanks, guns – were colossal. They are still colossal, even though the whole machine has had a terrible mauling in Russia.

Another debit item. The whole war production of the democracies has been slower than it ought to have been. Don't let's fool ourselves about that. It's true that during the months following Dunkirk, the British people probably achieved the most astonishing feat of war production known to history. But that doesn't alter the fact that the democracies as a whole have been slower in swinging into full war production than they ought to have been. This does not mean that there is anything decadent about the democracies. The truth is, there is something repugnant about this notion of total war, with human beings organised like communities of ants, to the democratic mind, and hence its slowness in abandoning itself to the idea. But we must have that full production.

Third debit item. This is the way in which so many countries, after seeing one terrible example after another of Hitler's methods, have still refused to combine against him, but have allowed themselves to be intimidated, over-run, then half-absorbed, one by one, as Mr. Churchill pointed out in his last speech. This inability to profit by experience has been staggering, and the Nazis must often have wondered at their good luck. Now, those seem to me the three great debit items: the size and power of the Nazi war machine; the comparative slowness of production among the democracies; the inability of the smaller European powers to combine against Nazism.

And now let's look at the other side of the ledger. What can be put to the credit balance? First, I think, the comparative failure of three out of the four Nazi weapons. These four weapons are the Army, the Air Force, the Navy and the propaganda machine. And the last three have been comparative failures. The Luftwaffe may have succeeded in Poland, the Low Countries and France, but it has so far failed against Britain and it is failing against Russia. Nobody denies that it has done enormous damage, but it has not been able, either in Britain or in Russia, to strike the really effective knock-out blows. Moreover, its losses have been on a stupendous scale. Not only in machines but, what is more important, in highly trained personnel. The loss of first-class Nazi pilots during the Battle of Britain alone must have been devastating. I wonder how many first-class airmen there are now in the Luftwaffe? Again, this air force was designed to destroy civilian morale. Here again, it has failed. Civilian morale both in Britain and in Russia is very high. This is a Nazi ace that has been trumped.

Now to the second weapon – the sea weapon. There can be no doubt that Hitler counted on this one, for he has referred to it specifically in more than one speech. We were to be knocked out in the Atlantic. We haven't been knocked out in the Atlantic. The losses there were at one time very considerable, but during the last few months they have been greatly reduced, whereas the Axis losses at sea, from the very same weapons that Hitler boasted of, have lately reached enormous figures. The total tonnage of shipping lost to the Axis powers now exceeds four million tons. Meanwhile, where is Hitler's navy? And where is Mussolini's?

And now for the third weapon that has largely failed. That is the propaganda machine. We mustn't under-estimate the importance of this weapon. After all, Goebbels is one of the most powerful persons in Germany. His expenditure must reach an astronomical figure in Marks. He employs an army of assistants. The maintenance of this gigantic propaganda machine must be a very essential and expensive part of the Nazi war effort. Well, what has it successfully accomplished during these first two years of war? It has done everything within its power to turn the people of the occupied countries against Britain. Has it succeeded? The growing severity of the Nazi decrees and orders in these countries proves beyond question that it has dismally failed. It has tried to drive a thick wedge between Britain and the United States, telling us that we are handing our empire over to America, and telling America that she is being tricked into fighting Britain's battles for her. Has it succeeded? No, once again it has dismally failed. Then, when it was decided to attack Russia, the whole vast machine began to churn out the old rubbish about Nazism saving Europe, and indeed the world, from Bolshevism. The idea was to make this typically unscrupulous and unprovoked Nazi invasion look like a crusade. Once again, the failure was dismal. Instead of whole armies of volunteers from the occupied countries, there have been nothing but a handful of Nazified youngsters who have volunteered for this service. The whole scheme has been a notorious flop.

And that isn't the end of its flops. Goebbels has had another and still more startling failure. For he has failed at home on his own ground. If the German people are still far from revolt, that is not because Goebbels has succeeded in keeping their morale high but because Himmler has succeeded in his task of maintaining his terror police, the Gestapo. If there is one single fact about which all neutral observers have been agreed upon, it is this: that the German people refuse to react as Goebbels would wish them to react to all his tall tales of victories. Right from the beginning of this war, these people have never shown any sign of enthusiasm. They still do what they are told to do, but they do it without inner conviction, as if suffering from a profound weariness. The machine blares out its news of gigantic successes here, of startling triumphs there, the trumpets blow, the voices scream victory, but the people don't come to life, still seem like so many sleep-walkers, and only ask each other in low, anxious tones when there will be peace.

And Goebbels dare not tell them the truth. He has to keep feeding them the dope of lying promises. Let him stand up and offer them nothing but toil and sweat, blood and tears, as Winston Churchill did our people. If he is ready to declare that the morale and will-to-victory of the German people are as strong as those of the British people then I offer him this challenge. The British people are free to listen to any broadcast they choose. They are welcome to listen every night, if they wish to do so, to the broadcasts in English from Germany. Now, if Goebbels is as certain of his people as we are of ours then let him remove the ban in Germany from listening to *our* broadcasts. If there have to be severe penalties to prevent his people from listening to our broadcasts or the Russian broadcasts then obviously he can't be sure of the German morale or trust his own people. And if he *is* sure and if he *can* trust them then I challenge him to remove those penalties. He can't have it both ways. He can't tell us his people are following him enthusiastically of their own free will and yet point to the chains that prevent them from doing anything else but follow him.

No, the fact is that his propaganda machine has failed at home just as it has failed abroad. Not because it is a poor machine. It is a wonderful machine – I wish I had it to play with – *but* the trouble is, it is fed with such shoddy stuff. It *has* to be fed with shoddy stuff. The Nazis have all the means to make out a magnificent case – except the case itself, which is so obviously dubious that it defeats all the elaborate machinery for exploiting it. If his propaganda department had all the world's geniuses working for it, it would still fail to convince the world that it would be better off if it had men like Hitler, Goebbels and Himmler doing what they liked with it. The terrible dilemma of this extremely clever little man is this, that try as he may, he can't make people like Nazis. They just won't have it. He can't even succeed in making Nazis like Nazis, with the result that there are growing dissensions in the party itself.

Well, there you have the credit side of these two years of war: that of Hitler's four great weapons, the Army, the Air Force, the Navy and the propaganda machine, all but the Army have been comparative failures so far. The Nazis know this, of course, even better than we do, just as they know what has been in their favour – those three items I listed on the debit side – and this explains, I think, why Hitler is tending to use his most successful arm, the enormous crushing land forces, more and more, and with a growing recklessness. Which brings us to another great credit item. This is the unexpected power of resistance shown by the Russian armed forces and by the Russian people. This has meant that the Nazi gains, which so far have brought them nothing, have been most dearly bought, the campaign having been fought at a ruinous cost in both men and armaments. No doubt the German High Command was prepared to make sacrifices, but not such sacrifices as these.

As for the German people, it must be just beginning to dawn upon them – for no matter how strict your censorship is and elaborate your arrangements for hiding the truth are, two million casualties cannot be kept a secret long – it must, I say, be just beginning to dawn upon the German people that no possible return, in materials, loot, prestige or anything else, that could be expected from even a successful Russian campaign is worth the price they are paying now, and that they have now hitched their wagon not to a star but to a disastrous whirlwind. You can't go marching behind a madman and expect to win. You may have apparent victories, you may claim all the battles, but because there is nothing in the deep centre of your leader's mind but a dark roaring chaos, the end can only be tragic for you. This indeed is the real gigantic tragic farce of our time, that when man has reached heights of ingenious invention and elaborate organisation unknown to the world before, he should find his destiny entwined with that of a single individual who has always been at odds with life, who has always shown himself unbalanced, untrustworthy, uncreative, motivated always by fear and hate; and that the darkness of one man's lopsided and tormented mind should have imposed itself upon all Europe, perhaps the whole world, so that, because we would not solve our problems decently, would not bring them into the light, we are compelled to live in this gigantic black-out. But all that at least we of the fighting democracies know very well, and before this grim ledger is properly balanced and the last line ruled, the Germans and all their jackals will have either perished or learnt their lesson too.

2 and 3 October 1941

Science and War

G ood evening. Now, as you all know, this last weekend, the scientists of the free world met in London for a special conference of the famous British Association. The subject of the conference was the Social and International Relations of Science. It was based, solidly as a rock, on the three following propositions: that science has social responsibilities towards the community as a whole; that the integrity of scientific thought and work can only be maintained in a democratic society; and that it is necessary that science should participate in the reconstruction of the world after the war. All free scientists realise now that what science has achieved, science should guard; in other words, that the vast discoveries of science should not be used as the instruments of any ruthless system of power politics. What the common mind has discovered should be placed at the service of the community as a whole.

Out of this conference has come a statement of the principles of scientific fellowship. Don't imagine, please, that because you aren't a scientist, because perhaps you don't feel particularly interested in scientific matters, that these principles are no concern of yours. They are of immense importance to us all. Their acceptance or rejection by the world may very well shape the rest of our lives, and the lives of our children and children's children. Here is the statement. *One*: The basic principles of science recognise fundamental human rights and responsibilities; they combine independence with co-operation; and they are essential factors in the maintenance of a worthy and advancing form of society. *Two*: Man depends for his maintenance and advancement upon knowledge of himself and of the properties of things in the world around him, and upon the use of this knowledge for the common welfare. *Three*: Representatives of all races, and all classes of society, have contributed to the knowledge and uses of natural resources, and to the understanding of man's relation to them. *Four*: Men of science are among the trustees of each generation's inheritance of ascertained knowledge. It is their function to foster and increase this heritage by faithful guardianship and service to high ideals. *Five*: The pursuit of scientific inquiry demands complete intellectual freedom, unrestricted international exchange of knowledge, and the progressive development of civilised life. *Six*: All groups of scientific workers are united in the fellowship of the commonwealth of science, which has the world as its province, and service to man, through the discovery of truth, as its highest aim. *Seven*: Any policy of power which deprives men or nations of freedom of thought and its expression convicts its supporters of an iniquity against the human race. *Eight*: As freedom to teach, opportunity to learn, and desire to understand are essential for the extension of knowledge, men of science affirm these principles and maintain that they cannot be sacrificed among civilised communities without the degradation of human life.

Now, there is nothing new and startling about these principles. Men of science have held them for some time. They have assumed that the world held them too. But that assumption was wrong. What is new and startling here is that it should be necessary to re-affirm such principles. And it is necessary to re-affirm them because ever since the Nazis came to power in Germany, a country that had long been recognised as one of the world's leaders in scientific education, research, discovery, those principles have been denied, and today they are denied wherever the Nazis have the power. In short, most of Europe has now been thrust back into the dark ages, so far as science is concerned. What is absolutely fundamental to true scientific knowledge, work, achievement, is denounced by official Nazi doctrine. Nor have the Nazis stopped at mere denunciation. From the very moment they achieved power, they have proceeded deliberately to wreck all the great German monuments and institutions of scientific knowledge and work. What should have been the German's greatest pride – that long list of Nobel Prize winners – was attacked at once. Men of the very highest achievements, whose names were revered throughout the civilised world, men like Einstein, Franck, Meyerhof, were turned out of their professional chairs, stripped of their honours and privileges, robbed of their possessions and could only take refuge in exile. Famous universities like Heidelberg and Gottingen, which had been beacons of learning, were plunged into darkness. No secret was made of the intentions of these half-educated brigands who were now in power. In January 1934, a Nazi spokesman at the University of Gottingen announced to the astonished world:

> *On this day we take this vow … We renounce international science. We renounce the international republic of learning. We renounce research for its own sake. We teach and learn medicine not to increase the number of known microbes but to keep the German people strong and healthy. We teach and learn history not to say how things actually happened but to instruct the German people from the past. We teach and learn the sciences not to discover abstract laws but to sharpen the weapons of the German people in competition with other people…*

In other words, science, like everything else, is to be placed at the disposal of the Nazi gang. It is, in short, to be prostituted. You can imagine the kind of man who was given the job. Nothing is more revealing than these Nazi appointments. The man responsible for sending Nobel Prize winners into exile and wrecking famous German institutions of learning was Hitler's Minister of Education, Dr. Rust. What were his qualifications? From 1909 to 1930, Rust was an ordinary schoolmaster at Hanover. He was then discharged because he had had several mental breakdowns and was thought to be incapable of filling even this modest post as a schoolmaster. But three years later, he was appointed by Hitler to be Reich Minister for Knowledge, Education and National Regeneration. The country of Einstein and Franck was to be regenerated by the ex-Hanover schoolmaster Dr. Rust. In 1937, he announced:

> *German history has brought to an end the peaceful period of scientific work. The Nazi revolution summons science to the decisive battle. Complete freedom of opinion and judgement are marks of the estrangement of the spirit from the eternal forces of nature and history. Freedom is not assured to science either by its abstractedness or by its independence of current events…*

Robbed of its fancy verbiage and reduced to a hard core of sense, this statement really means that Rust stands there as a mouthpiece of Hitler and the boys in the Berchtesgaden back room, and that they have the guns in their hands and that if anybody is fool enough to imagine he knows more about physics, chemistry, biology, medicine, anthropology and history than those boys with the guns know then let him look out.

In April this year, Dr. Rust opened some new schools for the training of future leaders and made it plain that he thought even less of real knowledge and genuine scientific achievement than before. 'It is the will of the Creator', he declared, 'that the earth should be a field of battle. It is the deepest conviction of Hitler that militant action is the fulfilment of Divine Law; and that only the individual and the people who fulfil this law can hope for the blessings of Providence...' Let's stop a moment to examine that astonishing statement. We know what militant action means to the Nazis: it means the ruthless bombing of open towns, the machine-gunning of refugees, the sinking of ships, the burning, blasting and torturing of human beings without regard to age or sex. This, according to Dr. Rust, is the fulfilment of Divine Law. Only the people who fulfil this law can hope for the blessings of Providence. Well, I prophesy here and now that the blessings of Providence for Dr. Rust and his murderous and blasphemous accomplices will sooner or later include the howling fury of outraged populations, to be followed by a choice between poison, the firing party or the rope.

But let us take another look at this speech of the Minister for Knowledge, Education and National Regeneration. The schools have been purged of all genuine scholars, scientists, teachers with free and independent minds and decent ideals; who takes their places? Dr. Rust can tell us all about that. 'There is no better instructor for this militant viewpoint of life', the learned Minister announces, 'than the fight itself. The best example of this is the group of fighting men around the Fuhrer who came into power together with him.' Here, of course, as shining ideals of youth, he is holding up as examples the unselfish Goering, the gentle Himmler, the truthful and compassionate Goebbels and other figures of saintly devotion. He goes on to say: 'The first teachers in our schools were exclusively proven leaders of SA and SS formations, from whose ranks teachers are still taken. In the future too, in the selection of the leaders of these institutions, the soldierly National Socialist attitude will always be decisive, and not the scientific qualifications...' All this, together with a will to victory from generation to generation, will produce a people who will be 'the master people of this earth...'Well, there you have it, plain enough. Never mind about scientific qualifications and the like for your teachers. What are needed are proven leaders of the SA and SS formations, in other words, proven blackguards from the jack-booted and brown-shirted ranks of storm-troopers and the like, proven and successful street fighters, looters, Jew baiters and torturers, and *Heil Hitler* robots. Out of this half-educated and brutalised mob will come the master people of this earth. Real knowledge will vanish; true science will disappear; the very desire for truth will quit the darkening minds of men. And it is that growing empire of darkness, cruelty and insanity we are fighting, and must ask every decent-minded man and woman in this world to fight with us. There can be no pact or truce with it. Either we destroy it for ever or it will destroy us, and all that we hold dear, for ever. Goodnight.

16 and 17 October 1941

Women in Germany

Good evening. I want to talk to you tonight about the position of women under the Nazis. The subject is topical for two reasons. First, this last week there was organised in Berlin a congress of women. Secondly, the Nazi propagandists, with their usual impudence, have been very busy lately telling enormous lies about the position of women in Russia, and calling Bolshevism the greatest enemy of women. The fact that this congress of women in Berlin and this propaganda campaign have arrived together is not without significance. Such things are never accidental in Nazi Germany. We may reasonably detect the hand of Goebbels here. That energetic little man is clearly worried by the morale of his womenfolk, as well he might be when sooner or later he will have to explain to them the stupendous losses of German manhood in the Russian campaign, and also have to explain to them why he cannot keep his promises to restore to them their sons, husbands, brothers, sweethearts. I have heard it said that when, at last, the German people do revolt, it will be the women who will make the first rebellious move. So something has to be done to keep the women quiet. There is a women's congress, assisted by whole reservoirs of eyewash, in Berlin. At the same time, the Soviet system is denounced as the greatest enemy of woman.

I mentioned impudence in connection with this latest propaganda move, and not without reason. For it is really an attack not on one of the weak places of the Soviet system but on one of its very strongest. This is actually a favourite Nazi propaganda trick and is based on Hitler's statement in *Mein Kampf* that little lies are no use; you must tell thumping big lies. It is really almost sublime impudence. If there is one thing certain about the British people, for instance, it is that they are tolerant and rather easy-going. So up jumps Goebbels and announces that the British are a violent, hard, cruel folk. If there is one thing certain about the Americans, it is that they have a genius for huge-scale, industrial mass production. So up jumps Goebbels and says that American production can be ignored, the Americans being a lazy, chaotic sort of people. Now it is exactly the same with the Russians. You might reasonably criticise the Soviet system on many grounds, but the one ground on which it can't be reasonably attacked is its relation to the woman question. Not only is it *not* the greatest enemy to woman but it is actually her greatest friend. The only discrimination between the sexes in Russia is one that favours women, in their capacity as actual or potential mothers. In the Soviet Union, two thirds of all the teachers, two thirds of all the doctors and a large proportion of the trained agriculturalists are women. More than a third of the industrial technicians are women. They are to be found in all the professions and important occupations and hold many official appointments of high rank. All this is, of course, common knowledge among well-informed persons throughout the world, and the fact that it is blandly denied by the Nazi propagandists only shows how much they rely on the ignorance of their audiences.

Three years ago, Professor Kirkpatrick of the University of

Minnesota published an impartial study of women and family life in Nazi Germany, and in that book he declares: 'The contrast with Communism is striking. In Russia, the fetters of law and custom were stricken with extraordinary suddenness from the limbs of women. The competent woman became the Russian ideal. Perhaps Nazism was driven to its stress on sex differences by an over-reaction against its hated rival.' Again, the care of mothers and children was one of the greatest achievements of the Soviet system. I was talking, the other day, with a woman who has specialised in the care of young children, and she spoke with great enthusiasm of Russian methods, and held that in some branches of this work, notably in the organising of crèches and nursery schools, the Russians were much further advanced than anybody else, and that we ourselves had much to learn from them. And it is these people, who have given women more opportunities than they have ever had before and have at the same time done so much for the care of mothers and young children, that are accused by Nazi propagandists as being the greatest enemies of women. This is typical Nazi impudence.

And now let us have a look at women in Germany. Here, once again, we come upon a bewildering assortment of paradoxes, a maze of contradictions, until the observer who lives outside the vast hypnotic daydream of the Germans hardly knows what to say. Nothing makes sense until you have taken hold of the essential clue, namely, that everything that is said is cool, unscrupulous propaganda, bent on creating certain states of mind without reference to the real facts, and that everything that is done is done for the benefit of a small, madly ambitious ruling group. The talk belongs to some fantastic illogical dreamland. The actions belong to the policy of the Nazi Party, which aims at power and has no other aim. It is really a waste of time examining in any detail what the Nazis have said about women, because there is practically nothing at some time or other they haven't said. They promised the women everything, just as they promised the farmers, the peasants, the industrial workers, the industrial magnates, the small shopkeepers, the large shopkeepers, everything against everybody.

What they actually did, as they rose to power, was to disintegrate the feminist movement, which had been very strong during the years of the Weimar Republic, which had begun by enfranchising women. In 1928, four enormous federations combined together some sixty women's organisations that had millions of members. Moreover, at this time, German women were well represented in many international women's organisations, such as the International Council of Women, the International Association of University Women, the International Medical Women's Association. This whole great structure of feminism stood in the way of the almost primitive tribal organisation that the Nazis wanted, and so they determined to remove it. They went to work first by fomenting jealousies and disagreements and encouraging and actively supporting all dissatisfied and rebellious members of these women's groups. Then, as soon as they arrived in power, the Nazis began to appoint their own leaders to such groups, with the result that many of the women's organisations had either to change their character and deny the principles that had first brought them together or to disband themselves. During the first year of the Nazi regime, many of the largest women's organisations were dissolved. By the end of 1933, it was possible to issue the following official notice:

> *The leaders of the Nazi Frauenschaft warn that no unsocial behaviour may take place in other associations. In case such should take place, the woman commissioner of the German Frauenschaft is to be given the facts. The commissioner of the province shall act in association with the German Frauenfront to restrain forbidden activity.*

This meant that German feminism had received its death blow. German women were now thrown out of responsible positions by the thousand. During the first two years, the number of German women teachers dropped by more than a third. By 1935, out of 6,000 teachers in higher educational institutions, only forty-six were women. A Nazi medical representative announced, 'We will strangle higher education for women.' German women doctors put up a fight, but during the first two years about 450 of them were removed, and this stupid policy was continued, until it was realised, too late, that national efficiency must inevitably suffer. Once the Nazis were firmly seated in the saddle, women disappeared both from positions of great responsibility and also from the councils of the nation. There were thirty-eight women members of the old Reichstag. Hitler's Reichstag of today has no women members at all. There are, of course, so-called Nazi women leaders, but they are merely the mouthpieces of the party policy in organisations dragooning women for the benefit of the party. German women disappeared from all the international women's organisations. They were kept severely within the tribal unit at home. Hitler has been in power over eight years. How many German women have made any name for themselves during these years? How many has the world heard about at all? Occasionally we have caught the name of some film actress or other. The rest has been silence.

At the same time that the Nazis were busy disintegrating the German women's movement, they were also busy spreading their own ideals of womanhood. We know what these were. They were the old 'Kinder, Kuche and Kirche' – 'Children, Kitchen and Church'. Woman was to be the recreation of the tired warrior. Woman was to stay at home. Woman was to bear as many children as possible, in order that the state should have plenty of young lives to hurl into the furnace of war. The Fuhrer, it seems, was essentially a lover of family life and young children, and photographs by the million of him talking and smiling to carefully selected peasant women and children were circulated throughout his empire. The fact that he was such an ardent lover of family life and young children that he remained a childless bachelor was not stressed.

And something more important was not stressed. When the Nazis first came into power, it was essential that as many men as possible should be employed, therefore women were turned out of innumerable jobs to make room for men, on the grounds that woman's place was in the home. But no sooner had the great war machine absorbed all manpower, no sooner was it seen that female labour would have to be employed on a very large scale, than it was announced that woman's place was not necessarily in the home but was also in the munitions and other factories, serving the machine that would ultimately destroy such family life as they had had. This is a very good example of the way in which Nazi policy, which goes in a direct line seeking more power, is covered by Nazi propaganda, which changes its own line to create new attitudes of mind. What has really happened to women in Nazi Germany is that they have been brutally made a convenience of – first taken out of good responsible jobs and then pushed back into inferior ones. Where the Russians promoted women, the Nazis have demoted them. The fact is, of course, that this insane power-seeking militarism is woman's worst enemy, ruthlessly disregarding all her own feminine values and always bent on using her contemptibly as a mere instrument. That is why I hope the first great blow to be struck at Nazism from inside Germany will come from the deluded and outraged German womanhood. Goodnight.

23 and 24 October 1941

The Black-Out

Good evening. We are in the middle of a world war – not a European war but a world war – so that at any moment another quarter of the globe may be involved. So it's possible that many of my listeners tonight may live in cities that are already planning defence against air raids, although such cities may be far away from the present combatant zones. Now, to such listeners I would say this: while you have still time to plan your air-raid defences and to make them as perfect as possible, take my advice and try to settle the black-out problem properly. That's something we haven't done in this country, with the result that we're paying a heavy price for what seems to most of us a very faulty policy.

Now, what's the object of blacking out a city? There are, it seems to me, two objects. The first is to avoid that vast pink haze in the sky which is thrown up by a well-lighted modern city, and which would serve as a beacon to raiding aircraft. The second object is to keep the city so dark that when the raiding bombers are actually over the place it is not mapped out for them by the lights below. Then, if they wish to do some accurate bombing, they are compelled to drop flares to discover exactly where they are. I have seen the German planes drop flares, but more often than not they didn't, simply because their aim was not to do some accurate bombing on carefully selected targets but to drop

bombs at random within a chosen urban area. But those are
the two objects of the black-out: to prevent a city from being
a beacon for approaching bombers and to prevent it mapping
itself out for bombers circling over it.

Now, these two objects don't demand the same kind of
black-out. For the first, you only need a modified black-out.
Obviously you can't have a blaze of neon lighting – as you have
down Broadway or in Piccadilly Circus here before the war –
but on the other hand you can have the streets, squares, railway
stations reasonably well lit, without throwing up this pink glare
into the night sky. I think I'd be happy at any time to live in a
city with just as much light as that and no more, because I've
always found huge glittering signs tiring and wearisome, and
once they begin ferociously to compete with each other in
winking gaudiness, the eye – or at least *my* eye – soon tires of
them. So this modified black-out wouldn't be bad at all. Now,
for the second object – that of keeping a city completely dark
when the bombers are actually above it – you obviously need a
very thorough black-out indeed, with the absolute minimum of
light showing. But, if arrangements are completed in time, it's
not difficult in most modern cities to have a modified black-out
until the actual *alert* – when the sirens go off, and when a few
switches are pulled and the whole city is hurled into the total
black-out. That, I'm told, is what happens in Moscow, and in
this matter the citizens of Moscow are more fortunate than the
citizens of London or any other city here. That is, to my mind,
the best way of tackling this problem. Unfortunately, it's not
the way we've tackled it here. From the very beginning of the
war we've adopted the system, with a few minor modifications
that I needn't discuss here, of having a complete black-out all
the time, every night, whether there are hostile aircraft about or
not. Even if no enemy bombers are reported as being anywhere
over Britain, this complete black-out is in progress and is rigidly
enforced. Vehicles carry lights, of course, but they are reduced to
an absolute and rather dangerous minimum.

I'll never forget my first acquaintance with this black-out in
London. It was during the first week of the war. I had arrived in
London from the country and was engaged to dine that night
with two friends of mine at a very pleasant little restaurant. As
it was still early September, we arrived at the restaurant when it

was still daylight. Then we had an excellent dinner and lingered over our coffee and cigars, so that it was at least two hours later when we decided to leave the bright convivial interior of the restaurant for the darkened streets. I say 'darkened streets', but that wasn't the impression I had. There simply weren't any streets. We might have walked straight into a gigantic bag of soot. There was nothing whatever to be seen. The darkness seemed so thick that you felt you could lean against it. Moreover, it was quite a strange sort of darkness. It wasn't like the darkness you find any cloudy night in any country lane, for somehow in the country there is really always a tiny bit of light filtering through, and once your eyes are used to the night scene you can generally find your way fairly easily. But in a big city, with tall black buildings all round you, it's a very different matter. It's a new and much blacker kind of darkness. The faint glimmer of the night sky is not reaching you, though you can look up and notice and admire the stars as you never could before. And of course in bright moonlight the effect may be really beautiful, and then you often feel you are seeing your city for the first time. But in London we don't have many nights of bright moonlight. Well, this first night of the black-out presented me with a most bewildering and terrifying experience. We went along – the three of us – like men suddenly blinded. We'd hesitate at the most familiar turning. All the usual landmarks had disappeared. Crossing one of the larger squares was a new and fantastic ordeal. I remember it took us nearly an hour to negotiate a distance that would have taken us not more than ten minutes' easy walking before. And this was the West End of London, a region I'd known intimately for years.

That autumn, I did a three months' tour of the country for the press. In some of the larger provincial cities that I didn't know very well, I had the most disconcerting adventures. I would plunge into the deep gloom and five minutes after leaving my hotel I would be hopelessly lost. Any idea of exploring the place would have to be abandoned. It was bad enough trying to get back to my hotel, which might be only a few hundred yards away. In those early months, the large railway stations in these provincial cities were so severely blacked-out, with only a few dim blue lights burning in their immense caverns, that it was a miracle how any late traveller ever found his right train. I would peer into these strangely hollow ghostly places and thank my stars I was doing my travelling by daylight. And while every morning I was cheerful enough, looking forward to another day's war sight-seeing – looking at camps, aerodromes, factories and so on – asking people questions and making notes of their answers and my impressions, very often before it was bedtime I would be feeling either grim or depressed, simply because of the black-out. It would create in me – and does to some extent to this day – a most unpleasant feeling of spiritual desolation. The most pessimistic long poem in the English language is by a Victorian minor poet called James Thomson, who died of drink, and it is called 'The City of Dreadful Night'. Well, it seemed to me, as this ferocious black-out descended upon me, that I was compelled to wander through a whole series of cities of dreadful night. True, the black-out is not quite as bad now as it was two years ago. There have been a few modifications. But now and again during these last weeks in London, when the days have suddenly become much shorter and the black-out has seemed as thick and impenetrable as ever, I've returned to my mood of two years ago. Curse this black-out, I've muttered, as I've left some cheerful interior for this vast wall of darkness.

And don't imagine that this feeling is peculiar to me. Nearly everybody experiences it, and nearly everybody mentions it. Indeed, I don't hesitate to say that of all the restrictions, limitations, irritations and vexations that this war has imposed on us, the black-out is the most unpopular. I have heard it denounced more often than any other feature of our wartime life. In the first place, this very heavy black-out that we insist upon in our large cities – and of course everywhere else as well – has produced a very substantial crop of traffic accidents. It is, indeed, very dangerous, and I would say more dangerous than any increase of danger from the air that would result from a modified black-out. Secondly, it keeps indoors a great many people who might benefit, educationally or socially, from going out at night. People who have had a long working day and feel tired, and perhaps don't trust their eyesight too far, often hesitate to venture out into the murk, to grope their way through the black-out, although there may be something not far away in the town that they would enjoy – a concert, a lecture, a discussion, a theatrical entertainment. Thirdly, it tends to slow everything up after dark, for neither men nor vehicles can move about with any speed and ease through this fixed gloom. Fourthly – and now we return to the point I touched on earlier, and it seems to me the most important point – this blacking out of everything once daylight has gone, this nightly descent into sheer darkness, this transformation of cities into gloomy canyons with ebony walls, does something to the mind and imagination. Many people, perhaps most people, are not strictly conscious of this reaction, which probably has most of its effect just below the level of consciousness. But that it *is* affecting millions of people here, I'm completely convinced. It's as if these Hitlers, these power-crazy outcasts who are now sacrificing whole armies and spreading destruction and ruin all round them in order to satisfy their lust for power and their desire for revenge, had somehow contrived to hurl the whole lot of us, every night, into the gloom and misery and chaos of their own minds. This blacking out, which must now turn nearly the whole continent of Europe into one vast peninsula of unrelieved gloom every night, is part of their revenge. They have spread darkness, they have extinguished light, over thousands of miles. This is their kind of life, and they have compelled us all to live it with them. And it is this, I believe, that people hate in their heart of hearts. It is the vast growing darkness of Hitler and his kind. It's like a deep black stain creeping over the fair surface of the earth. Light itself is a kind of defiance to these blackmailers, bullies, torturers and murderers, who are all crying, with Macbeth, in their dark hearts, 'Out, out brief candle!' That is why, if I had my way, I would risk, until experiment proved me wrong, more light in our cities. And that too is why we must have more light in our minds. Wherever the swastika goes, the mental black-out begins; Goebbels hangs up the dark curtains; Himmler extinguishes the lights; and the voice of Hitler screams in the deepening gloom. More light, I say, more light. Goodnight.

6 and 7 November 1941

American Isolationism

G ood evening. Now here is a question I have been asking
myself lately, and it's a question that some of you are
better able to answer than I am. Do these prominent American
Isolationists ever *read* anything about Nazism? Or we can
turn it into another and larger question. Do they really know
what Nazism is, and simply pretend they don't, or don't they
really know? I can't tell from the quotations from their articles
and speeches that reach me over here. They may be genuinely
ignorant. They may be pretending. What is absolutely certain is
that they cannot be talking and acting out of a full knowledge
of the subject. They still talk about the Nazis as foolish people
here talked about them several years ago. 'No, I don't like them,'
they say, 'but that's no reason why we should fight them. Let's
just leave them alone.' And in reply to that, I say that it is exactly
because of such talk as this that Hitler has risen from an obscure
beer-hall demagogue to become supreme dictator of more than
half Europe. For ten years, one foolish set of persons after
another has said, 'I don't like them, but let's leave them alone,'
only to discover, when it was too late, that though they might
wish to leave the Nazis alone, the Nazis had no intention of
leaving them alone.

I have some extracts from speeches by prominent Isolationists
in front of me now, and with the sentiments most of them
express I am in thorough agreement. But the trouble is, those
sentiments have nothing to do with the case. The arguments
would be sound arguments if they began with the realities of
the situation. But they don't. It's just as if the whole time they
were talking about a situation that involved a pussycat when
we happened to know that it involved a man-eating tiger. One
prominent Isolationist says, I see, that he is opposed to war
because it means ruin, blood and tears and so forth. But does he
think the rest of us *like* war? I was an infantry soldier for four
and a half years during the last war; a great many unpleasant
things happened to me, and I saw still more horrible things
happen to my comrades. Our Isolationist can't tell me anything

about modern war. I have children growing up among the sirens and bombs and incendiaries of this war. Does he imagine that I think that's amusing? He can't be more opposed to war than I am. But there's one thing worse than taking your chance in war and that is existing in contemptible and abject slavery. We'd rather be dead than live in a world completely dominated by the Nazis. So, probably, would our friend. But how does he propose to stop the Nazis dominating the world? By making speeches saying that he doesn't like war? I hate being tossed about in small boats, but I wouldn't make a speech about it during a shipwreck. I ask him one plain question: does he or does he not believe that the Nazis seek to dominate the world? If he does believe it then I suggest that his whole argument falls to the ground. If he really doesn't believe it, and is not merely doing a bit of wishful thinking – and nobody has gained more from other people's wishful thinking than Hitler – then I suggest he takes some time off to acquaint himself better with the aims and beliefs of Nazism.

Then there is another famous Isolationist who, I see, declares that 'keeping the USA at peace and free from foreign wars is the most noble and patriotic service that an American can render the Republic'. Now, there is only one thing wrong with that solemn statement, but unfortunately it is fatal. What is wrong is that it doesn't apply to the realities of the situation. It is thinking that your neighbour is having a little trouble with a cat of his, when the truth is that there's a man-eating tiger who may be leaping over your wall any moment. Any American in his senses wants to keep America out of *foreign* wars. But how any man in his senses can honestly talk about this present conflict as a *foreign* war completely beats me. It is being wilfully blind to what is really happening in the world. It is bringing a stagecoach mind to describe a world of automobiles.

Our Isolationist, in this extract, goes on to say that he hates dictators, and denounces Nazism, Fascism, Communism, Imperialism – in fact, all the -isms – and while he was about it, he might have denounced realism too. The point now is not what he hates and denounces but what he is prepared to do about it. Denunciations don't stop German panzer divisions. You can't argue the Luftwaffe out of the sky or the U-boats out of the water. People who talk like this are just cold meat for the Nazis.

They've thrived on them for years. There are men starved, beaten and bleeding to death at this moment in concentration camps who were just as good at denouncing as he is. Our Isolationist may be a monument of sincerity, and be saying exactly what he believes, but, if so, then he simply does not know enough.

Of course, the Nazis will be only too eager to prove that so far as America is concerned, this is a foreign war. The Nazis have always worked that trick. What is the trick? It is to make sudden violent moves, which apparently have limited objectives, declaring at the top of their voices that that is all they want, while at the same time every one of these moves is part of a vast plan, for which now there is a mountain of evidence, to subdue not merely Western Europe, not merely all Europe and the Near East, but eventually the whole wide world. Just remember how every time Hitler has made one of his lightning moves, he has also announced that after that he would be satisfied. He admits this to be his method. You break the spirit of resistance by first making comparatively small demands and then, as your opponents' will is weakened, making much bigger demands, finally taking everything you want.

Nazism can't stop now. There is nowhere where it can draw a line. Why? Because it isn't merely challenging some temporary political and economic settlement but is challenging our whole civilisation. That challenge is implied in everything it says about itself, in everything that has been taught to German youth during these last years. The Germans are the master race. They are superior to all other peoples. Hitler is not simply the leader of the party in power but a prophet, a saviour, representing some mysterious Teutonic deity. Every action, no matter how violent, cruel or treacherous, is justified so long as it serves the purposes of the Fuhrer and the Reich. The Poles are to be exterminated, the Russians, the Czechs and others to be enslaved, France to be turned into a kitchen garden and a brothel, and so on. Things have been done within this last twelve months that have not been done before for a thousand years. To read the briefest and baldest record of this Nazi tyranny is to feel sick with horror. Foreign wars indeed! In the spring of last year, without a word of warning, the full German fury was launched on peaceful neighbouring countries. Cities like Rotterdam, against which the Nazis had no grievance whatever, were murderously bombed and their citizens butchered. In August 1939, Nazi Germany signed a solemn pact with the Soviet Union. In June 1941, again without a word of warning, that same Soviet Union was invaded in full force and with appalling ferocity. Foreign wars indeed! The whole continent of America has been honeycombed by the most unscrupulous Nazi agents, themselves part of a vast organisation of espionage, sabotage and potential invasion. There are no limits to the ambitions of these men. Why should there be? Ten years ago, some of them were almost down-and-out, shabby adventurers and back-room intriguers, laughed at for their tall talk. Now these same men hurl enormous armies across Europe and into Asia and Africa, own vast fortunes, have the power of life and death over millions, and behave like half-crazed war lords of the dark ages. Their maddest dreams are coming true. And then people like our Isolationists talk of their challenge to our whole civilisation, the most dangerous it has known for a thousand years, as if it were something like a golf match. Foreign wars indeed! 'Shall we go in for the tournament this year? No, I think not. Too expensive!' As I have said before, it is not for me, or for anybody here, to tell America what it ought to do, or even to air our outside opinions on the domestic politics of the United States. But, as I have also said before, many, many times, this is a world conflict, a fight to the death between civilisation – or, if you prefer it, potential civilisation – and a new and terrifying barbarism, which has already destroyed or attempted to destroy all the higher values and standards we recognise wherever it has seized power. Therefore, I feel I have the right to denounce any American public man who talks such twaddle about foreign wars and tries to persuade his audiences that they are living in the year 1900 and not in 1941.

In the extracts I have before me, one Isolationist takes a different line. He declares that he does not want Germany to win this war but that the democracies can't win it, so that what he has constantly advocated is a negotiated peace. Now, let's take the lid off that and have a good look at it. How do you negotiate with the Nazis? I haven't the least doubt they would be ready to negotiate. They've always been ready to negotiate. There is nothing they like better, except invasion, than signing pacts. They will sign anything at any time. By now there must be a ton or two of beautiful parchments exquisitely sealed that they have signed. Solemn pacts, agreements, covenants, signed with gold pens, photographed and filmed, toasted with hock and champagne. I seem to remember Chamberlain bringing one back with him, triumphantly, from Munich. I don't know what the sort of paper they use for these peace treaties and pacts is worth these days, but what I do know is that the peace treaties and pacts themselves are worth even less, are, in fact, worth nothing to the other side. They are always worth something to the Nazis, however, because they give them time to plan new conquests, to equip more panzer divisions, to manufacture bigger bombs. This particular Isolationist has always appeared to know more about the Nazis than the rest of us. If he knows how to make Hitler keep his pledged word then he should let the world into the secret. Isn't it all quite simple? If the Nazis were the kind of people you could negotiate with then there would never have been this war at all. What made this war inevitable was the fact that, after so many tragic failures, it was made plain that Nazi Germany had outlawed itself clean outside the world of negotiations, of sensible co-operation, of dignity, honour, truth, of peace, and had decided to live by alternating acts of treachery and force, using exactly the same methods to subdue the world that the Nazis successfully used to seize power in their own country. And I challenge any Isolationist to deny those facts. And I further declare that they are falsifying the issue. Goodnight.

18 November 1941

Gestapo

Nearly every two or three weeks during the last six months, we have read that Herr Himmler, chief of the Gestapo, has paid an official visit to another country. He has visited Norway, Denmark, Holland, Belgium, France, Italy, Spain and, I think, Romania. Not long ago I read an account by a neutral journalist of the arrival of Herr Himmler in a restaurant in one of the occupied capital cities. Suddenly, there was a stir, there was the tramp of storm-troopers, a flicker of fear travelled across the faces of all the Germans present, who rose anxiously to their feet – and there entered, surrounded by his bodyguard, an unimposing figure with a rat-trap face: Heinrich Himmler, chief of the Gestapo.

Why should there have been this extraordinary manifestation of fear? Why does this unimposing Nazi official move round half Europe in an atmosphere of fear and trembling and anxious obsequiousness? The head of your police department or ours could not, even if he wished to, create this sinister atmosphere round himself. What is Herr Himmler's secret? The answer to all these questions is to be found in the character of the gigantic department controlled by Himmler, the Nazi secret political police, the dreaded Gestapo. This force existed in embryo before the Nazi Party achieved power and took over the state, for Himmler had already organised a political intelligence service, and also there already existed that strong-arm corps known as the Schutzstaffel or SS men. In 1933, Goering, then Prime Minister of Prussia, made use of both this intelligence and espionage service and the SS men to establish, at first only for Prussia, a National Socialist Political Police – Geheime Staatspolizei – which soon became known by its abbreviation: Gestapo. In April 1934, Himmler was appointed chief of the secret police for the whole Reich, and now the Gestapo had all Germany in its grip.

What are the powers of the Gestapo? They are for all practical purposes unlimited. Even Nazi writers on legal affairs admit that owing to the nature of the work of the secret police for the preservation of the National Socialist State, which of necessity reaches into all strata of society and covers all the activities of German citizens, orders of the Gestapo cannot be challenged in a court of law. The ordinary citizen has no appeal against the actions of the Gestapo to any independent public tribunal. These policemen are called upon to justify their actions only to themselves. In all political matters, affecting the security of the state, as distinct from ordinary crime, they are the sole judges of what action shall be taken. This may not sound too bad until you remember that in the opinion of the Nazis there is practically nothing that cannot be considered to have a political bias, that every possible move made by a citizen may be judged to affect the security of the state, and that therefore this gives these secret police arbitrary and almost unlimited power. Here is a translation of part of the statute of 1936 defining the scope and status of the Gestapo:

> *It is the duty of the Secret State Police to expose and to oppose all collective forces which are dangerous to the state, to collect and evaluate the results of these findings, to inform the government and to keep all authorities informed of all evidence. The chief of the Secret State Police, in agreement with the Minister of the Interior, decides which individual matters are to be given to the Secret State Police.*

This practically amounts to giving the Gestapo a blank cheque, which may have to be honoured by any and every wretched citizen. Ordinary legal processes go on, there are judges and courts and lawyers, there are elaborate codes of law, but this vast body of ruthless men is completely free of any challenge by these processes, codes and courts and is at liberty to prove that politics and the security of the state enter into any affair, and therefore in practice can do what it likes.

This may explain what has often puzzled many of us, namely, that all the Nazi leaders, who ten years ago were poor men, now seem to have a multitude of splendid possessions, great town houses, magnificent country mansions, large estates, forests, shooting lodges and so forth. For men who keep telling the world that they represent the Have-Nots and that they are fighting the pluto-democracies, these men appear to have done pretty well for themselves. Indeed, it would be interesting to tabulate a list of the personal possessions of our leaders, of Churchill, Bevin, Morrison, Alexander and the rest, and of the Nazi leaders, Hitler, Goering, Ribbentrop, Goebbels etc., and to compare them. It would soon be obvious who had been feathering their nests. Which brings us back to the Gestapo, who can take action as soon as they suspect that any person has been – or even could be – dangerous to the state. A great many German citizens who happen to have been the owners of fine houses or coveted estates have been proved by the Gestapo, to their own satisfaction, to be dangerous to the state, and they have been summarily arrested and their possessions instantly confiscated. After that it would be easy for a prominent member of the Nazi Party to accept the loan of such possessions or to acquire them at a bargain price. And this may help to explain how men who ten years ago owned nothing but a gun and a brown shirt now possess so many pleasant things.

In any event, this unchallenged supremacy of the secret police, their constant over-riding of ordinary legal processes and decisions, clearly turn Nazi law into a sinister force. If round every corner waiting to pounce there are unscrupulous men who can arrest you on a charge that has only to be proved to the satisfaction of their own superiors and not to anybody representing your fellow citizens then strictly speaking there is no law, the state as a guarantor of personal rights is a mere mockery, and you are back in the days of Genghis Khan.

And it is this existence under the oppression of the terrible instrument that decent European citizens, who have known something like civilisation for a thousand years, are asked to accept as life under a *New Order*. A New Order indeed! It is the oldest order known to unhappy mankind – plain crushing despotism. This is really a pyramid system, with complete freedom at the apex and none whatever at the base. At the top is Hitler, who can do what he likes, with nobody to say him Nay. Next come the principal members of the gang, who can do what *they* like, so long as they don't offend their Fuhrer. Next come less important members of the gang, who can do what *they* like so long as they do not conflict with their superiors. So it goes on down the scale, with subservience to the man above and bullying for the man below, until we reach the base of the pyramid, composed of ordinary citizens, who have no liberty whatever and must merely obey everybody's orders.

This horrible system would not be possible without the huge octopus power of the Gestapo, spying everywhere and striking at once with relentless severity. There is even a Gestapo within the Gestapo, a mysterious organisation known as the Sicherheitsdienst or Security Service, whose members are distributed everywhere, spies to spy on spies. It reminds us of:

Big fleas have little fleas – on their backs to bite 'em,
And little fleas have lesser fleas – and so ad infinitum.

It suggests a nightmare vista of unending suspicion and insecurity.

The striking force of the Gestapo consist of two specially trained sets of young men. First, the SS shock troops, who enlist for four years and are kept in barracks. These young men, who are taken from the pick of Nazi youth, are more like soldiers than policemen, and indeed often follow immediately in the rear of the invading German armies, to do the mopping up and to police the newly conquered territories. They must, of course, be extremely numerous now, and be a formidable army in themselves, though it should be noticed that this is an army that is not exposed to the wear and tear of front-line action. In other words, it is not the Nazi elite that suffers all the casualties at the front. They are kept intact in the rear, if necessary to beat up their fellow citizens. And if the ordinary German is still capable of thinking for himself, this sinister fact should make him think quite a lot. The Nazis like to make war, but chiefly not at their own expense.

The second specially trained contingent consists of young men enlisted for twelve years and known as the Death's Head Corps. These fine young fellows, splendid specimens of Nordic youth, have been trained with great care and 'hardened' for their special task of looking after the concentration camps, where they have amused themselves for some years now, in their superior cultured German fashion, bullying, starving, beating, flogging and torturing to death their wretched prisoners. The record of what these young men have done, these ignorant lads deliberately corrupted by sadistic leaders, is one of the blackest chapters in modern European history, and is enough by itself, without the assistance of all the other acts of faithlessness, aggression and tyranny of this Nazi Party, to make any thought of co-operation with or tolerance of Hitler and his party quite impossible to any decent-minded people. The air of Europe will not be fit to breathe until the last of these young brutes has vanished from the scene. So much for the public personnel of the Gestapo. Of the army of secret spies, which operates everywhere, we can say nothing, beyond the fact that it exists and grows more numerous every day.

In Germany and German-occupied territory, the Gestapo takes hold of the public in three different ways. It may merely warn the citizen, telling him that it has its eye on him and that he had better be careful. As there is no way of challenging this, the opportunities for blackmail here are obviously unlimited. Then it may take the citizen into what is called 'protective custody', which is simply the arrest and detention of anybody it is convenient to arrest and detain, whether any offence has been committed or not. Then finally, there is the concentration camp or, what is probably preferable, death. And against the threat of these horrors there is no appeal. All manner of decent folk in Norway, Holland, Belgium, France, are now making the acquaintance of this benevolent 'New Order' of Hitler's, and if they ever had any doubts about what it is worth, they have certainly lost them now.

But the Gestapo also functions outside the boundaries of the Reich. You may have seen one of its members this morning. Their task abroad is a double one: first, to collect information, which they do most thoroughly; and secondly, to create unrest, with particular reference to the organisation of those activities known now as Fifth Column. Diplomatic and consular services are frequently used as a cloak for these Gestapo activities abroad. The German Embassy always has the largest possible staff. All kinds of pressure is brought to bear on many foreign citizens by the Gestapo agents, who have even resorted to kidnapping. Behind this is the most impudent bit of legal fiction ever resorted to by any government, for earlier this year a decree was set forth declaring that German penal law applied to everybody everywhere, not only Germans outside Germany, but even to you and to me and everybody. For all we know to the contrary, sentence may have been already passed upon us. State megalomania can go no further. Unless these people are checked, the whole world will be a madhouse. Goodnight.

8 and 9 December 1941

The Kitchen Front

I have always believed that it would be impossible for us to win this war without asking considerable sacrifices and many changes in our national habits. We could not expect successfully to challenge a great power that has been organised for years, with extreme efficiency and ruthlessness, as a vast fighting machine, and yet make little or no change in our mode of living. It was one of the mistakes of the Chamberlain government in the early months of the war not to insist that these changes would soon be necessary. In spite of the inborn conservatism of the British public in general, most people were only too ready to meet any demands made upon them, and indeed there was often much grumbling that more demands were not being made, that there was too much pretence in official circles that everything was still more or less normal.

This pretence was, I always felt, psychologically unsound. It is obvious that under the conditions of this bestial business known as 'total war', with its blockades and black-outs, rationing and bombing, life must be quite abnormal. What is the use of pretending that things are more or less the same as usual if the average householder finds his whole world plunged into almost complete darkness round about five o'clock and must then for the next twelve hours be ready to meet the attacks of raiders dropping high-explosive and incendiary bombs? In my opinion it does not help the ordinary man or woman to accept the constant challenge of this danger and discomfort if he or she is encouraged to pretend that life is almost normal, apart from these considerable drawbacks. Life under these conditions is clearly anything but normal, is wildly and terribly abnormal, almost crazy. Therefore, in my view, it is better to admit this at once, to throw away all these pretences, and to be ready to lead a life fantastically different from any existence known to us in peacetime. The slogan, instead of being 'Everything as Usual', should be 'Nothing as Usual'. Apart from the demands made upon us by our gigantic war effort, even on those psychological grounds I have always advocated the maximum sensible interference with our normal lives instead of the bare minimum. And I think most people here have felt that too. I have heard more grumbling about the government *not* interfering than about official interference. You people have often said, in effect, 'Come on, shake it all up. We don't mind.' And they should have been shaken up from the word go, as indeed of course some of us have been.

To take my own case: most of the work I do now is quite different from the work I was doing before the war; I do not live – cannot live – in either of the two houses I lived in before the war; my whole mode of life is quite different. And I don't mind about this at all; I consider myself lucky on the whole that I am having such a complete change, and that it enables me to stand the strain of the war better, in spite of the fact that I lead a very exhausting sort of life. No, I am all for the general shake-up, for changing people's occupations, backgrounds, habits, whenever this should be necessary. After all, we are not, as a people, too changeable, volatile, fickle, too much given to running after new things. Our faults are all the other way. We so easily become too easy and lazy and complacent. We sink into ruts. We become too fixed in our habits, like persons who age too soon. Young folk are often told that soon they will have to 'settle down'. There has always been too much and not too little 'settling down' in England. This makes for stability, ease and comfort, and a certain husbanding of nervous strength that enables the British people to weather crises that would wreck some populations. It explains why, as I have pointed out before, we are the last people in the world who can safely be challenged in a so-called war of nerves. Compared with us, even the Germans could be regarded as a crowd of potential neurotics. Put this wholesale 'settling down' into a routine and the conservative habit of mind has its dangers. You cannot be encouraged at one moment to continue without making any drastic changes and then asked the next moment to whiz round and go at full speed in the opposite direction.

I mention these points because tonight I want to say something about our food situation. It is no secret that we shall have to cut down our scale of living. This is not going to be an easy winter. Germany is now able to use ports facing the Atlantic, from Norway down to the Bay of Biscay, as submarine bases. On the other hand, because Southern Ireland insists upon being neutral in this war, we cannot make use of advanced bases there and are therefore very severely handicapped. In addition, in spite of our recent successes in the Eastern Mediterranean, the influence of which will soon make itself felt, the convoy duties of our Navy have been immensely increased and extended. We could do with a great many more destroyers. Recent sinkings, though no worse than they were during the third year of the last war, have been considerable. And every ship lost means not only the loss of that particular cargo but also all the other cargoes that ship could have carried subsequently. Still operating within the rather severe limits of the 'Cash and Carry' rule, our imports of foodstuffs from the United States are necessarily restricted.

Now, our Ministry of Food, as I told you some months ago when discussing its work in some detail, has done and is still doing a very good job. The trouble with this Ministry just now is not that it is faced with a general shortage of essential foodstuffs but that it is now having to challenge those habits, that innate conservatism of the British, which I mentioned at the beginning of my talk. For our people as a whole have fixed and very narrow ideas about food, which is one reason – indeed, the chief reason – why so many visitors to this country always complain about our food. Our two chief faults are that both as cooks and as diners we are extremely unenterprising. We don't like to make experiments in eating. We can go on eating the same sort of dishes year after year without ever dreaming of having a change. This is not true, of course, of every man Jack of us, for some of us here, and I certainly count myself one of them, like experimenting and insist upon having gastronomic adventures. But the people in the mass here are terribly unadventurous about food. That is the first fault. The second is that as a people we dislike, more I think than any other civilised people in the world, eating communally. I suppose there must be fewer restaurants per head of the population in Britain than in any other European country. If we are compelled to eat out, we submit to it, but our preference is always for eating at home. This explains why, outside our larger cities (and there isn't much to be said in favour of most of them), it is often impossible to obtain a decent meal in a public place. Everybody is busy eating at home. Whereas in most civilised countries, a man could often ask his friends to have dinner with him in an hotel or a restaurant, here he would ask his friend to dine with him at home. That is the situation, then: that as a people we are unenterprising and unadventurous in our cooking and eating, and, secondly, we have never taken kindly to communal feeding but definitely prefer to eat at home. And it is precisely these habits that are making things very difficult just now for our Ministry of Food, who if they had the very same supplies for another sort of people would have no difficulty in solving their problems.

The reason is this: that the Ministry has not to contend with a general shortage of essential foodstuffs but chiefly with a temporary shortage of one particular kind of foodstuff. Now, with a people who were interested in changing their diet, in having adventures in the kitchen and the dining room, this temporary shortage of some particular kinds would not matter very much, because such people would tell themselves that this was a good opportunity to lay off the familiar ingredients and to try something new. For there are always good available supplies of some essential foodstuffs. This brings us to the second consideration, that of communal feeding. With some kinds of food more abundant than others, it is easier to adjust consumption to supply in community kitchens, organised on a big scale, than it is in 2,000 separate shops and little kitchens. Again, there must be no waste. But now, with all the goodwill in the world, it is impossible to prevent some wastage in 10,000 small kitchens, no matter how each housewife tries her best to be economical. But in a community kitchen, scientifically organised, this wastage can be reduced to an absolute minimum. It is also far easier in such kitchens to see that the people who have to be served by it are all having the right sort of nourishment, a properly balanced series of meals. This, of course, particularly applies to the one main meal of the day – call it dinner. If it is certain that everybody is at least getting one good, hot, well-cooked, nourishing meal a day, apart from snacks earlier or later in the day, then something will have been achieved.

Again, evacuation has created special food problems. For example, the men who have stayed behind in the more dangerous areas because they have jobs to do there have to have their meals prepared for them. Their wives ask who is to do this providing and catering. If it looks as if their men will have to fend for themselves then many of those wives say that they would rather stay with their husbands and do *their* jobs of cooking the meals than be sure of safety elsewhere. It is very natural that they should take this line. But if community kitchens are established in such areas then it is no longer necessary for conscientious wives to take this line, for they can be evacuated, often with their children, with an easy conscience, knowing that the food problem will be solved for their menfolk. But at the other end of the evacuation you may have a similar problem, for if thousands and thousands of women and children have arrived in a reception area, it may be very difficult to feed all these extra people cheaply and well. Here again, the community kitchen would settle the difficulty.

All this does not take into account enemy action, but where there has been heavy bombing, it has been found necessary to establish communal feeding, because all the normal services of supply, gas, electricity etc. may have been seriously interfered with, and catering in the usual private fashion may be absolutely impossible. This is, of course, understood by everybody, and in most badly bombed areas, such community kitchens and feeding centres have been established at once, but they have had to be done as a rushed emergency job and are looked upon by most people as a temporary expedient.

But it will undoubtedly be better for us in every way if community feeding can be set going almost everywhere during these next few months – and here, unfortunately, we come up against that prejudice, which I have referred to already, against eating in public. The Ministry of Food has already opened several establishments of its own, in which good, nourishing meals can be obtained at very cheap prices, but what is needed now is an enormous extension of the scheme, backed by ample public support. I am all for it myself, not only because our war effort demands it, as I have already shown, but also because I think, war or no war, it is a step in the right direction, breaking down a prejudice that has made us such poor and dull caterers, as so many visitors can testify. Out of this war emergency more community feeding centres may come afterwards, something that will add to the amenities of our urban life here. Our task here, then, is to try to make our people become more experimental and adventurous in their home catering, and more willing to take at least some of their meals in public. The task of our well-wishers overseas, especially our friends in the United States, is to see that a too narrowly restricted Cash and Carry rule is not allowed to hamper the war effort of a people who are now fighting the world's battle for the future freedom of mankind and the harmonious development of all our physical and mental resources.

11 and 12 December 1941

America Comes In

I spent last weekend at the small town of Droitwich, where my wife was staying a week or two to benefit from the brine baths there. We were out of our hotel on Sunday night and it happened that we had not heard the news over the wireless. So when we returned to the hotel, I said to a pleasant elderly woman – the type of elderly woman one finds in all such hotels – 'Oh, was there any news tonight?' She replied, quite calmly and quietly, 'Oh yes, I think there was rather important news. The Japanese have been bombing Manila and Hawaii.' I jumped about a yard into the air. Somehow it just would be such a calm elderly lady in a small hotel in an inland resort who would announce to me, just in that cool voice, that the other half of the world had just been set afire.

Since then, of course, the news from the Pacific has taken precedence of all other war items, in spite of the fact that the battle in Libya is going forward and the Russians are pressing on. I happen to have been travelling about the country since Sunday and everywhere in trains and hotels and restaurants and offices and shops our people have been discussing at length every bit of news that has filtered through the smoke that still seems to cover this vast new theatre of war. There has been none of the excitement of the mere spectator in the minds of our people that you overseas should so suddenly find yourselves in the violence and uncertainties and horrors of modern war. We have had bad news just as you have. Perhaps in a way that is just as well. It means that from the outset a bond of common suffering and sympathy in this particular struggle has been forged between us. Nobody is going to pretend that, quite apart from the loss of gallant and highly skilled men, these naval losses are any joke. They are of course very serious indeed. I would, however, ask my American listeners to remember that this has always been the way of naval warfare, in which nothing happens perhaps for a long time and then something tremendous happens almost in a flash. We had it in the last war. Only two days before the Armistice, on 9 November 1918, our battleship *Britannia* was torpedoed within sight of Gibraltar. Then, during the opening phase of this war, we lost the battleship *Royal Oak* and the aircraft carrier *Courageous*.

Nor should this highly efficient, lightning and of course thoroughly treacherous attack of the Japanese be regarded as yet another example of Nazi strategy. Actually, the whole Japanese attack, both on sea and land, is almost a replica of her strategy in the war with Russia in 1904. We should see behind this method of attack the figure of the famous Admiral Togo and not that of Hitler, who, like the German leaders of the last war, has never been able to launch a series of seaborne invasions under cover of naval forces.

Nor should it be thought, except in terms of a very short-range policy, that Japan has now done very well. The Japanese have gained the immediate advantage presented to them by the adoption of methods that have outraged the civilised world. But they have outraged that world. By this one vast treacherous and murderous stroke they have unified not only North America but practically the whole continent from Alaska to Patagonia. They have converted the New World into one gigantic determined opponent.

The bombs that fell out of the blue last Sunday are probably the most fateful pieces of explosive of our time. They did more than set ships and barracks afire. They blew away, once and for all, illusions with which many of us have struggled, without success, for years now. On Saturday night, people were still talking nonsense, the kind of silly nonsense we had heard for years, and by Sunday night, after those bombs, it was dead and gone for ever. Some of us, who didn't pretend to any special knowledge and wisdom, said years ago – I know I go back to 1935 myself and have it in print – that war between the great democracies and Germany, Japan and Italy was inevitable. Sometimes we went further and, pointing first to China and afterwards to Spain, and then to Hitler's corroding tactics in Central Europe, we said that from the point of view of these three predatory powers, who hardly made any secret of their greed for power and their unscrupulous determination to gain that power, the war was already in existence then.

It is my own considered opinion that a great many decent and not altogether stupid people didn't believe us, denounced us often as sheer trouble-makers, simply because they didn't want to face the grim truth. Englishmen, when their American friends pointed to the horrible ruthless Japanese invasion of China, tried to pretend that this was merely a local affair, of no great interest to people on this side. On the other hand, Americans, when their English friends pointed to the rocketing ambitions of Hitler and Mussolini, were often inclined to mutter something about other people's quarrels and to hint that Europe had always been a quarrelsome place anyhow.

Now, the biggest target of those bombs that began falling last Sunday was probably this hill of rubbish. The explosions blew clean away the smoke from the tragic face of our modern world. What remained, plain to be seen, was the real set-up. What is that set-up? It is conspiracy, the most dangerous the world has ever known, on the part of comparatively small groups of power-crazy men, who happen to be the absolute masters of unfortunate millions of slaves; a conspiracy to dominate the world at all costs, to make an end of what can reasonably be called civilisation – that is, Christian ethics, a reasonable liberty, sensible co-operation, freedom of thought and speech, all the democratic devices for talking it out, the rights of common men to an individual way of life.

These people that we are now fighting aren't linked together as you and we are linked together. There is between them no great common bond of sympathy. Their ways of life are anything but identical. The Germans consider the Japanese a lower race, hardly better than monkeys. The Italians hate the Germans, who despise them. The Japanese dislike everybody but themselves and have always repaid the instruction they have had from the white races by ingratitude and treachery. Their contribution, in modern times, to world civilisation has been almost nil. No, in this great armed camp of the enemy there is no real unity of peoples, no growing understanding, no deepening sympathy. All that has happened during these past few years is that the masters of these toiling drilling masses have formed themselves into a gang, to challenge once and for all any possible world system of decent democratic order. And let me add that in my opinion, up to now they have gained far more by our weakness than by their strength. But then we have been at a disadvantage, the same disadvantage suffered by an ordinary peace-loving quiet citizen who walks home with his stick and pipe one night while the gangster waits round the corner with a gun and a club.

But now that disadvantage is done with. Last Sunday ended it for ever. We know now exactly what the set-up is. It has been written on the sky for us in fire and smoke, and on the very ground in blood. Now comes, at last, the showdown. We are united as these people can never be united. We know exactly what we are fighting for. We are fighting so that our way of life shall not be destroyed and so that we shall be left in peace to improve that way of life.

The wretched Germans who perish now by the million far into the frozen interior of Russia – what are they fighting for? Why, they don't know, and rightly don't know, what they are doing there. The miserable Italians who hurry to surrender themselves in East Africa, in the Libyan desert, and now in Russia, they don't know what they are fighting for, or even what they are doing there. Now hundreds of thousands of little men, brothers and cousins to the hundreds of thousands who disappeared for ever into the wastes of China, are being flung upon beaches and into jungles all over the Pacific, where eventually they will mostly meet a violent end – and do they know what they are fighting for, or what they are doing there?

The only people who do know are Hitler and his gang, Mussolini and what may remain of *his* gang, and the mad military clique in Japan. These people dispose of vast armed forces, make use in violence and treachery of every modern technique, but the fact remains that essentially they do not belong to our modern world. They are all throw-backs. They belong to the world of Genghis Khan and Attila. What are they doing here, then? I'll tell you what they're doing. They're challenging us and everything we hold dear. It is just as if they were the mad puppets employed by a force that said, 'I'll compel you people of the great democracies to test your convictions and beliefs and then, if necessary, to work, to fight, to make sacrifices, for those convictions and beliefs.' And we have all accepted that challenge. You don't need to be told, for we have spent many, many hours here telling you how we on this side accepted the challenge, how the people in the worst and deadliest hour of all suddenly stood up, inspired by a new faith or the re-discovery of an old one, how the most relentless and evil form of this challenge, the heavy nightly bombing of civilians, only made them more determined to meet the challenge. You all know about that, and at once responded, in your own generous fashion, to every story of that great communal courage and act of faith.

That's our part of it. Perhaps it was all a bit slow, as is our way. But now, this very week, has come your turn. And how quickly, how resolutely, with what immediate unity, you have accepted the challenge! Let me say how that instant unity and that fine blaze of indignation have been admired here. 'America?' I heard a railway employee cry on a train yesterday, 'America? Why, she'll wipe them Japs off the map before she's done with 'em.' It would do your hearts good – though I'm certain your hearts don't need any good done to them – to see the confidence in you that shines everywhere here, for our ordinary folk, though they may know nothing about figures of potential steel production and facts of that kind that spell disaster in the end for the Axis, have a tremendous respect for the ultimate might and majesty of the United States.

So there we are, all in it together, knowing at last without a shadow of doubt who the enemy is and where he is and what he is up to, and knowing too who our friends are and what there is to be done between us, and, not least, knowing on each side of the Atlantic what we are fighting for and why the fight is on. What did it? Bombs did it. Treachery did it. Murder did it. No dubious issue here. The front may be 20,000 miles long. The first strokes may tell against us. But now we are all together, and know exactly where we are, and that is our first great common victory.

25 and 26 December 1941

Christmas

It has been hard work finding Christmas presents this year. Toys have been scarce and expensive, for in the old days most of our cheap toys came from Germany and Japan. It is an ironical fact that these two countries, which are almost insane in their demand for power and have behaved with a revolting cruelty unknown for centuries, should have specialised for so long in the manufacture of cheap toys. Was the money we used to pay them for these toys instantly converted into torpedoes and bombs? Did they rub their hands, after every cargo of children's playthings had been disposed of, and tell each other what magnificent instruments of violence, destruction and death they would now be able to afford? Did the very men who designed these brightly coloured little toys spend their spare time applauding the most shocking plans for wholesale treachery, looting and murder?

Anyhow, toys have been scarce and expensive. Luxurious things to eat, boxes of candy and the like, have not, of course, been obtainable, so there has been no chance of falling back on them. Girls and women like things to wear, but now you must give up coupons for most of these, and the supply is naturally limited. I bought my daughters some pretty scarves, for which I had to give up a few of my own clothing coupons; but, fortunately, I had some to spare, not being a man with any passion for adorning himself. My small son handed us a list of presents he wanted that was on a grand, pre-war scale of opulence, but, like the good, sensible chap he is, he has been satisfied with much less. For the small children in our hostels, we managed to collect some little gifts and also contrived to rig up a Christmas tree or two, the first many of them have seen.

In some ways, I prefer this rather spare and diminished Christmas of wartime to the much more lavish affairs of peacetime. I had begun to be very suspicious of them. Too much advertising, too much commercial enterprise altogether, about *them*. We were rushed into buying things we did not want much too early. There were too many high-pressure campaigns, and they began too early, usually in the opening week of November. It began to look like a racket. The genuine goodwill and kindness of the season were almost buried under a gigantic heap of catalogues, advertising, booklets, hints, reminders and bills. Father Christmas had the calculating look of a keen debenture-holder. Even the snow, on this side, was artificial. It was only the fact that for young children the magic still worked, and the further fact that I was the father of a family, that prevented my becoming as cynical and unresponsive as Old Scrooge.

But then the barren years before the war were favourable to the development of cynicism and unresponsiveness, not only about Christmas but also about many other equally delightful and sensible institutions. We were all ready to de-bunk everything. We were the knowing ones. We knew it all. We couldn't be taught anything. Perhaps it was high time we were challenged and thoroughly tested. For there were coming into power, in such countries as Germany, Japan, Italy, men whose cynicism and unresponsiveness left ours far behind, men who had de-bunked all humanity's attempts at decency, fair-dealing and kindness, men who really were the knowing ones, who knew it all, who couldn't be taught anything, men who were quite ready to dope and enslave whole populations, who regarded truth and honesty and mercy as mere weaknesses, who gave torture and murder an official standing, who were determined to grab power at no matter what cost to the rest of the human race. These men were not playing at cynicism. They lived in a hell of it. In a sense, we may be said to be fighting their despair. If they should win, that despair of theirs will capture the whole world, so that men might indeed lose hope for a thousand years. But we know they cannot win. Faith in common humanity will triumph in the end over despair.

Meanwhile, the restrictions of wartime have brought us a new kind of Christmas, spare, diminished, stream-lined; and, as I said before, I think I prefer it to the old one, even though the present allowance of food and drink is obviously not quite adequate to the occasion. Whatever this new Christmas may be, at least it no longer comes under the suspicion of being a gigantic commercial racket. So far as we can celebrate Christmas, we celebrate it for the right reasons. We wish to give happiness to our children. We want to spend an evening or two with our families and old friends. We celebrate, in our various ways, the birth of our religion. I understand and sympathise with those people who declare that our modern world cannot successfully pretend to be truly Christian. I think most of us are aware of our deficiencies in that respect.

But it is one thing to be poor Christians, faulty men and sinners; and it is quite another thing to be anti-Christian, to despise the ethics of the cross, to hate the Sermon on the Mount. To behave in this fashion is to be a kind of Satanist, which is indeed what many of the Nazi leaders are. What is it they admire? They have told us at some length. They admire pride, violence, treachery and cruelty. They have actually developed systems of training to eradicate from their picked youth any embarrassing suggestion of the opposite qualities – modesty, honesty and mercy. Take a look some time at Milton's *Paradise Lost*, and read his magnificent account of the demon leaders in Hell, and you will be reminded at once of the Nazi chiefs. The whole history of Nazism is an appalling record of treachery and cruelty. That is why if these men succeeded in gaining the whole world, they would still never know a moment's peace and happiness, simply because they could never trust each other and would expect to be stabbed in the back.

In the same fashion, these Axis partnerships, which are celebrated with such flourishes, must be extraordinarily uneasy affairs. How far can Germany and Japan trust each other? Not a yard, and of course they know it. Indeed, the Nazis' racial theory of supremacy, which in some mysterious manner assumes that the Creator intended his world to be ruled by the Teutonic branch of the Aryan race, makes any genuine long-term alliance between Germany and Japan a complete impossibility, because the Nazis regard the Japanese as a very inferior race, whose claim to anything like equality is merely absurd. The Japanese, of course, are well aware of this, and of what its consequences would be, in the event of a total Axis victory. Thus we can see what an uneasy partnership this must be. But then this uneasiness must run through all the Axis ranks, and for this good reason – that it is admitted by the leaders of those ranks that treachery, duplicity, faithlessness, lying and stabs in the back are an essential part of the policy. Now, these same weapons can be used at home just as they have been used abroad; and we know for a fact that they *have* been used, for already both in Germany and in Italy certain military leaders have died in very suspicious circumstances. And I fancy we have not heard the last of these mysterious deaths or disappearances. There will probably be more and more of them.

The German people used to be very fond of celebrating Christmas, but what sort of Christmas can they be having this year? They have been told by Hitler, with an effrontery that is shocking in its callous lying, that their casualties in Russia have been almost negligible. The campaign may not have succeeded

– and even Hitler cannot pretend that he has captured Moscow, arrived at the Caucasus and destroyed the Red Army when he has obviously done nothing of the kind – but, he has told them, so far it has been fought with comparatively few losses. Now, we know that a conservative estimate puts the figure of German *dead* alone at about a million and a half; and not all the censorship and Gestapo tricks and Goebbelisms can successfully pretend for long that a million and a half dead men can be reckoned at under 100,000. It simply can't be done. If so few have been lost then why do we never hear from our Wilhelm, our Heinrich, our Franz, and what has become of the three boys who lived next door, or the two men at the butcher's and the four who left the baker's? Hitler has staked everything on his belief that you can fool *all* the people *all* the time, but Lincoln, who said that that was just what you couldn't do, was the wiser man.

Again, not only has one loudly anticipated triumph after another failed – for weren't they to be in London by September 1940 and in Moscow last October? – but now the German people are waking from their brief dream of sudden glory and much loot to discover that rising around them on every side, like a terrible glittering wall of swords, is the implacable hatred of all the people they have oppressed. They know now that they are hated as no nation has been hated in Europe for hundreds of years. They have sown dragon's teeth. No doubt more and more hostages will be shot, more mass executions will be ordered, and the Gestapo and storm-troopers will be urged to commit more atrocities; but no matter how massive and formidable your military machine is, you cannot slave-drive a whole continent.

It has been pointed out by Germans themselves that they tend as a people to be haunted by a strange sense of doom; they are forever hearing the horns and trombones sounding the doomful themes of the twilight of the gods. How they must be haunted now! How the black ravens must be gathering in their dreams! They have contrived at last to set the Pacific in a blaze, but what comfort does that bring them, when once again they find themselves at war with America? What is it to them, huddled in their comfort-less homes, still without news of their husbands, sons, brothers, still without the promised triumphs and the easy quick peace, to learn that the Japanese have made landings here and there, bombed this and destroyed that? Their Fuhrer promised them swift, glittering successes, easy conquests, cheap glory, and his solemn assurance that never again would they know the endless black casualty lists of the last war. Well, he has kept his word in one respect. They do not have the endless casualty lists. Those have been kept from them. But the casualties, the endless line of dead men, the gaps in every home, are there again. And now they are worse off even than they were in the last war, for they are even less respected and more deeply hated, and the last shreds of honour are gone. We on our side can keep what remains of our old Christmas with hearts and minds at rest, knowing that our way of life is not worse but better than it was, that we fight to set men free. But they have to keep Christmas in the shadow of Anti-Christ, hearing themselves cursed in thirty different tongues, and at heart knowing themselves to be chained to a machine that would enslave men. The little Christmas trees they stare at are a mockery. They are wet with tears and crimson with blood.

22 January 1942

Women at War

Our Ministry of Labour has many headaches, but I imagine that easily its largest and most nearly permanent headache is the Woman problem. It is not so much that women in themselves are so much more difficult to handle than men, or even that they are less interested in the war effort; the trouble is simply that the whole business of calling up women for the women's services or for war industry is infinitely more complicated. Women have so many more domestic ties and responsibilities than men. This fact has been brought home to me in the hostels run by the war charity company of which I am chairman. During the last few weeks we have lost the services of several valuable assistants, not because they disliked the work and wished to go away but because various feminine responsibilities and obligations claimed them elsewhere. Thus a very useful married nurse, whose husband is in the Army, had to leave because she was having a baby. Then our only bookkeeper, a girl formerly employed in a bank, had to return home because her sister had had a very severe nervous breakdown and her mother sent an SOS. One of our best nursery school heads has had to leave us because her mother, now old and ailing, asked her to come back home to be near her. So it goes on. And the Ministry of Labour officials, who are generally harassed but not unsympathetic men, must now have a nightmare perspective of the complications of female life.

There is, of course, a very big drive going on to obtain the largest possible number of young women for both the war industries and the women's services. Over three million registered last year and are now being drafted into war industry or the services. It is unfortunate that the Auxiliary Territorial Services, always known as the ATS, which needs the most recruits – though even now it is about a million strong – is the least popular, for most girls prefer the dark blue uniform of the Naval service, the WRNS, or the lighter blue of the Air Force branch, the WAAFS, to the khaki of the ATS. Actually, most of the girls in all three services do more or less the same kind of work – namely, office work, cooking and waiting at table, motor driving, looking after stores, tailoring and various lighter technical jobs. But for some reason or other – perhaps because the khaki is not so becoming as the two blue uniforms, or because the Army seems to have less glamour than the Navy and Air Force, or because there are ten ATS girls to every one in the other two services – girls are not so eager to join the ATS. On the other hand, I have found after talking to girls in the ATS in various parts of the country that, once they are in, they don't dislike the life. At first perhaps they don't like the regulation clothes and the discipline and the bit of drill they do. In point of fact, most of them, after doing a little drill and some regular physical exercise, getting to bed in decent time and eating reasonably wholesome food, look both healthier and prettier than they did in civil life. And this is a fact that has not been stressed enough in the recruiting campaigns, which, so far as I can judge as an outsider, have not been conducted with very much skill and intelligence.

Nowadays, of course, you see these maidens in uniform, usually walking in pairs with their little fingers entwined, all over the place. I shouldn't like to say how many different feminine uniforms you see in a day's travel here now. You go, we'll say, to the railway station. On the way, you pass land girls, who have a kind of uniform. You also notice a woman postman, in uniform, and perhaps a women bus conductor or two, also in uniform. Driving through the town, you see nurses in their familiar uniform, then girls working for the Red Cross, in a dark blue uniform, then probably several older women in the dark green and maroon uniform of the WVS – the Women's Voluntary Service. You might also, if it's a large town you're driving through, notice a policewoman in *her* dark blue uniform. There is also, to be seen here and there, the distinctive khaki uniform of the women who work in the Navy, Army and Air Force Institutes and Canteens. If there's an aerodrome in the neighbourhood, you observe the greyish-blue of the WAAFS – the Air Force girls. At the railway station, you notice the women ticket collectors and porters, also in uniform – and very natty some of these young female railway workers look too – and altogether there are about 15,000 of them. On the platform, you are sure to see the khaki of the ATS – the Army girls – various ranks, including lots of girl subalterns with nicely powdered noses. On the train itself, you might see several feminine uniforms you had never noticed before, and if your destination is London then there, before the day's out, you would see still more mysterious feminine uniforms, some of them suggesting that Ruritania had now joined the anti-Nazi front and is admitting dashing blondes and glittering brunettes into its dragoons and hussars. Incidentally, I give very high marks – for obtaining a generally picturesque, military but essentially feminine effect – to the uniform of the American Red Cross over here.

Yet all these girls in uniform are a mere handful when compared with their sisters in overalls – and very fetching some of them look too! – the girls and women in the war factories. I must have seen hundreds and thousands of these at work, helping to make aeroplanes, shells, instruments for guns and planes, time fuses, gas masks, parachutes and all the munitions of war. I have watched them at their benches at all hours of day and night. I have listened to them laughing, singing and cheering at their lunch-hour concerts in their canteens. I have seen them pouring out of trains and buses, swarming up the roads, to begin their work.

You would imagine from some occasional newspaper reports, nearly always based on a few exceptional cases, that these girls in the war factories earned very high wages, but although most of them are earning more than they were capable of earning before the war, their average wages are probably round about three pounds a week. And many of them have a very long day because it may take them a couple of hours to get from their homes or lodgings to their work and then another couple of hours to return at night, which means getting up in the black-out and returning home in it in the evening, and hardly seeing any daylight until Sunday. Again, a great many are not living at home because they are working in enormous new factories that have been built well away from the old industrial towns, so that these girls and women have to find lodgings for themselves, often in areas where accommodation is very limited.

This has become such a problem that our Ministry of Supply is now building hostels near some of its larger factories. I went over one of these hostels only the other day. It was still being built – the largest assembly room, which would serve excellently as a theatre, was not yet finished – but I saw enough to give me a good idea of what was happening. This particular hostel was designed to accommodate about 2,000, mostly women and girls, and was not unlike a military camp in appearance, with rows of solidly built huts, each containing twenty cubicles – two girls to a cubicle – and bathrooms, wash-houses etc. Only about 400 women and girls were already living there. I had lunch with some of them – not many, because most were then at work in the factory and they would eat their lunch there – and it was a reasonably good lunch, and everybody looked cheerful. On the walls were notices advertising forthcoming hostel dances, film shows and so on, all of which, I was told, were very popular. The charge for board and lodging – not including amusements, though these are only a little extra – is twenty-two shillings and sixpence – say, about five dollars, which of course is very cheap.

I'll admit that camp life on this scale, even with all these conveniences and comforts, would never be my choice – I dislike a hard existence – but it is worth remembering that a great many of these women and girls not only don't share this distaste but like nothing better than living with crowds of others. This is proved by what they did in their holidays before the war, when they nearly always made for the most crowded seaside resorts, and latterly were beginning to patronise with enthusiasm various holiday camps not unlike this hostel I saw. In fact, the man who was rapidly popularising the holiday camp idea among the workers, the man who owned most of the largest holiday camps round our shores, Mr. Butlin, a former showman with a flair for camp organisation, has recently been appointed head of the Ministry of Supply's hostel department. So these women and girls are not likely to suffer much while they are still under the charge of their favourite holiday provider, Mr. Butlin. This was a very shrewd stroke by the Minister of Supply.

And indeed it was high time there were a few shrewd strokes. The appeal to women has not on the whole been very well managed. There has been far too much rather vague nagging, which women soon resent. Sometimes – I am referring now to what happened months ago – strong appeals were made over the air and in the press for women and girls to volunteer for work in the war factories, but without any clear-cut arrangements having been made to deal with the volunteers as soon as they arrived at the Labour Exchanges, with the result that soon the enthusiasm and then even the patience of the volunteers evaporated, and large numbers of disgruntled women and girls returned home and announced that there they would stay. It is not that they were unwilling to help the war effort. On the contrary, they were all too eager to help it. But they were badly handled.

Now, it's more than likely that some of you will soon have – if you have not already had – the job of recruiting women and girls for various war services. Do you mind if I give you a little good advice? First, then, do nothing publicly until you have made definite arrangements to deal at once with the women who come forward to volunteer. Perfect these arrangements first. Then, when everything is cut and dried behind the scenes, and the whole machinery of distribution is ready, launch with all the force at your command a sudden, sharp, strongly emotional appeal – over the air, in the motion picture theatres, in the press, at flag-wagging meetings – telling the women they are urgently needed. Then give them the few necessary facts – that they can sign on at such a place, that they will be put to such and such work, roughly for so many hours at such and such a rate

– definite instructions, unmistakable facts. Then the women, only too anxious to respond to the emotional appeal, also know exactly where they are, and, your organisation being all ready, when they rush forward, you are all set to deal with them. But don't ask for them and then look as if you don't know what to do with them. Don't drearily nag at them. Don't encourage them to lose patience. Remember that few of them have not some responsibilities and obligations they must sacrifice. They know already it is their war as much as yours. They want to help – bless them! Best of all, perhaps, let women themselves manage the whole campaign.

27 March 1942

Colonel Blimp

We might call my subject this week The Life and Death of Colonel Blimp. Most of you know as well as I do who Colonel Blimp is, but for the sake of those who don't, I'd better explain that Colonel Blimp is a famous creation of our great cartoonist David Low, who used this figure – shown as a bald-headed, elderly, fattish man with a large military moustache – to symbolise what he considered to be a stupid, old-fashioned, ultra-conservative or reactionary point of view. Colonel Blimp was first created several years before the war, but it is during the war – and especially during these past few months – that he has been mentioned so often, and not only by speakers and writers in the press here in Britain but also by similar persons in the Dominions and United States. Thus it has been freely said that our whole war effort has suffered from the presence, in positions of authority, of too many Colonel Blimps. It is not a figure of speech I use myself, as some of you may have noticed, just as I never use the phrase 'the old school tie', though not long ago an angry man wrote to me to say how tired he was of my using it, which just shows how, once you are thoroughly angry, you never stop to examine the evidence.

But as we all more or less now have some idea who Colonel Blimp is, what he stands for, and even find it difficult to get away from references to him, I think it is time I had something to say about him. And here let me add that Colonel Blimp was a man of very strong likes and dislikes, and that among his strong dislikes was myself. But if he couldn't be fair to me, that's no reason why I shouldn't try to be fair to him. For example, here's a story that I like, about something that happened only this week. A friend of mine is the secretary of a progressive group that sends out statements and circulars on problems of the war and the peace. Its most recent circular, which was sent out in large numbers all over the country, made a decided attack on the Blimps and had on its cover a cartoon by David Low showing the funeral of Blimp. At the same time, this circular appealed for contributions to help in its work. Well, among the replies my friend the secretary received was the following:

> *Thank you for your circular. Unfortunately, I am one of the Blimps of Blimperdom – and I am now too old to change – but I gladly send you the enclosed cheque for ten pounds in order to help you to give me and my like a decent funeral with all possible speed, and which I trust will be enthusiastically attended by all those who have youth on their side. Good luck to you!*

Now, that letter seems to me as important as it is amusing and charming. It's important because I believe it is in some respects typical. What is happening is that the Blimps are becoming aware of their Blimpishness and are changing or – if they feel they cannot change – are gradually retiring into the background and modifying their claims to advise and lead us.

Why are the Blimps, who so steadfastly refused to change or allow anything else to change, now at last allowing themselves to be converted or translated? Have we anti-Blimps become more persuasive? No, I don't think so. In my view, two recent sets of events in this war have done the trick, shaking the Blimps as no arguments of yours and mine could have done. The first set of events took place – and are still taking place – in Russia. The Blimps, who of course always had their own view of Russia and the Russians, were quite convinced that the Soviet would never hold out against the tremendous onslaught of the German armies. But all last summer and early autumn they heard how the Red Army resisted all attempts of the Germans to destroy it, and how it exacted the maximum price in men and materials for every town and village the German armies captured. Then ever since, they have learned how the Red Army has struck back, with ever-increasing force, at the invaders, compelling them to yield village after village, town after town, district after district, and also compelling the German leaders to throw in more and more reserves of men and war materials. They have also learned how the Soviet people, whom they had previously thought of as mere sullen or deluded slaves, have risen to height after height of endurance, courage and brilliant organisation, battling and toiling day and night for the republic which they felt to be their own precious possession. There was simply no denying these facts, and unfortunately they contradicted everything that Blimp, who is a simple soul and never very well-informed, had come to believe. That made him think a bit. He didn't particularly want to think, but there was no help for it – he simply had to think. Doubts were born at last. Perhaps the fellows at the club hadn't known it all. Perhaps old So-and-so, supposed to be a bit of an authority on all this Bolshevik stuff, had been wrong at the time.

Well, that was one set of events. Now we come to the other: our reverses in the Far East. Now, the Blimps always thought they knew about the Far East, because they were frequently just the chaps who went out to these places. East of Suez, you may say, was their territory. And one reason why they often wouldn't listen to the rest of us was that they felt they'd knocked about the world, knew their India, Malaya, China and the rest, while the rest of us had merely been doing some fancy reading and writing at home. They knew all about 'natives', as they always insisted upon calling them. They knew all about yellow men, brown men, black men. They knew all about the empire. When Kipling cried, 'What do they know of England, who only England know?', they all loudly applauded.

And let me say here that I've always felt that cry of Kipling's was very mischievous. The trouble with many of the Blimps was that they themselves may have known a good deal about the empire but often they knew precious little about England herself. It was this ignorance that often made them so dangerous.

Frequently, they left home as young men to do duty, as soldiers, commissioners, police officers, in distant parts of the empire. When they came back on leave, they returned to old haunts or to where they could best amuse themselves. After twenty years or so of this kind of life, they would retire on a pension to some pleasant rural part of this island where they could get some reasonably cheap hunting, fishing or shooting. Generally, there was nothing to take them into the industrial parts of the country, in which the majority of our people live and work. At the age of fifty or sixty, many of them knew no more about industrial England than they had learned at the age of fifteen. The most gigantic social and economic transformations might be taking place and yet they would know little or nothing about them. They weren't necessarily stupid men or unsympathetic men. Nine times out of ten they got along very well with people of all kinds with whom they were actually in contact. And they had an intense love of this country, nourished by years of exile from it. The trouble was, too often they didn't understand all that had been happening to this country and its people. They didn't know enough.

Then again, some of them couldn't help being disappointed because after spending years perhaps in distant tropics eagerly looking forward to their retirement in this country, they found the reality far below their expectations. They were active and probably strong-minded men, used to responsibility, and they found themselves out of employment, back in a country that perhaps they suspected they didn't understand, rather bored, sometimes apt to be bad-tempered or soured. Sometimes I've felt that they deliberately didn't try to understand the way the world was going in the years before the war, for fear that the reality would make them feel too uncomfortable. They hoped rather than believed that all this shouting and bullying and marching about of these Nazis would turn out to be nothing much in the end, just more German nonsense. As a class, this war soon hit them very hard because of the mounting taxation. It was obvious that their comfortable old life was gone, and probably gone for good.

But if all this – and more – were necessary to save the country, they were ready to take it. For, you must understand, it is not the Blimps, at least as I distinguish them, who would ever want to sell out, as certain types in France were ready to sell out. For my part, I would never question their genuine and very deep-seated patriotism. There was nothing wrong with their hearts. It was always their heads that were at fault. They just didn't know enough and wouldn't even try to learn. Yet it always seemed to me that their quick anger when you hinted at all this was very significant. It suggested to my mind that beneath an apparent complacency they were already secretly disturbed by the way the world was blowing up all over the place and behaving in ways quite beyond their comprehension. It's not the absolutely cocksure man who soon gets angry if challenged but the man who's no longer quite sure and is trying to persuade himself, as well as you, that he is.

So there Blimp was, secretly becoming more and more uncertain. And Soviet Russia gave him a surprise. Then came our reverses in the Far East, which hit him very hard because they were undoubtedly in his pet department. Events East of Suez simply weren't going to plan at all. His world really was vanishing. You must remember that these reverses were far more surprising to him than they were to the rest of us, who guessed what must inevitably happen once Japan suddenly unmasked her guns. It stood to reason that we must face a period of serious setbacks, simply because we couldn't bring enough men and material to the vast distant area in time. But Blimp, having been living not in the present but in the past, in which such disasters simply couldn't happen, had to endure one terrible shock after another. Now he was compelled at last to admit that his world no longer existed, that a great page of history had been turned, that we were now at the beginning of a new era and must therefore face events and subsequently control and initiate them as if we too were new men.

But there was still health and life in Blimp. He didn't want to bury himself in the ruins of his shattered world. He loved this country and had a real affection for nearly all the people he really knew and didn't just imagine he knew. He has always talked a lot, perhaps too much, about 'carrying on'. So now he will carry on. But I said my subject was the Life and *Death* of Colonel Blimp. Well, he will carry on, but not, I think, as Blimp. The man who wrote that letter to my friend the secretary said, you remember, 'I am now too old to change, but I gladly send you the enclosed cheque for ten pounds in order to help you to give me and my like a decent funeral with all possible speed.' But of course he was wrong. He wasn't too old to change. When he wrote that letter, he'd already changed. There may be a funeral, but the coffin will be empty. Or it may simply contain a large military moustache of old-fashioned cut and a few discarded prejudices. So goodbye, Colonel.

3 April 1942

Share the Luxury

If only the poets and dramatists and novelists of the Axis powers went to work in the same wild way as their propagandists do, what wonderful works of imagination they would give us! I was thinking this today when I happened to see some extracts from an account of London that had appeared in the Turin newspaper *La Stampa*.

Incidentally, it's worth pausing a moment to consider the fantastic travel background of this stuff. Now, this description of London, we are told, comes from the Stockholm correspondent of this Italian newspaper, and this correspondent is supposed to be quoting Swedes who have just returned from London. Then this copy of the Italian newspaper found its way to Lisbon, and it was brought back from Lisbon by the friend of a London editor. So that, if everybody is telling the truth, you get this story going from London to Stockholm, Stockholm to Turin, Turin to Lisbon, and then from Lisbon back to London. And this is the kind of mad world we're living in. No wonder it's so hard to discover the real truth about anything.

But unlike these various gentlemen in Stockholm, Turin or Lisbon, I can at least tell you the truth about London. And it's very different from this description of London published in the Italian paper, which is a fascinating bit of invention. It conjures up for us a London that is darkened, deserted and forlorn, just like the 'City of Dreadful Night' in that extraordinary pessimistic poem by the Victorian James Thomson. We read how 'the silence round Waterloo Station is unbelievable', how most of the hotels 'are closed for lack of visitors', how most of the famous restaurants 'no longer cook meals', how in Regent Street 'a thousand shops are closed' and 'only one restaurant is open; but what a depressing sight it is with never more than three or four customers'. And so it goes on. This is a quite accurate description of London at any time between two and five in the morning. As a description of London at any other time, it is simply a work of the wildest imagination. I say this almost with regret, for there is to me a certain grave charm in this picture of a gigantic deserted city. I believe I would find a melancholy pleasure in wandering up and down a Regent Street, an Oxford Street, a Piccadilly, in which hardly any shops were open, and there were hardly any passers-by, and the solitary restaurant had never more than three or four customers. My grumble about London is that nowadays all the restaurants – and they seem to be as numerous as ever they were – are packed to the doors, so that it is very difficult to find a free table, and you're compelled to book a table hours ahead, a thing I'm always reluctant to do. As for the hotels being closed for lack of visitors, the truth is they are nearly all open – for some, of course, have been taken over by the government for use as offices etc. – and have never been so full, I believe, in all their history. The traveller who arrives in London these days without having booked a room well in advance will have a miserable time of it trying to find accommodation. Opera, ballet, concerts, straight plays, musical shows and vaudeville are all in full swing, pretty much as in peacetime. We have at present twenty-eight theatres open in the West End of London.

Actually, this description of a mournful, deserted London, which was of course printed in an Italian paper to persuade the miserable Italians that somebody was even worse off than they are, comes very ironically just now, because for the last few weeks there has been a great deal of criticism of this luxurious living, in Parliament, in the press and in public meetings, and it has been suggested in many different quarters that a stop should be put to it. You will probably remember that Sir Stafford Cripps in one of his first public utterances here, after his return from Russia, called for more austerity, and it was this remark of his, more than anything else, that gave the signal for this storm of criticism to break. Moreover, this condemnation of luxury in wartime hasn't been made a political issue. It comes, I repeat, from many different quarters. Some wealthy Conservative Members of Parliament have been as insistent that this luxury should cease as Labour and Socialist Members have been. It has been asserted over and over again lately that the fact that this kind of life should still go on in the West End of London is detrimental to our war effort and to public morale.

Now, I must confess that on this question – as on some other questions – I find myself in agreement with neither party, but in partial agreement with both, that is, the people who say 'Let it alone' and the people who say 'Stop it'. It seems to me that neither party has examined the problem of luxury in wartime with sufficient thoroughness, and that men on both sides have tended to indulge their own particular temperaments. And I don't apologise for asking you to consider this problem with me, because it isn't really a local problem, merely affecting the West End of London, but is a problem that every community that finds itself engaged in total war will have to consider. If most of you haven't come up against it yet, I think you will soon find that you will come up against it. There is, in fact, no escaping it. So let's consider it carefully together.

To begin with, nobody in his senses would defend for a moment the kind of luxury that could only exist at the expense of the war effort. If, for example, thousands of fit young men who ought to be in the armed forces were being employed in luxury hotels, restaurants, theatres etc., the result would be a monstrous and indefensible situation. But that, of course, is not the case here. Such luxury as we have only comes into existence, so to speak, after the war effort has had its full quota of manpower and materials. This is true even of foodstuffs, for the fancy foods still served in expensive restaurants exist in such small quantities that it would not be worthwhile to ration them on a national basis. All this luxury may reasonably be considered an *extra*. And there is, of course, in reality less and less of it as time goes on. And those who defend it would say:

> *Why bother with it? Let people who can afford it enjoy what's left of it. Total war is a dreary business for most people, so why deliberately make it drearier? Why shouldn't people be allowed to enjoy what remains of*

the colour, spice and variety of life? They won't fight and work any the worse for an occasional pleasant night out.

That, I *imagine* – and I must be cautious here, for I haven't come across any public statement of his on the subject – is what Mr. Churchill would say if pressed for his opinion. The opponents of this attitude, and of course they tend to be men and women of a more severe temperament, and in some instances may actually belong to that queer group of persons who really dislike seeing other people enjoy anything they can't enjoy themselves, say something like this:

> *That's all very well, but even assuming that the existence of this luxury life doesn't take anything directly from our war effort, and we doubt that, the fact remains that its continued existence is really a menace to our war effort. For what is the use of continually telling people that our situation is very serious, that gigantic efforts and sacrifices will have to be made by everybody, when we will allow this sort of easy, luxurious, expensive, life to go on? It looks as if we don't mean what we say. If we are serious, if this is a great solemn moment in our history, then let us behave accordingly, sweep away all that remains of this easy living, this expensive dining and wining, this dancing and extravagant nonsense, and insist upon everybody living austerely. Then at last people will have no excuse for not realising what is at stake and for not making the gigantic efforts and sacrifices that we demand.*

That is the other argument. And, I repeat, though I agree in part with both arguments, I don't agree entirely with either. I don't advocate either complete non-interference or complete abolition. I believe there is a third possible course, and I believe also that it is one that would best help the war effort, so I ask those of you who may find yourselves soon facing the same problem to give this possible solution your careful consideration. Now, my objection to this luxury is not that it exists at all – for I agree with those who say they cannot see why we should deliberately stamp out all that remains of the colour, spice and variety of our ordinary life – my objection to it is that as conditions are it tends to be enjoyed, day after day, by *more or less the same set of people*. That, to my mind, is really what is wrong with it. It simply isn't true, of course, that most people here enjoy too much luxury. The fact is, most people don't have enough, and could well do with rather more fun and games. No, what is wrong is that a few people still have far more than their share of the pleasant things that are left. I think it would be absurd to close down hotels just because they are too comfortable and well-managed, shut up restaurants just because they still contrive to serve good dinners, and darken places of amusement just because they're still amusing. This seems to me wrong-headed. There is no point in dreariness and discomfort for the sake of dreariness and discomfort. I don't believe that people who are bored will fight and work the best. On the other hand, I can't see why more or less the same set of people, who happen to have the money and be on the spot, should have all the colour and fun that's left.

What I suggest, then, is that luxury should neither be left alone nor abolished but should be brought into intimate relation with the war effort itself. It's the people who are doing most for the war effort that should be allowed to enjoy what luxury is left. The airmen and sailors and soldiers on leave should have their full share of it, and the men who've done particularly well and have had the toughest time should be given special privileges here. Let them have the softest beds and the fattest dinners and the most amusing shows – if they want them. Let the war factories compete for the foremost place in production, and inside the factories let there be competing teams of workers, and then give the winning teams a short holiday and a roaring good time. Let the official who's worked day and night on some terrific job of organisation have a break and take himself and his wife to the best that the city can offer them. In short, keep what luxury is left, what colour, spice and variety of life remain, but no longer allow them to be bought by the first comer with the price in his pocket, but turn them into rewards and privileges. I don't say this will be easy to organise. But I'm certain it's worth trying.

17 April 1942

What Is Needed for War

It's generally considered here, by the people who know about such things, that the American government radio feature *This Is War* is the best radio programme of its kind that has yet been produced. We are grateful for the chance of hearing it ourselves and of passing it on to more and more listeners. The subject of this radio programme is, of course, the all-important one of total war. During the last two and a half years, some of us here have written and talked a great deal about total war. It's a conception foreign to the minds of the peace-loving peoples of the great democracies. They haven't been subjected for years, as the people in the Axis countries have, to intensive propaganda treatment to familiarise them with the idea.

Again, we must remember that to the Axis dictators and the military cliques who surround them, total war is really the line of least resistance. It is easier for them to make war than to live in peace. That's why they must be destroyed, for we can only co-operate with people who *want* to live in peace with their neighbours. But total war automatically solves or disposes of problems that the Axis dictators simply don't know how to deal with adequately on a peacetime basis. Hence their assumption from the start that war is inevitable, and that on the whole it is a good rather than a bad thing. All this has given them certain advantages. They learned to play the terrible game of total war far earlier than we did, and always welcomed it, whereas we in the democracies came to it reluctantly. This reluctance is natural and right and does us credit. But it mustn't be carried past a certain point. And we all know very well – and we in Britain woke up to it at Dunkirk, and some of you saw it the morning of Pearl Harbor – that our sheer survival as democratic citizens now demands that we think entirely in terms of total war – that is, the complete organisation of the whole community to wage war in the most effective manner.

This means that we must rid ourselves of many of our old ideas. For example, total war is a very different thing from the old romantic conception of war. It means that we must serve the war effort in what is our best particular capacity. A doctor must be a doctor and not go flying fighter planes. A skilled mechanic must work with machines and not go shouldering a rifle. A woman who is a good caterer should do some official catering and not try to become a nurse. We must decide – or let others decide for us – where and how we can be most useful, and not, as in the romantic conception of war, where and how we can be most dashing and picturesque. If we can serve the war effort best by putting on uniform then let us put on uniform, but if we can't then our splendid appearance in uniform is merely a piece of self-indulgence. Many people imagine that unless they are hurling themselves into immediate danger, they aren't helping the war, whereas in actual fact they may be just a nuisance and an added responsibility in the danger areas and would be much more useful and patriotic if they were back home planting potatoes or working a lathe. The proper attitude towards danger in wartime is to try to disregard it one way or the other. And indeed one of the many ironies of this war is that lots of dashing young men who've gone looking for danger have never yet found it, while all manner of timid elderly ladies have suddenly found themselves in the middle of danger they never wanted and have behaved magnificently. Actually, this war will probably be won not by heroism but by good organisation, hard work and constant small self-sacrifices, often of a very dull kind.

Failure to co-operate in total war is frequently due simply to a lack of imagination. So many people don't realise what kind of world they're living in now. They have an entirely false and dangerous sense of security. 'It can't happen here' is their slogan, whereas in this world and in this war, it can happen anywhere. These people neither understand the height and depth of the menace nor appreciate the terrific effort we shall have to make to put an end to that menace. They tend to think of this war as a sort of tiresome interruption to their ordinary life, as if a drunken man had come to lodge in the house. We still have quite a number of people of this kind in Britain, and in my view the government could have done a great deal more than it has done to blow away their cosy illusions.

But that would mean giving a revolutionary interpretation to the events of the last ten years, and the conservative mind isn't prepared to do that. I still come across middle-aged, comfortable couples here, tucked away in hotels or country houses, who imagine that because they're paying their taxes and their bills, they're doing all that's necessary. It doesn't occur to them that if they're making no direct personal contribution to our war effort then because they have to have food, fuel, service of many different kinds, they're no better than expensive passengers in a ship that can't afford to be carrying any passengers. On the other hand, I must admit that just as more could be done publicly to challenge the attitude of mind of such people, so too more could be done to find suitable war work for them to do. In all the democracies, I think, we need much more of a 'Burn Your Boats!' attitude of mind in our leaders. They should tell their people that if they lose this war then they lose practically everything, but that if they win it then they can go forward to reconstruct the world and make it look a far more civilised place. Far too many people, especially among the more comfortable classes, are either clinging too hard to the past or trying, at the expense of the immediate war effort, to make certain of their future. It should be made plain to them that clinging to the past is idiotic folly, and that dodging present commitments in order to get a mortgage on the future is cheating, sabotage and treachery, and should be treated as such. The kind of genial swindling of the public that used to be considered 'smart business' should, in total war, be instantly rewarded with a long term of imprisonment with hard labour. A man who uses his wits against the interest of the community in total war is like a man stealing water in a besieged fortress. In fairness to most of our own people here, however, I must point out that they have generally been several months ahead of the government in their demand for further increases of rationing and far more restrictions. Too often have we heard some polite government spokesman apologising for some wartime restrictive measure that most of his listeners have been demanding for the past six months.

Again, in total war, though real equality of sacrifice is quite impossible, the fewer obvious inequalities there are, the better people will feel. This is particularly true of those sections of the public that cannot help feeling they have been badly treated in the past and are suspicious of fair words after they have heard so many harsh ones. If a government takes away the hard-won rights of one class, it should, if it is wise, make at the same time a spectacular raid on the privileges of the other classes. If it should be proposed to coerce labour then that is the moment to be equally ruthless with capital.

The psychology of total war deserves the most careful attention of governments and their expert advisers. The greatest mistake – and it was made here in the early part of the war, and I doubt if we're free from it yet – is to encourage people to regard their wartime life as merely a drearier and more restricted version of their pre-war life. This, in my view, is absolutely fatal. It checks any enthusiasm; it manufactures boredom, it discourages self-sacrifice, and it creates in the public mind a false picture of the war itself. It is particularly bad for young people, who are bewildered by it and often become suspicious. Youth isn't wedded to a comfortable routine, is nearly always contemptuous of it even in ordinary times. What youth dislikes is a dreary monotony, lack of opportunity for adventure, excitement and for making use of its own creative energy, and any persons or situations that suggest youth is unimportant. What it likes is to feel necessary and important, to lead and be led, to make full use of its energy, and to see the future glowing and brightening before it.

Now, the Russians seem to me to understand the psychology of people engaged in total war better than anybody else. So far as I can gather, they try to make everything highly coloured and dramatic. Their people are made conscious of themselves as spectacular and heroic figures. Work in a war factory there seems to have been made as exciting as a horse race. They make full use of the competitive spirit, which I have actually heard denounced by officials here. If they have to do without something pleasant, and they have had to do without many pleasant things, they try to turn this restricting into a large gesture of self-sacrifice.

Nor does all this contradict what I said earlier about total war being very different from the old romantic wars, when you could often afford to disregard your usefulness and merely be dashing and picturesque. The ground plan of total war, its use of us as manpower, must be strictly utilitarian and indeed even scientific, and to this we must submit, agreeing to do, as well as we can, what it is thought we can do best for the war effort. But once that ground plan has been laid down, and the walls go up on those solid foundations, that's no reason whatever why all the colour and fun and romantic ardour should disappear from the scene. On the contrary, this is where all the possible colour and fun and romance should be introduced, where all the people should feel themselves to be taking part in a terrific historic drama. And for the sake of variety, to avoid staleness and boredom, this drama should be deliberately divided into successive acts. Every few months the people engaged in total war should feel they are taking part in a new act. Thus I think that all the United Nations should now be plunged into a new act or chapter called the First Offensive, or something of that sort, and everything that is planned, done and said should have an intimate relation with the First Offensive, so that it appears as if an entirely new spirit is animating the free peoples at war. I believe actually that that spirit exists among the people themselves, but the huge drama itself should be set in motion. To this such a fine radio programme as *This Is War* would make an excellent and, we would hope, a typical contribution.

14 and 15 May 1942

Who Are the British?

Now, here is an extract from the letter of an American woman to a certain English woman writer. I am going to read this extract slowly and carefully because it's important that you should take it in. 'I wish', says this American woman to her friend here,

> *I wish you would help us to see some clear picture of England as it really is. For instance, on the same day that I read J. B. Priestley telling of the new England which is arising, without class distinctions and with a real solidarity of aim, I received a letter from an English friend living in a country house, all about the garden and the shortage of staff and the difficulty of keeping the lawns right, and saying, 'After the war there will be a good deal of unemployment so there will be no staff difficulties and life here will be delightful.'*

*Which is real? Both are honest people seeing the world
each from his point of view, but which is England?*

So much for the American correspondent. She wants to
know which is the real England – the England I have so often
described to you, the England that is rapidly losing its class
distinctions and achieving a common purpose, or the England of
her friend in the country house, who looks forward to plenty of
unemployment after the war 'so there will be no staff difficulties
and life here will be delightful'?

Now to begin with, how much does this person in the country
house – and I now assume it's a woman – know about England?
Does she know as much about it as I do? I don't hesitate to say
that she doesn't. Ever since this war began, I've been travelling
up and down this island of ours. It's been an essential part of
my job, moving around and seeing what people were doing – in
factories, camps, aerodromes, large cities, small towns, villages.
I've addressed meetings of every size and description, from
thousands of workers assembled in factory canteens to small
groups in drawing rooms. I used to have a regular weekly radio
audience here of about fifteen million people, and thousands
and thousands of them used to write to me. I've spent uncounted
hours in railway trains, hotels, restaurants, canteens, workshops,
asking questions and answering questions. There isn't any *kind*
of people, from members of the War Cabinet to taxi drivers,
railway porters or schoolboys, with whom I haven't discussed
our war problems. I don't believe there's any book of first-rate
or even second-rate importance about Britain in wartime that
I haven't read. I've spent hours studying the reports of such
investigating groups as Mass-Observation or the Institute of
Public Opinion. But I mustn't go on. The point I want to make
is that when I tell you or anybody else what is happening here
and what the ordinary British people are thinking and feeling,
I'm not merely guessing.

No good lady in a country house can match my wartime
experience because if she could, she'd no longer be a good lady
in a country house but would be doing a job in the war effort.
And my guess is this – that that woman who wrote to her friend
in America and said that after the war there would be plenty of
unemployment and therefore no staff difficulties and so life here

would be delightful, that woman hasn't one thousandth part of my experience and knowledge of wartime England. In fact, I don't believe she knows anything about wartime England at all. Furthermore, she doesn't know anything about this war. She doesn't know what it's about, how it came into existence, what it means, how it can best be fought, or anything else about it.

And if anybody thinks that she and her kind represent England then there's a simple test, which I shall be delighted, for my part, to undertake with her. Let there be collected, in any part of this island, a fairly representative audience of our people. Then I will gladly appear before this audience and tell it freely and frankly what I think is happening here, namely, that the inevitable pressure of total war, which must mean either a dictator's war or a people's war, is rapidly ironing out class distinctions here and compelling us to think in terms of a common purpose. I will do this providing that this country-house woman follows me on the platform and tells the same audience, also freely and frankly, that she is looking forward to plenty of unemployment after the war so that she can find again plenty of cheap, docile labour to work for her in her house and garden, and that that state of things will be delightful. And I declare here and now that she daren't do it. That audience would howl her down. There isn't a public man in this country who dare get up and talk such drivel. I don't say that such things aren't said in private, to a few equally idiotic intimates. But I do say that nobody dare talk to the people themselves like that. Mr. Churchill once said, 'What sort of people do they think we are?' And I say to these persons, 'What sort of people do we think we are?'

Of course I've met these ladies and gentlemen in country houses who talk such callous nonsense about unemployment. They're not quite as bad as they sound. In their own little circle, they may be quite decent – kind-hearted persons, anxious to help the people around them. Their trouble is that they haven't any imagination and they simply don't know what's happening in the world. Strictly speaking, they aren't living in this world at all, their minds never having caught up with the terrific march of events. They probably stopped thinking for themselves somewhere about 1910. They still regard this war as a kind of brief interruption in a quiet, settled existence. They haven't the least notion that the world has really been in a state of wild revolution for years and years. They've never taken a proper look at anything. They're living in a dream. They're like the last of the dinosaurs, still crashing and blundering about the place but really on their way to extinction. None of the people who are *in* this war, and not merely dreaming on the edge of it, talk this sort of nonsense. You don't hear it in the camps and aerodromes, the factories and workshops. Nobody visits the people in their shelters during a blitz and tells them to stick it because very soon the war will be over and then they'll be unemployed and ready and willing to serve as footmen, housemaids and under-gardeners, in order that the English country house may flourish in all its ancient glory.

And isn't it about time some of our American friends understood a few things about the English people? I've talked to you before many a time about the character of our people, and began to imagine any further talks on the subject weren't necessary, but apparently they are. Now listen! The English are a slow, rather lazy-minded people, always reluctant to make changes. They're very good-humoured, want to avoid trouble and fuss, and are very difficult to rouse. It's hard to make them very enthusiastic, and equally hard to depress them. They're not a bit like lions, which are gorgeous and rather temperamental beasts. But they are, in the mass, extraordinarily like bulldogs. You know what a bulldog's like. It's a slow, sleepy sort of dog, and if it knows you well, you can do anything you like with it. I've seen children in a family that owned a bulldog just dragging it about and rough-handling it in the most startling fashion. But once a bulldog makes up its slow and sleepy mind that it doesn't like you and that you're up to no good, then that bulldog gets a grip on you and *never lets go*. That's what the Germans and Italians forgot, though they know it now all right. After the fall of France, the whole world imagined that Britain would sue for terms. But it never occurred to the mass of the British people, any more than it occurs to a bulldog to let go. And I believe there's one German who in his queer intuitive fashion understands this, and his name is Adolf Hitler, who showed in *Mein Kampf* that he had some notion of what the British character was like and then allowed himself to be misled afterwards, by people like Ribbentrop who had no insight and had never really come into contact with the ordinary people here.

And another thing. Don't be deceived by second-rate novels and films about England. The English people don't consist chiefly of hunting squires and hat-touching villagers. They are mostly people who live in industrial towns, very similar to your own industrial towns, people who work in factories, iron foundries, coal mines, ship-building yards, wool and cotton mills and the like. They're mostly fairly tough people who do fairly tough jobs. And because *we* grumble about our war production – and remember we're born grumblers – don't imagine that it isn't a man-size war production, for, believe me, it's the most gigantic effort ever made by forty-five million people in the history of this world, and it had to be improvised and brought up to full strength at a time when the German Army was twenty-one miles away, when we were raided day and night, and when we stood alone and defied the world's greatest military machine to do its worst. These are the people I'm talking about, the little bulldog people, and I say that here and now they have two ideas in their heads. The first is that Hitler is going to be defeated even if it should take us the rest of our lives to do it. That bulldog grip won't let go. The second idea is this – that after Hitler *is* defeated, *things aren't going to be the same as they were before the war*. If we've fought and toiled and suffered so that democracy shall survive, it's going to be a real democracy, and there isn't going to be a lot of unemployment in order that women in country houses should have plenty of cheap labour to employ, and if women in country houses don't like it, they can lump it. I've no particular grudge against country houses and the people who own them – as a matter of fact, I own one myself – but nobody can reasonably expect the ordinary folk of this island to go deliberately back to an economic and social system that had ceased to function properly before the war.

My own belief is that if this woman in the country house is prepared after the war to co-operate with the rest of us in really tackling the job of reconstruction here, producing as rapidly and lavishly for peace as we've done for war, re-building the battered ugly towns, re-housing large numbers of the people, seeing that every child has every opportunity to grow up strong, healthy and decently educated, then she is perfectly right in thinking that life will be delightful here. But if she thinks it will be delightful because the towns will be crowded with unemployed, because the men who are now manning the guns and the girls who are now making them will be driven into her service for any wages she chooses to offer, because all her old privileges and class prejudices will be confirmed, then I can tell her here and now that she is going to be sadly disappointed. Democratic England has arrived, and she'd better make up her mind to live in it like a sensible good citizen.

22 May 1942

Social Experiments

I have just been reading in one of the weeklies an article by our Julian Huxley, who has just spent five months lecturing and travelling about in the United States. One point he makes in this article seems to me very important. He says there has been a good deal of criticism of the administration in the United States, because, the critics say it is wrong to undertake social experiments in the middle of a war. Now, I know this kind of criticism very well. We had a great deal of it here at one time, chiefly from similar types of minds. If you pointed out that a great deal of rapid social reorganisation was necessary, you were accused of trying to 'play politics' in the middle of a war, of taking advantage of the national emergency to hurry through measures and policies that represented the point of view of a section of the community, of menacing the necessary national unity by advocating class interests and so forth. It is for this reason that I propose to deal with this particular type of criticism.

The internal affairs of the United States are no concern of mine, and I stick to my opinion, which I emphasised here some weeks ago, that we in the Allied nations would do well not to try to interfere in each other's affairs, to leave each country and people to settle their own internal problems, and so to refrain from criticism. Therefore I make no comment on what is happening in the United States. But on the other hand it would be absurd not to give each other the benefit of our own direct experience. If, for example, the United States is now going through a stage of war experience that we have already known, is in fact busy building up as quickly as possible a national effort towards total war, and we on this side already know what that means, what difficulties are encountered on the way, what obstacles will have to be faced, then I say that it would be absurd for us not at least to offer a little advice based on our own experience. We are co-operating to do one gigantic job, and if we can save each other from mistakes then so much the better.

Very well then. It is my experience that the attitude of mind that protests against social experiment in the middle of a war, that condemns new social organisation as 'playing politics' and taking advantage of a national emergency, is an attitude of mind that is liable to be extremely harmful to the war effort. It tends to prevent government moves that would make the country better able to wage total war. While protesting against other people 'playing politics', it is itself 'playing politics' and often in the most dangerous way at the most dangerous time. It is itself thinking in a limited sectional fashion. It is considering the war problems from a fatal pre-war point of view. It doesn't understand the situation its country is in and doesn't know what total war means.

That, I think, is plain speaking, and now I will justify those blunt comments. It is simply no use anybody saying it is wrong to undertake social experiments in the middle of this war, because you cannot fight this kind of war without undertaking the most gigantic social experiments. That is one of the most serious mistakes Britain and France made at the beginning of this war. They hoped to get by without making any real changes, and of course they couldn't do it. There were some influential people in France who preferred the Nazis to any real social changes, and we know the kind of existence they've created for themselves and their people. Britain woke up after Dunkirk and then tore into the job, with most of her people ready to make any changes as long as they were good for the war effort. But of course we had these critics who said the rest of us were 'playing politics', taking advantage of the national emergency, indulging in class prejudices etc. etc. And some of those people, by making noise enough, did prevent or at least postpone some things being done that badly needed doing, and needed doing not because of anybody's economic and political theories but because of the war itself.

Let me give you an example from my own experience. In the summer of 1940, when I was doing a weekly Sunday night talk on the air here, I described a large empty house I had seen, a house whose owners had gone overseas, leaving us to protect their property for them, and I said that such houses should be requisitioned for the use of people bombed out of their own homes, and that their gardens should be used for growing vegetables. Well, I received dozens of angry letters, most of them from people in in comfortable country mansions, telling me that I ought to be ashamed of myself for saying such things, that I was a wild revolutionary, a Red, and all the rest of it. These people meant no harm. They were simply people who hadn't started thinking about the war, hadn't the least idea yet what this war amounted to and what demands it would make on us, whereas I was trying to think in terms of the war. I knew very soon we should need all the housing accommodation we could find, that thousands would soon be homeless because of the bombing, so that we might as well start by making full use at the earliest moment of all the accommodation we could find. It was all perfectly obvious to anybody who gave a moment's real thought to the subject. And, in point of fact, after a great many evacuated bombed-out women and children had had to put up with pretty bad conditions for several weeks, our authorities began to take the necessary measures. And during the next twelve months, thousands and thousands and thousands of houses were requisitioned for this and other purposes. All that yapping and screaming at the time of my broadcast couldn't prevent the authorities from facing the inevitable fact.

Now, if I'd said in my broadcast that those empty houses ought to be taken over by the military, nobody would have objected. As a matter of fact, my own house in the country, not an empty house but one being used, was requisitioned and taken over by the military at twenty minutes' notice, with what inconvenience you can just imagine. I said nothing about that. Why should I? Nor would any of those people have minded if it had been a question of the military taking over the houses. What they didn't see – couldn't see because they hadn't begun to think about the war properly – was that in this war there is no essential difference between the military and the civilians.

For what happened in the autumn of that year, 1940? The Nazis made a great attack on us, but it was an attack, through heavy indiscriminate bombing, not on the military but on civilians. So that it was clear that finding accommodation for the victims of those air raids was an essential part of the war effort.

My point, then, is this – and I don't care how many times I repeat myself because this has to be driven home – that in those countries that have not been preparing a long time for total war, as Germany and Russia have, this war demands, whether you like it or not, an elaborate social reorganisation, and if you pretend it doesn't, and successfully oppose these changes, then you are holding up your country's war effort, sabotaging its chance of victory, and actually helping the enemy. The Britain of 1942 bears no resemblance to the Britain of 1939. The whole economic and social structure is being changed. These changes aren't due to the fact that the men who lead Britain are enthusiastic social revolutionaries who have been longing for years for this opportunity. On the contrary. Most of them are dyed-in-the-wool conservatives whose natural tendency is to resist any attempt at change. But Mr Churchill and his colleagues have been led to take these measures by the sheer logic of the facts. They're determined to win the war, and gradually they have discovered that in order to win the war they must make these changes, just as a boxer must go into a strict training to give himself any chance of winning a fight. A system that may be good enough for peacetime – though I have always doubted it – is clearly not good enough for wartime. It just won't work.

Now, you can go one of two ways, for there is an alternative. You can line up the nation behind the war effort as Hitler does: that is, by vastly increasing all the forces of coercion, not only by ordering people about but also by putting a whip to their backs or sticking a gun in their ribs. It is quite clear that more and more the German war machine is being run on these lines. The whip is being cracked louder and louder. And more and more guns are being stuck into their ribs, even in the army itself, while the Gestapo is being heavily reinforced and armed, and being given machine-gun posts everywhere, to deal with the civil population. That is one way of dealing with it, and it isn't our way or yours. But that only leaves the alternative road open, and along that road you are compelled to bring the social system nearer some sort of equity, not because you have set out to reform the country but simply because the sheer deadly necessities of the war effort demand it. You have to see that men are properly employed now, because manpower is precious. You are compelled to cut down inessential work and concentrate on essential work for the same reason, that materials and manpower must no longer be wasted. If there should be a shortage of essential supplies – food, clothing etc. – then you have to ration these supplies, to make sure that everyone gets a fair share of them. So too, you cannot now afford to have large masses of people who are undernourished, suffering from bad health and unfit to co-operate in the common task. Again, you have to make the fullest possible use of the nation's ability, without any reference to a social or economic class system. The barriers of class are now seen to be a bad liability, so that anything that helps to remove them is contributing to the common effort. As you need everybody's enthusiastic help, you must make it plain to all and sundry that this is their war. Try to fight total war as rugged individualists and you are out, and from that time on, under the Axis lash, will be neither individualist nor very rugged.

But I'll go further than this. So far I've argued that the successful waging of total war demands social experiments and changes not for their own sake but for the sake of creating a real war effort. And this can be proved by what has happened in Britain. Nevertheless, I go further than that. The Nazis and the Japanese and their assorted quislings are fighting for an idea. It is a loathsome idea, that of the complete domination of the war by certain groups, but it's still an idea, and whole battling hordes of them are dazzled and inspired by that idea. The Russians have an idea and know exactly what they're fighting for. And we in the great democracies must have an idea, must be equally inspired and enthusiastically co-operative, and obviously that idea must have some connection with the notion that men must have the chance to become free and equal. Therefore any changes that we make that bring us nearer to that notion will set that idea shining in men's minds, so that men will fight harder and work harder and sink all their petty differences to achieve the great common purpose.

18 June 1942

War Conditions

Every time I have any talk with anybody who has just returned from America, he or she always asks me to stress in my broadcasts what war means to the average British citizen. I am always told that folks overseas still do not understand our war conditions. They imagine, I am told, that we are still living one kind of life when in fact we are living a very different kind of life. 'You ought to make all this quite clear,' these people just back from America say to me. And I reply that I thought I *had* made it clear. I've been doing these overseas radio talks now for two years – with one or two breaks, of course – and from first to last I've tried to explain as truthfully as possible what life has been like here. I've never consciously made it sound better or worse than it actually is. I believe the truth to be the best propaganda. If it isn't then there's something badly wrong with your cause.

Now, I can't believe that any regular listeners to these talks of mine could possibly believe some of these fantastic notions of our wartime life here. But of course everybody doesn't listen to these talks. Therefore, I suggest this. I am going to correct – I trust, simply and forcibly – some misconceptions that I am told by our most recent arrival from America are fairly common overseas. Now, will you oblige me – and do great service to our democratic cause – by passing on these corrections of mine? If it means politely but *firmly* correcting a neighbour then please don't hesitate to do it. If it means writing a friendly note to a newspaper or magazine editor, please don't hesitate to do that too. For remember – though it is easy enough and innocent enough to get these wrong notions of how the British are taking the war, our common enemy, who is a master of these tactics, has a most powerful interest in both originating and spreading such reports, in the hope of driving a wedge between the nations ranged against him. Thus correcting these wrong impressions is itself a little necessary war job.

So here goes. First, rationing. Now, I myself read an article some months ago in a famous American weekly that gave quite a false impression of rationing in England. I don't mean that the writer deliberately misrepresented the situation, but I do mean that in order to be amusing and dramatic the writer distorted the whole reflection. Thus, for instance, he suggested that because second-hand clothes are not rationed as new clothes are, and he had found one or two shops that were really selling new clothes that passed as second-hand clothes, therefore this rationing of clothes was a farce. This is completely misleading. Clothes rationing here is not a farce at all. It has worked well. Nobody in my family, nobody I have ever talked to, has ever tried to get round the clothes rationing by buying second-hand garments that are really new ones. It might be possible to do this – on a very small scale indeed – but it's obviously quite impossible to do it on a large scale, because no trader could obtain the necessary large supplies. I have no hesitation in saying that this suggestion was nonsense.

As for the rationing of food, it is true that at one time a fairly large black market existed, which enabled the well-to-do to eat pretty well, but that black market is rapidly dwindling. And – it must be remembered – it never did affect the country at large very much. It operated chiefly in and for the West End of London. And I do wish American and other press correspondents, who naturally stay in the West End of London, would stop assuming that the West End of London is Britain. It is just as much Britain as Fifth Avenue is the United States. Probably the best way to give you some notion of our food rationing is to be directly personal about it. Now, I'm not a poor man, and – as you may guess from my appearance or even perhaps from my voice – I am a man who enjoys a good dinner, so that you may bet your boots that I am going to take my share of any decent food that's going. Now, I have had just *one* small piece of steak, about three inches square, in the last twelve months. I have not had a single lamb or mutton chop. I don't think I've had even one square inch of fried ham. In normal times, I eat plenty of fruit, but now, of course, there just isn't any fruit. We give our oranges to our children. I haven't tasted an orange for over a year. Cream vanished long ago. I have a sweet tooth, but I don't suppose that I have a bit of dessert that seems to me anything like sweet enough more than once every two or three weeks. We aren't hungry, and we're all pretty healthy, but except on a few special occasions dining is no longer much of a pleasure. All the best food, especially the best meat, goes to our men in the services, and of course nobody grumbles about that. And for the most part the children here are reasonably well fed. There are fewer under-nourished children than there were before the war. So much for rationing.

Now for transport. This is getting tough, and if you feel like grumbling about your new restrictions, just remember ours. Unless you can prove to the authorities that a small allowance of gasoline is urgently necessary, you don't get any gasoline at all now. From now on, there's no such thing as private motoring in this country, and anybody driving an automobile can be stopped and asked to justify the trip he's making. Any use of gasoline for purposes of pleasure will get you into trouble at once. Taxi cabs and bus services have been cut down and are being cut down still further. Nobody knows much more about this – or suffers much more – than I do, simply because I am always travelling about the country. When I broadcast to you, like this, I have to do it late at night, and I'll tell you how I get to and from the studio – I walk; for though I am supposed to be doing a fairly important piece of national service, I am not allowed the use of a car nor even any gasoline. At three in the morning, I walk. Our train services have been cut down too, with the result that most long-distance trains are very crowded indeed. Travelling to the Midlands the other day to make a speech, I had to stand five hours in a packed corridor. Furthermore, I never take more baggage than I can manage to carry myself, because porters are scarce and I don't like to demand their services when other people – women with children – need them more than I do. And I haven't had any food on a train for months and months. We take a few sandwiches with us now, and as there's nothing to drink, it's thirsty work getting through them.

Next, hours of work. It stands to reason that we couldn't have mobilised so many men and women and raised our war production to such a stupendous height without enormously increasing our hours of work. Most people are working at least one and a half times the amount they worked before the war. In addition to these long hours, nearly everybody is doing some other job of national service. Men are either in the Home Guard or in the National Fire-Watching Service, which means that much of their dwindling spare time is given to the war effort. Women and girls too have all taken on a hundred and one voluntary duties connected with ARP or Red Cross or the Women's Voluntary Service. Most people are hard at it from morning till night at least six days a week. I don't myself consider this any great hardship. In point of fact, the best way to get through a period of total war successfully is, to my mind, to be as busy as possible doing what you feel are useful jobs. To hang about wondering what the news is or where your friends are is undoubtedly the *worst* way of getting through this grim period. If you're in it, you might as well be in it up to the neck.

Now, about the black-out. I was astonished to learn, the other day, from a man who had just returned from the United States that 50 per cent of the Americans he talked to didn't realise that we here have a nightly black-out, which really is a black-out. But of course we do. We have had an almost total black-out, from dusk to dawn, for thirty-three months now, and most of us have forgotten what outdoor lights look like. I for one am quite used to finding my way about London in an ebony darkness or at best a faint glimmer of starlight. The people I am sorry for are the people who have to drive after dark, for you must remember that our headlights are dimmed almost to extinction, so that it is impossible to see more than a few yards ahead. And out in the country – because there still might be an invasion – there are no signposts to tell you the way, so that unless you know the road quite intimately you simply cannot drive at night. All this is still necessary. It is true that for the time being the Luftwaffe cannot organise the big raids of the blitz period, but you must remember that some part of Britain is being raided nearly every night, and nobody knows where an enemy plane or two may appear. And of course we have always to be prepared for raids on a much larger scale, for mass bombing as a retaliation for our huge new raids.

Finally, I must ask you to remember what we are paying for this war. Nearly all the workers in the factories are now having to pay income tax for the first time in their lives, and in addition our indirect taxation – such as the duties on sugar, tobacco, liquor, and the heavy purchase taxes on goods of all kinds – is very high indeed. The combined income and surtax on larger incomes has reached a truly fantastic proportion. I am no millionaire, but I lived very comfortably before the war. Now, it would be quite impossible for me to live at that rate now – even apart from rationing and all the other restrictions – simply because it would be quite impossible for me to earn enough money to leave me enough, after paying taxes, to live at that rate. I couldn't do it even if I earned a million dollars a year. The tax on really large incomes goes up to 97 per cent. Nobody can have more than about 25,000 dollars a year to spend because whatever the rest may be, it is taken in taxation. Most of us who entered the war having various heavy commitments are compelled to meet those commitments by drawing on our savings. No matter what we may be earning, we are living at a loss. No matter how successful we may have been before the war, we realise that we shall have to start all over again after the war. There is nothing to grumble at in that, for if I thought that the bad old world can be replaced by a new and much better world I would be delighted even if it meant that every single thing I ever possessed had vanished with that old world. We are beginning to understand at last that national wealth consists of resources and labour and not of financial figures in books, which may mean that at the end of this war we shall realise that if the world has developed its resources and organised and improved its labour then the world is potentially wealthier than ever and that men have only to co-operate sensibly, and to stop snarling, plotting and grabbing, to enjoy that real wealth.

Meanwhile, please accept my assurance that the people of this island are geared as never before in their history to fight this war to a finish. I believe our fighting men have never been tougher. I believe our workers have never before made such colossal efforts. I believe our whole civilian population is gladly making the innumerable sacrifices demanded of it willingly and thankfully. And though we may differ on this problem and that – for we are not driven hard but a company of democratic men and women with minds of our own – I believe that never before as a nation have we been so single-minded and so devoted to our common task – the complete extinction of Nazism, Fascism, Japanese militarism, and all such enemies of the free mind and the loving heart.

Registering for Service

I've just been to one of the Ministry of Labour offices to register for national service and thought you might like to hear about it. Yes, men born in 1894 – the forty-sevens and forty-eights, the old guard, the men of the last war – must now register for military service. This doesn't mean that we're liable to serve in the armed forces, and I must say from the look of us this morning, that decision is a very wise one. If you armour-plated a few of us, we might do as tanks, but we'd never be nippy infantrymen of today. In this war, fighting soldiers have to be fitter than they were in the last, when we often hung about in trenches for months at a time and led the life of rats and moles. Our boys are now superbly trained and so, by the look of those I've seen, are your boys too.

No, the reason for making us forty-sevens and forty-eights register ourselves is to make sure we're doing essential work. If, in the view of Ministry of Labour officials, who are experts, we are not doing essential work then, after a further and more elaborate interview, we're able to be transferred to some job that's more necessary to the war effort. For example, a man arrives who is the cashier of a certain firm – let us say the Eureka corset company – and it has been decided that keeping corset accounts just isn't good enough, then he is interviewed and persuaded that he would be better employed keeping the accounts in some war factory or at least with some firm doing more essential work.

So am I doing essential work? If the Ministry of Labour doesn't think so then you may hear my voice no more, and perhaps I shall disappear into some gigantic factory whose rate of production should go down considerably once it has me on its staff. As a matter of fact, if I couldn't be persuaded and had to be given an order to change my occupation, I could still plead before a special manpower board, composed of experts who are not themselves Ministry of Labour officials and so take a disinterested view. But I wouldn't plead, being a proud fellow. Very few men do, in point of fact, and most people do not need to be given an order to change their job but are easily persuaded at the interview to volunteer for something more essential. But the registration is compulsory and can be regarded as a kind of conscription. Meanwhile, the Board of Trade is rapidly closing down all unnecessary businesses – has in fact closed thousands of them – but that takes longer than examining the cases of individual employees, so the Ministry of Labour, which has plenty of drive, calls for higher and higher age groups to present themselves.

The business of registering is not ideal. It was, in fact, disappointingly brief and straightforward from the point of view of a man wanting to do a radio talk about it. I went to a branch of the Ministry not a long way away from the Houses of Parliament. I'd like to be able to tell you that it was a magnificent building, worthy to represent a proud nation in arms, but the truth is that although it was reasonably clean and workmanlike, it was shabby and drab and needed a few good coats of bright paint. I gather that the Ministry of Labour is aware of this shabbiness and drabness in its buildings and is anxious to make them look more representative of the work they are doing. Some of the posters I saw there were very good indeed and I look forward to the time when the buildings themselves are equally attractive. I went upstairs to the department allocated to us middle-aged men and saw there other fellows about my shape and size and wearing the same slightly worried look of all responsible fathers of families. Up there, I sat at a title table with an official who was smart, grey-haired and amiable and, as I guessed rightly, came from Wales. He entered on a space on a card my National Identity card number, put down my name in full and my address there and announced to the British government, after I had prompted him, that I had two children under fourteen dependent on me. (Nothing was said about the older children, who seem to cost a little more.) Then he put down that my profession was that of author and broadcaster and that I had no regular employer but was a kind of one-man business. And that was all except that in return for giving those few details about myself – and I'd have gladly given him plenty more – he gave me a little slip that said:

This registration of men of your age will show what they are doing and how many can properly be spared from their present work. If it seems possible that you are one of those who could undertake more vital work, you will be asked to come for a selection interview when the whole question can be fully discussed. In the meantime, if you feel that you are not serving your country best in your present job, let the Employment Exchange know at once, but do not throw up your present job. They will tell you what to do. It may be best to leave you in your present job, but if not, the Exchange will try to find you more vital work either locally or in another district.

I don't know how this strikes you, but it strikes me as being very sensible and realistic and I know there must be lots of men who leave those Employment Exchanges and wish that our peacetime economic affairs had been conducted in this sensible and reasonable fashion, instead of looking half the time like a kind of gigantic dog fight for some sort of job and a living.

After having done my duty as a citizen, I was shown round the rest of the building, which contained separate rooms for the registration of young men for military service, of juveniles of both sexes, and of women. I was shown where women have their selection interviews, and I may say that being a sex that likes a bit of privacy, they have those interviews, with women officials of course, very privately and cosily behind screens. This calling up of women for national service is, I need hardly tell you, a ticklish business, compared with which the calling up of men is merely a brief, hearty, routine affair. Incidentally, about seven and a half million women have been registered. No compulsion to serve can be applied to the wives of men in the fighting forces, though naturally those wives who have no children to look after and are not running a household are encouraged to find war work, and large numbers of them are doing such work. All women with serious domestic responsibilities, not merely those looking after husbands and children but also those who take in boarders or evacuees, are considered to be already doing national service, though some of them find it possible to undertake part-time war work. The remainder, who are liable for national service, are handled with tact and discretion, discuss their circumstances at these selection interviews, are given an opportunity to decide what kind of essential work interests them, and have an opportunity to appeal against decisions that seem to them unfair. The number who do appeal is very small indeed. It is only the comparatively tiny number of sheer dodgers who are given a sharp direction by the Ministry officials.

There is a very genuine attempt to tackle the huge unwieldy job of mobilising the nation's manpower in a reasonable and human spirit, so that no man or woman feels that he or she is dealing with nothing but a gigantic machine. As Mr. Ince, the Director of Manpower for the Ministry of Labour, said in a recent speech, 'I realised that the problems I was being called upon to face were human problems and could only be dealt with successfully if they were dealt with on the basis of human values.' It should be understood that our Ministry of Labour is not a government department that simply takes and does not give anything. It is not merely a machine for swallowing the time and energy of the citizen, an immense modern equivalent of the old press gang. A great deal of the Ministry's power is exercised not in calling up men and women but in seeing that when they are called up, especially in industry, they have a square deal. Thus, under the essential work order, which applies, as its name suggests, to those concerns doing very essential war work in mines, docks and so forth, workers are guaranteed a minimum weekly wage, or in the case of pieceworkers a guaranteed daily wage, provided that the employee is there ready to perform any reasonable service. In concerns affected by this order, no employee can be discharged, nor can he leave his employment without each side giving a week's notice and obtaining the special permission of the Ministry of Labour official dealing with such cases. In all essential industries, casual labour has been abolished. Men can't be put out of employment during a temporary lull, and one of the worst evils of the old economic system has therefore been banished.

Again, the Ministry of Labour now insists upon a certain standard of welfare in all concerns above a certain size. It is not merely a matter of providing reasonably safe and healthy conditions of work, for our old Factory Acts and their Factory Inspectors have long taken care of that. This new welfare is real welfare. Because we have had to transfer large numbers of men and women to essential war jobs, we have rightly insisted that they shall be employed under civilised conditions, and from the first the Minister of Labour, who is of course Ernest Bevin, a famous trade union leader, decided that he would not exercise his powers to direct men and women to employment away from home unless he was satisfied that proper arrangements for their welfare existed. These arrangements are not even confined to those inside the factories, but also apply to conditions outside, to arrangements for housing, travelling and feeding. Inside the factories, the new welfare arrangements include much-improved feeding facilities – canteens providing good hot food being found everywhere now – extended personnel management and welfare provision and more medical supervision and factory nurses. The Ministry has now established special courses in labour management at all of our universities. I have myself met and talked with many of these personnel managers at various big factories and always found them enthusiastic about their jobs and as keen as they were efficient. This has made a great difference during the war. And it will make even more difference after the war, for such economic and social experiments cannot be abandoned. We may often be slow to take the right road in this country, but once we have taken it, we rarely turn back.

And now I'm going to make a small bet with you listeners. I am going to make a statement, quoting it from the highest authority, about the mobilisation of our manpower, and to any listener who writes to me assuring me that he or she is not surprised by it because he or she knew it already, I will send you a personal letter of thanks – and apology. And here is the statement – quoted, I repeat, from the highest authority, the Minister of Labour himself: 'No country in the history of the world has mobilised its manpower to such a point as we have done in this war.' Now, I'll bet that surprises most of you. But it's true. We have mobilised for national service, in one form or another, a greater percentage of its citizens than any other country in this war. Germany may have called up a bigger proportion of its men, but it has not been able to mobilise its womenfolk as we have done. Even Russia, in spite of its tremendous war effort, has not reached our percentage of total mobilisation. The Dominions of the British Commonwealth – Canada, Australia, New Zealand, South Africa – have done magnificently well, but they have not mobilised their people on this scale. The population of the United Kingdom between the ages of fourteen and sixty-five is roughly thirty-three million. Out of that thirty-three million we have registered twenty-three million. This means, in effect, that out of all our people, except the very young and the very old, two out of every three have been registered for national service in one form or another, and this includes women as well as men. Finally, let me make this point. Although the government has now enormous power, freely voted to it, none of this mobilisation would have been possible without the eager co-operation of the mass of the people themselves. It was they who wanted to see the nation mobilised for the destruction of Nazism.

4 September 1942

Three Years of War

This is for me no ordinary talk but a very special one. I have two good reasons for saying this. The second reason I will leave until later, but the first one should be obvious. This is an anniversary. We have now been at war for three years. On 3 September 1939, our government, with the full approval of all the people of this country, gave Nazi Germany an ultimatum, which Hitler ignored, and so we declared war. Remember this. The British people had not then been attacked. They were apparently in no immediate danger themselves. They didn't want war and had done everything possible to keep the peace. But the Nazis had proved themselves intolerable. They could not be reasoned with. They made solemn promises and broke them as soon as it was convenient to break them. It was impossible to do anything more with such people on a peaceful basis. They intended to get everything they wanted either by threatening or by using force, and therefore they would have to be resolutely opposed by force. A world in which this megalomaniac screamed his demands and threats every few months and then moved his armies again was not a world that decent men could tolerate any longer. So the British people, who don't like war and never pretend that it is the highest of man's activities, went to war – not because their possessions had been attacked, not because they were invaded, but for an idea. Please never forget that. The Britain that found herself standing alone in the summer of 1940, that defied all the devilry that Hitler and Goering could imagine, had gone to war for an idea, the idea of the sensible co-operation of states and their citizens, an idea that had been flouted over and over again by Hitlerite Germany.

These German gangsters, who had come to power in a country that still thought of war-making as man's chief activity and of the soldier as the chief member of the community, had all the big battalions and the big squadrons, and so they were supremely confident and didn't hesitate to boast and trample and plunder and murder. They are not so confident now. If they do even more desperate things, that is because their confidence has turned to a terrible ferocious despair. We were called upon to face seventy million Germans who were organised down to the last button for war, a country that had been on a war footing for years. We had, while invasion drew nearer and the enemy bombers roared over us, to organise ourselves, first for sheer defence and afterwards for attack, and over and over again in these talks I have tried to give you a picture of that vast hurried organisation of ours, the mobilisation of the whole nation for the armed forces, for war production, food production and the like, and I don't propose to repeat all those facts and figures now.

I still believe that the magnitude of our achievement is not sufficiently appreciated. We have made mistakes; there may have been faults of organisation and leadership; there may have been a lack of both imagination and exact knowledge at times amongst us; but the fact remains that our people themselves have proved to be as miraculously productive as they have been wonderfully stout-hearted. When they have agitated, they have agitated not for less work but for more work, not for fewer sacrifices but for more sacrifices. No country in this war has called up a bigger proportion of its citizens for national service than we have. Don't be misled by our constant criticisms of ourselves – and I think I have done my share of such criticising – for we like to speak our minds and dwell on our faults – for the fact remains that the war effort of the British people has been – is – terrific.

And remember this, please, that we have been in this war now for three years. For the past year or so, our troops have had to slog away at their training, our workers have had to slog away in their factories, without anything very dramatic happening near home, in a kind of anti-climax after the stirring Battle of Britain, and this has not been easy. Though we may be fond of under-statement and appear not to relish the dramatic, we are anything but a robot people who want nothing but an appointed task, but at heart are easily moved, quickly respond to a challenging and dramatic situation, and tend to become bored by sheer routine. This, then, has not been an easy time for us. It is significant that the other week, when the news of the great Dieppe raid was announced, we were told that production here immediately jumped to a new high figure. This didn't surprise most of us. The opening of a second front, near home, will make terrific demands on our people, but I am convinced that the mere challenge and drama of it will enable our people to meet those demands.

Just lately I have been thinking a good deal about the last war, putting my mind back five-and-twenty years. Now, the corresponding period to this in the last war was the late summer of 1917, when we had also been at war three years. I had been in the trenches during the second half of 1915 and the first half of 1916. But then in the summer of 1916 I was buried by the explosion, so close at hand that it disturbed my dreams for years, of a giant trench-mortar shell, with the result that I returned to England for a long spell of hospital and convalescence and after that, light duty. So it happened that during this corresponding period in 1917 I was still here in England, for I did not return to France until the following year. And I have been examining my memories of that period at home here and then comparing them with my impressions now. There was then, after three years of war, a cynicism, a staleness, a feeling of disillusion, of grim weariness, both among soldiers and civilians, that has no parallel here in this country now, when people are still zestful, eager, ready to demand further sacrifices, more fighting, more work, and completely undivided, as they certainly were not in 1917, in their determination to rid the world of this Nazi madness.

The difference is really most marked. The spirit of the nation is functioning on a higher level altogether. These soldiers of ours now, untried though many of them may be, seem to me to be physically and mentally of a far higher calibre than our battered and half-cynical troops were then. There is an entirely different spirit among our civilian population, which tended then to be either wearily indifferent or cynically engaged in making as much money as it could out of the war. The big towns are not the same, the folk in the country are not the same: there is now a toughness, there is a zest, there is a potential enthusiasm, waiting for the first news of a victorious advance to burst into a steady flame, all entirely absent then. Not here will you find that grim weariness and deepening disillusion of 1917. But I'll tell you where you will find it. You'll find it in Germany, where by all accounts news of either victories or defeats appears to leave the people silent and outwardly unmoved, as if they felt that nothing of their true selves could share any longer in this gigantic insanity. Every account I have read by neutral observers of the spirit of the Germans reminds me of that grim weariness of 1917, when all the zest and resilience appeared to have gone.

And I say that these are the same old Germans, in spite of Hitler and all his Nazi propaganda. Hammered and shaped by their superb powers of military organisation, they will go on and on giving a good account of themselves, perhaps blasting their way forward here and there, with the last energies of despair, but sooner or later, when we have hit them time after time where it hurts most, when it is no longer possible to put into operation plans worked out to the last detail years before, when their huge iron tide has ceased to flow and has begun to ebb, then they will begin to crack – and to crack badly. That will not be next week, or next month, but if we batter at them with all our strength, putting our total energy into each stroke, as if – what is indeed the solemn truth – we were fighting for our very lives, then sooner or later it will happen, and these people will learn again, and let us hope once and for all, that free men, who have never planned conquest, who enter war reluctantly, almost shrugging their way into it, make the most formidable opponents.

In this great final effort, which is still before us, the chief burden will have to be borne by the British Commonwealth and the United States – in fact, *by us*. China has been fighting for years and years for her cause, which is also ours. The desperate and indeed inspired resistance of Russia, which is rapidly bleeding her, has eaten into the manpower and production of Nazi Germany and blunted the edge of its blade. But now, let us make no mistake about this, it is our turn. From now until the final collapse of these mad empires of treachery and murder, if the English-speaking peoples don't do it then nobody can do it.

You on your side are rapidly gearing up the great machine of war production and assembling and sending out magnificently equipped armies and air forces. We here are waiting the zero hour. Does that term zero hour mean much to you? It means a lot to me, for in the last war it meant the very second of attack, when the scaling ladders were all ready in the trenches and we stood before them, glancing at our watches, when the barrage would lift and roar into the further distance, when there would tremble on our lips the command 'Time! Come on, boys! Over we go!' And this is it. The zero hour of the great English-speaking democracies. You can feel it in the very air here. The time cannot be long now. And I say this, that when the hour does come, no better armies will have ever left these shores – for I consider these boys better at their new trade of fighting, tougher and more skilful, than we ever were; and no people who ever lived on this island will be more ready, more eager, to sacrifice whatever should be needed than the people here now who are toiling to support those armies.

And everywhere now here you hear a sound that must haunt the uneasy dreams of Hermann Goering and his swaggering Luftwaffe. You hear the sound of war planes, from furious Spitfires streaking across the sky to the giant four-engined bombers with their terrible loads of destruction. Yes, more and more war planes, until this island is beginning to look like a gigantic aircraft carrier. Well, they screamed and threatened and bullied us into playing the dreadful game this way, and now they shall have all they asked for, and more for good measure, so that when the last of these planes has done its work, no man will be mad enough to plunge the world into aerial warfare again. The eagles gather and scream, and over the Rhine the twilight deepens, and soon that doomsday which is foreshadowed in the mind of the Teuton will break, and the dark empire of Hitler will be nothing but an evil dream.

I said that I had a second reason why this was for me no ordinary talk but a very special one. It is this. Except for a few short breaks, I have done these *Britain Speaks* talks for well over two years now, and it has been both a pleasure and a privilege, for your innumerable kind messages have shown me that I was not speaking to the empty air. Instead, I like to think that during these years when I have been compelled to remain here at home, I have in fact made more friends overseas than I ever did during my travels. But it is time you had a change, so no more *Britain Speaks* from me, though perhaps later I might return to the microphone. Thank you for listening, for telling me how you listened, for many kindnesses. And good luck!

23 and 24 December 1942

Christmas 1942

This is our fourth Christmas of this war. Some of you may very well feel that under these present circumstances we had better stop trying to celebrate Christmas. We are engaged – let's face it – in a gigantic task that involves the maximum amount of destruction and killing. Most of our families are scattered, and there are persons very dear to us who are in constant danger or, at least, are far away, enduring much hardship. We haven't the time, the money or the opportunity to create and then enjoy the kind of Christmas we used to have. The piles of presents can no longer be bought; the rich Christmas food is no longer obtainable; the necessary people to have fun with may be hundreds or thousands of miles away; and many of us are too busy, too worried and anxious, perhaps too deeply sorrowful, to achieve the old festival spirit. Better give it up, eh?

No, I don't think so. I feel that we should do what we can to pay at least some small tribute to the Christmas spirit. The attempt will do us good. Then again, the children, to whom this season is pure magic, must have their Christmas. Down at our children's hostels in the country, all the women and girls on the staff have been busy for weeks cutting out, stuffing and sewing dolls and animals – very strange animals too, some of them – to give the children Christmas toys, in place of those missing from the shops here; and these home-made toys will give just as much pleasure and happiness to the little children as the most expensive and complicated gifts of the pre-war Christmases. I feel, in fact, that this so-called austerity Christmas is much nearer the real thing than the easy and lavish Christmases we had before the war, because they seemed to me to be degenerating into mere routines of lavish spending and astute commercialism, whereas now it is not simply a matter of throwing money about but rather of giving time and loving care, giving in fact more of oneself, to make Christmas possible. Again, the war has taken millions of young men and girls, who are not too far removed from the wistful anticipations and eager responses of childhood, a long way from their homes and all the old magic of Christmas, and if we have some of those young men and girls in our neighbourhood, as most of us have, then here too is an opportunity for us to achieve the Christmas spirit, simply by bringing a little happiness to others.

These are good reasons why we should still keep Christmas, but they are not the only ones, nor to my mind the most important. Christmas is the festival of birth and re-birth. Something strange and wonderful has happened; and an unknown star blazes in the sky, wise men travel from the East with gifts, shepherds hear angelic voices; a certain child is born, and now the Kingdom of Heaven is at hand. All this hopeful symbolism was characteristic of the times, 2,000 years ago. There were innumerable small sects celebrating their mysteries; there were prophets and preachers everywhere in the Near East; there were constant rumours among the Jews of the Messiah. Men waited for a sign. Why was this? Chiefly, I think, because men felt themselves terribly in need of some new and more profound revelation. The world was beginning to look a very evil place indeed, controlled only by those dark devils and demons whom we can regard as symbols of men's unchecked, reckless, unconscious drives, of primitive instincts raging like tigers. Cruelty, deceit, a boundless sensuality, were to be found everywhere, from the circuses of Rome to the smallest Galilean village. The whole Mediterranean world had been divided and impoverished by the great civil wars of Rome. Judea had suffered under the criminal quisling regime of the Herods. This was a time when at any moment there might be a massacre of the innocents:

In Rama was there a voice heard,

Lamentation, and weeping and great mourning,

Rachel weeping for her children,

And would not be comforted,

Because they are not.

It was a world in which everything that was gentle, mild and good seemed destined to suffer and then vanish, and only the brutal, the treacherous, the cruel, could survive. And even they could not survive long. For there was a widespread feeling, especially among simple ordinary folk, that the world was coming to an end. Nor was this such a foolish belief. Any world in which the destructive or sterile elements dominate the creative elements is, in effect, coming to an end. For, notice, the world is really kept going, is endlessly re-created, by the quiet, patient folk in it, by the mothers rearing their children, the peasants tilling the fields, the craftsmen, the scholars and poets and artists, the mild saints. These are the creative elements, and *not* crazy emperors and their satellites screaming with blood-lust in the circus, drunken armies burning and looting and raping, uproarious Antonys and Cleopatras, lecherous, scheming Herods and the like. It is faith, hope and love that keep the world going. So these men of 2,000 years ago felt that doomsday was just round the corner. Yet most of them did not feel entirely lost. They felt that the world could be redeemed yet, if the right voice spoke the right words. They looked for a faith. And then, in one tiny corner of that world, there came one 'who was moved with compassion for the multitude', and 'the common people heard him gladly'. It is that arrival which we celebrate at Christmas. And if we were fighting now for any possible gain, it would be the idlest mockery to celebrate Christmas in the middle of such a war. But we are fighting for a very different reason. *We are, in fact, fighting to prevent the world being put back to where it was before the first Christmas.*

That, anyhow, is how I see – and have always seen – this war. It is not fundamentally a war between so many of us and so many Germans, Japanese, Italians and their allies. It is not fundamentally a struggle to see which *nations* shall win. It is a battle to decide whether we can build a civilisation based on 2,000 years of Christendom – and here, in my opinion, it does not matter if we are actual Christian believers or not – or whether every lamp lit during those 2,000 years shall be extinguished and a barbarian darkness be spread again over the face of the earth. If our enemies win then, as I see it, even the values themselves – the very ideas of truth, justice, mercy and the rest – will disappear, for they will be deliberately blotted out of men's minds.

We on our side are not particularly good men. We are ordinary, weak, sinful human creatures. Constantly we fall far short of what we know to be the most desirable conduct. But at least we are facing the right way, we're looking towards the light and not towards the darkness. Consider, for example, this question of brutality and cruelty. Now, nearly all armies at war behave, at some time or other, brutally and cruelly. We should expect that, even if history didn't emphasise the fact over and over again. But now we are fighting men who begin with a deliberately conceived, quite cold-blooded policy of brutality and cruelty. And that is a very different thing. That is what I mean by facing the wrong way, looking towards the dark. This is not ordinary human weakness but evil itself. It is devil-worship. It is selling your soul for power. If it should triumph then the real world, as we know and value it, would come to an end.

If any of you regard this as an exaggeration, I should like you to consider what is happening now in those parts of Europe where the Nazis are in complete control. There is a deliberate, highly organised, systematic mass murder of the Jewish people. We are told that two million of these people have already perished, and that now a further five million are in danger of extermination. Most of you are probably already familiar with the revolting details: the drives through the Polish ghettoes; the old people and crippled taken to cemeteries and then shot; the fiendish loading of the rest into railway trucks, where, so terrible is the over-crowding, above half die of suffocation; the slave camps for the comparative few of the young and strong who survive. There was a Jewish mother in Paris who, when the police came to take her away to camp, threw her six children and then herself out of the window. If that happened in Paris, we can imagine what has been happening in Central Europe, where all hell has been let loose against these wretched innocent people. What have these people done that such an avalanche of misery should descend upon them? They have done nothing except, through some twist in his strange, tortured mind, aroused the hatred of this man Hitler. The craziest Roman emperors – the men who were described by their contemporaries as 'monsters' – never loosed such misery and cruelty on their people.

But notice how everything that disfigured the world that saw the first Christmas, the world that was darkening and coming to an end – the sacrificing of whole armies for whims and crazy ambition, the slaughter of helpless peoples, torture, slavery, huge cold cruelty – has now rapidly returned to this world of ours, but on a much vaster scale than the ancient world ever knew. In a few years, half Europe has slipped back whole centuries. The idea of a world redeemed by faith, hope and love has vanished. The cruel old gods, symbols of the relentless, unconscious drives of archaic man, have come lumbering out of the Germanic forests. And it is this we are fighting – and if the war lasts a hundred Christmases, we must go on fighting it, for there can never be any truce with it.

That is one significant difference between this war and the last. In the last war, in spite of the disapproval of all the High Commands, there were on the various fronts at Christmas – as I know, for I saw it for myself – often a temporary lull, quite deliberate, that sometimes amounted almost to a truce. The reason for that was that it was still felt that this was a war in Christendom, and the spirit of the old festive season operated for both sides. But there are no such lulls and temporary truces at Christmas in this war. The gulf is now too wide. We fight so that our own Christmas and all that it stands for shall endure at all.

If we see the war in this light – and I for one have never been able to see it in any other – if we see it as a gigantic struggle for the future of the whole world and the soul of man, then certain things will, I think, inevitably follow. Thus we shall not waste time and energy worrying about paltry considerations of national prestige. We shall not try to *use* this war for any smaller end of our own. We shall emphasise over and over again our common ideals, and be always guided by them, expediency or no expediency. We shall not imitate for any purposes the yapping and snarling and hate-mongering of the enemy. We shall fight to destroy not only the power of Hitler and his Nazis and Fascists and the Japanese war lords but also the diseased, rotten world that could allow them and their armies to grow and prosper. It is perhaps not without significance that we are all singing now 'I'm Dreaming of a White Christmas'. We shan't have a white Christmas this year but dark, blood-stained one. But we are fighting for a white Christmas.

30 and 31 December 1942

New Year Resolutions

Wmet about New Year resolutions? Do you make them? I used to try my hand at it, now and again, in the years before the war, but I never went in for anything elaborate – no complete reformation of my character – but just a little improvement here and there. That wasn't because I imagined myself to be almost perfect, but for the contrary reason, that I knew I wasn't capable of enormous self-improvement and so just made the best of a pretty bad job. Which showed, of course, that I had reached years of maturity. When we are young, we imagine we are capable of being anything and doing anything. I remember that in my teens I couldn't decide whether I was going to be a great musician, a great writer, a great actor or a great something else, and didn't really much care so long as the greatness was there; whereas now I know I am a writer and nothing else, but don't know – and, to be frank, don't much care – if I'm a great writer or a little one, a prophet or a modest entertainer.

If there were no war then I shouldn't be thinking and talking about New Year resolutions. But a war on this scale changes our whole situation most profoundly. We are not the same people we were. Many of us are leading quite different lives. As people engaged in the grim task of total war, we can't pretend to any maturity. We are young and uncertain but hopeful again. Therefore, I feel, not strictly as private persons but as a people fighting a war, we can allow ourselves to consider a few New Year resolutions. And here are some good resolutions that seem to me well worth considering. The first is, that in 1943, we should all try hard to cultivate the extremely necessary virtue of steadiness. Yes, that's what I said – steadiness. This war has lasted long enough now to reveal much of its essential character. What is that character – that is, as seen from our particular angle? Isn't it a curious alternation of long periods of apparent dullness, when nothing much seems to be happening, with sudden short periods of colossal drama? Just when you think everything is sinking into a dreary stalemate, the whole scene suddenly comes to life and something tremendous happens. The campaign in Libya is a good example of this. Last summer, Rommel suddenly attacked, and while we are still rubbing our eyes and hardly believing our ears, he is sixty miles from Alexandria and it looks as if we have lost Egypt. But he is checked at El Alamein, and then nothing seems to happen, and you begin to feel nothing will ever happen again there. But then Alexander and Montgomery suddenly attack, and while we are rubbing our eyes again, Rommel is in full retreat, his army in ruins, Egypt is safe and it is Tripolitania that is in danger. There is of course a sound military reason for these dramatic alternations. In this war, an offensive demands long and careful preparation, and this preparation is kept secret, so that it seems to us that nothing is happening. On the other hand, once an offensive is launched, with its full weight of armour, the whole movement is much faster and more destructive than similar offensives in previous wars: hence the sudden tremendous drama. And I think we may be certain that this is likely to be the character of this war to the very end. Now, I believe that these peculiar alternations between nothing happening and too much happening must be met with great steadiness of mind. We can't allow ourselves to sink into apathy or despondency during the periods of preparation, nor must we allow our minds to be whirled between deep depression and giddy exaltation during the sudden dramatic periods of unexpected defeat or victory. The steady mind is what is wanted throughout. Therefore, I say, let our first good resolution as a fighting people be to cultivate the virtue of steadiness.

The next resolution I suggest is one that is not entirely unconnected with the first, because steadiness of mind is needed here too. The second resolution could be framed something like this: that under the sudden intoxicating sense of victory we will not go back on what we thought and felt and decided during the times when there were no victories. That's probably not very clear, so I'll explain what I mean. It seems to me that when a great many people find news of victories rolling in, they begin to change their mind about what they thought and felt and declared before such news was possible. During the dark days, when the Nazis had grabbed nearly all Europe and the Japanese began grabbing half Asia, stung by these defeats and humiliations, these people surprised some of us by admitting openly that the old pre-war world was simply not good enough and that we had to fight for the opportunity to create a new and better world. But I have noticed, even already, when the tide has only just begun to turn in our favour, that some of these people are changing their attitude, are beginning to hint that after all the old pre-war world wasn't so bad, and that our successes prove that we were all right all along. Have you noticed any of this? I find it disconcerting, not because there is much of it about yet but because it should be noticeable at all at this early stage. For it is possible, and I think more than likely, that during the coming months we may have huge dramatic successes, dwarfing anything that has happened in our favour up to now. What are these people going to say then? And are *we* going to change and then drift with them? We must fix firmly in our minds this thought: that it was not the pre-war apathetic democracies that could defeat the Axis – for actually those democracies were outwitted and outplayed by the Axis – but it is the new wartime democracies, battling their way towards a new and better world, that are now defeating and will ultimately destroy the aggressive, power-crazy military dictatorships. If you go back then you go back to the state of things that produced this war and will inevitably produce other wars. This is common sense, but there are people who only admit its force when they themselves are feeling insecure and no victory is in sight. It is the old story: 'The devil was sick, the devil a monk would be.' Once they find themselves flushed with victory and the danger of defeat is past, then they tend to return to old habits of mind, to old prejudices and narrow convictions, and so want to put us to where we started from. This tendency must be resisted both in ourselves and, through us, in others. Victory should be a liberating force. That, then, is number two.

The third good resolution I suggest applies strictly to us

English-speaking peoples. We are scattered throughout the world, in many widely different communities, and although we enjoy the use of the same language, just because we can understand what is said without any great effort, often we disagree simply because we don't make any allowance whatever for the differences that exist. In short, we behave exactly like members of one family. We are impatient, we are touchy, we can get on each other's nerves. I've no need to labour this point. Most of you are probably rather tired of hearing talks on this subject. But what I am going to say now – bringing me to this third good resolution – has not, I think, been over-laboured; and it is this. The best way we can help to promote the mutual understanding of all the English-speaking peoples in this war is to take it easy and not overdo it. Don't let us all start trying to settle each other's affairs. At the moment we've neither the time nor the energy nor the right opportunity. Full and frank discussion of all our problems – and indeed all our shortcomings – will be very necessary, yes – but at the right time. And this isn't the right time. We've too many other things to do. Let's settle the Nazis and the Japanese first, long before we start a gigantic English-speaking, wide-world debating society. I don't think anybody can accuse me of a desire to avoid open discussion, to soft-pedal awkward topics, and I've done as much criticising and grievance-ventilating as the next man. Some of it is necessary even now, but each branch of our English-speaking people must do it for themselves. If Americans are going to be busy criticising English affairs, and the English busy criticising South African, and the South Africans busy criticising Australian, and the Australians busy criticising American affairs, we shall soon be all over the place, and nobody will gain except Goebbels and his staff, who incidentally are busy themselves encouraging this type of discussion and criticism. We must take each other on trust. Our fighting men do it all over the world, and are glad and proud to do it, though their very lives may depend upon it. The least we can do is to follow their example. We must say: 'These people are all right, and with them we can win this war. True, I don't understand, I don't very much like, one or two of the things they have done, but we can clear all that up later, if it should be necessary to clear it up. But for now, let's get cracking together.' This doesn't mean we must take no interest in each other. If I believed that, I shouldn't bother coming to the microphone every week to offer you these talks, which try to reflect a fairly average British point of view and to give you glimpses of wartime Britain. This great common war effort will in fact create much good understanding and a far greater knowledge of each other. But, I say, let it go at that for the time being. Leave the mutual criticism, the arguing, the thrashing out, until later, until the Nazis have vanished and the Japanese have learnt their grim lesson – and then, if necessary, let it rip. So that's my suggested third good resolution.

My fourth is simple enough. Let us remember that though our English-speaking peoples, strengthened by this new understanding and mutual trust, must inevitably play a great part, perhaps the leading part, in the creation of the post-war world, there are a great many other people in this world too and it is as much their world as ours. For example, there are the Russians, the people who have done most to break the force of Nazism on land. There are the Chinese, who have been in this war longest and were fighting and suffering when the rest of us were merely glancing at the newspapers. There are all the people of Europe, many of whom have suffered more than we have in this common struggle. There are, to name no others, all the folk in the vast continent of South America, who, though remote from most of the conflict, are watching every act of the drama with intense concern, realising that their own future depends upon its outcome. We are all world citizens and world-builders from this time on, and so must take a world view. Therefore we must widen our knowledge and enlarge our sympathies. The narrow view is out of date, and as dangerous as a 100-year-old locomotive on a main railway track.

These, then, are my suggested New Year resolutions: first, steadiness of mind, because this war particularly demands it; secondly, no weakening of the indignant desire to change the world just because now the victories arrive; thirdly, the cultivation of a trustful and not narrowly critical habit of mind among us English-speaking peoples; and finally, a resolution not to forget that we are not all the world and that, although we may have to take the lead in creating the post-war world, we shall soon be joined by comrades from everywhere, and so must take the global view in peace as in war.

6 and 7 January 1943

Total Mobilisation

I'm addressing this talk to my friends Jack and Sophie Burden, with whom we stayed for three winters in Wickenburg, Arizona. But of course the rest of you can listen in.

Dear Jack and Dear Sophie – Your fine long letter arrived the other day, and the whole family took turns in reading it. A grand budget of news. And now you can no longer meet guests at Phoenix or run them in and out by car because there's not the gasoline to do it; and Sophie goes careering between Wickenburg and the ranch on her bicycle; and there are young men in uniform to be seen round the drug stores – well, well, well. We're always wishing we could come and see it all for ourselves. Every month, quite regularly, U-boats or no U-boats, we receive our copy of *The Arizona Highway* and stare at its excellent photographs of desert and mountain and canyons in a sort of nostalgic mist.

I'll give you our news briefly. Jane is still running five children's hostels and works at it from the time she wakes until long after she's gone to bed – quite a full-time job still. Angela has just spent fifteen months touring the camps and aerodromes with a theatrical company and goes out again shortly. Barbara is doing very well at the School of Architecture – we're going to need plenty of architects soon, as you can imagine. Sylvia is now a dispatch rider with the WRNS, and in a tough place too – almost a front-line job. Incidentally, when Mrs. Roosevelt was over here, Sylvia on her motorbike spent a proud morning acting as one of her out-riders. The others are still at school. And I'm writing a big novel about an aircraft factory, rehearsing a new play, helping to plan a film, preparing an important official booklet, doing these and other broadcasts, and generally slogging away. We still haven't a house of our own, live out of suitcases, but contrive to collect most of the family at holiday times. On Christmas Day, Jane and I cooked the whole Christmas dinner – for seven of us – ourselves, and made such a grand job of it – turkey, pudding and all the trimmings – that we do nothing now but boast of it. If, after the war, you should want a hard-working couple in the ranch kitchen, you might let us know.

Meanwhile, I wish we could show you England in wartime. It's curiously deceptive. I've just travelled up from Cornwall to London, a good long journey for this small country, and most of the way it looks as green, quiet and peaceful as ever it did. There was an American officer – from Texas – in my compartment – we see Americans everywhere here now – and he was remarking how quiet and peaceful it seemed. But, as I pointed out to him, this apparent peacefulness and quietness is very deceptive. I said, 'I don't know if you read in our papers the other day how a man dug up an innocent-looking little length of piping. Unfortunately, he started to examine it a bit too thoroughly, with the result that it exploded and killed him. Well, that's England as it is now. It *looks* quiet and peaceful, but actually it's stuffed with TNT. And detonated and ready to explode almost at a touch.' For example, travelling by train you don't see many aerodromes, though you notice a great many planes roaring across the sky, but as a matter of fact there are aerodromes everywhere, as you soon discover when you try to spend a quiet night with anybody in the country, for ten to one the house is near an aerodrome, and machines are roaring over the roof half the night. This island has been described as a gigantic aircraft carrier, and it's not a bad description. It's also the advance base for the grand attack on the Nazis. And it's also a huge arsenal and workshop. I know a good deal about that side of it because I've spent a lot of time visiting factories of all kinds, but especially, just lately, our aircraft factories – because of my novel, y'know. We're turning the stuff out, day and night, like mad.

And to my mind, the very finest job we've done is this wholesale mobilisation of the entire nation, not only for the armed forces but also for the war factories, all the essential services, and the land. Chaps, like you, Jack, and women like you, Sophie, are, after a very short preliminary training, now busy here turning out parts for planes, tanks, guns. I expect by this time you've heard about the almost miraculous achievement of our production, which is, for the size of our population, the very highest in the world. But the point is this – and this is why I say this mobilisation of manpower is our finest job – that we've turned the whole industry of the country upside down and inside out, set millions of men and women to work on new jobs, without losing the elasticity, the give-and-take, the inner freedom, which properly belong to democracy. The powers of sheer coercion have been there, but they've hardly had to be used at all. The people, of course, have met the authorities more than halfway, but the authorities themselves have behaved sensibly, humanly, wisely, with the result that we've retained the *spirit* of a free-and-easy people while changing the form, the outward shape, sharpening the whole industrial system into a spearhead. That's a great thing to have done, I feel, and it's important not only for wartime but for peacetime too. We've learnt a lesson of the utmost possible value.

And – by thunder! – you and we and those grim Russians advancing through their snows, the whole fighting crowd of us, are going to teach the Nazis and then the Japanese a lesson too. I don't include the Italians, because, frankly, if you leave out Mussolini and his little gang of headquarter Fascists, the rest of the Italians don't need the lesson by this time, because – poor devils – they *know*. They've already had far more than they can take – their empire gone, their armies melting away, their industrial cities in ruins, their whole economic system paralysed, their country held down by the Gestapo. They wish they were out of it – the game's altogether too rough and tough for them – and in my opinion very soon they will be out of it. Poor old Musso – in the summer of 1940, when he thought the war was in the bag, he was the big tough boy and asked for the privilege of allowing some Italian squadrons to share in the bombing of London. He was granted this privilege, but no sooner had his Italian bombers arrived above the Thames than the Spitfires and Hurricanes fell on them like furies and blew them out of the sky. And how, when the great Stirlings and Lancasters unload their giant bombs on his factories, he screams that we're a nasty cruel people and says that Rome ought to be regarded as an open city.

But of course the Germans and the Japanese are a very different matter. They're much tougher and can take a great deal more. And it's my belief they're going to have to take plenty before this year is out. Both of them have now lost nearly all the advantages given them by the long start they had over us. For instance, two years ago we were trying desperately hard to cope with the Luftwaffe, the strongest air force in the world at that time. But now the Luftwaffe is trying desperately hard to cope with our air forces, and clearly not succeeding. If the Nazis have enough planes in one place to do the job then they find they haven't enough in another place. If they rush planes to Tunisia then the Russian front suffers, and so does northern France, where your terrific Flying Fortresses are doing notable execution.

A real second front is already looming up in the Mediterranean. This means a tremendous strain on the Nazi transport system, which is already over-strained. But that's not all, for that transport system is being pounded day and night by our planes and yours – engine shops, railway yards, locomotives, all more precious than gold, are going up in smoke and flames. The crushing defeat of Rommel's Afrika Korps has completely protected the huge southern flank of the Russian armies, and it was to attack this flank, and to secure the oil of the Caucasus and after that the oilfields of the Middle East, that Hitler hurled so many of his best divisions into the furnace of Stalingrad, a name that must seem to him like something heard in a nightmare. Once we have secured the Mediterranean, not only can we attack Hitler through southern Europe but we can also rush munitions to Russia and India and China.

In the meantime, Hitler, who appears to have quarrelled with his best strategists, has to fight it out, through the hell of winter in Russia. His chance of shortening and so strengthening his lines there has gone. The colossal German Army, designed and trained for lightning offensives like the blitzkrieg, is now everywhere on the defensive. The Germans can fight stubbornly on the defensive, but nevertheless their armies are nothing like so formidable in defence as they are in attack, if only because the strength of the German military machine lies in its detailed preliminary staff work and very thorough organisation. Everything with them is planned long in advance. But once you are absolutely on the defensive, you cannot work to previously prepared plans, because situations constantly arise that have not been considered in advance. Furthermore, there is the question of morale. The German soldiers will fight hard and endure hardships and make grim self-sacrifices so long as they still feel that their armies are winning victories and are invincible. But once they are everywhere in retreat, this necessary confidence soon begins to dwindle, and will soon disappear altogether, and then morale will take a nose-dive. They've not reached that point yet, of course, though occasional recent items of news from the Russian front do suggest that German morale there is not quite as good as it was, and it will certainly not improve during the next three months.

Meanwhile, they have to hold down half Europe, filled with people who are becoming increasingly defiant. The nearer the Allied armies approach to these peoples of the occupied countries, the more actively defiant they will become and the more difficult it will be to control them. Just when Hitler will want to take his garrisons away from these countries, to fight his battles elsewhere, his Quislings will be clamouring for more troops to keep order in their territories. This is probably happening already. Hitler has not only a badly battered transport system on his hands but also far more demands for men than he can possibly fulfil. And yet he's not yet felt the full weight of British and American armies, neither on land nor from the air, where our combined bombing fleets will soon be terribly destructive. He has to meet that full weight this year, and for my part I doubt if he will be able to take it.

As for Japan, after the brilliant opening successes, due to long preparation and elaborate treachery, it seems to have halted too long between three separate lines of action – to attack Australia, to invade India or to go for Siberia. Japan has waited to see which course would pay best, and has, I suspect, waited just too long. With the Germans in retreat both in southern Russia and in Africa, the Japanese position, with half their army tied up on the mainland and the other half scattered in small pockets all down the Pacific, is nothing like so good as it was, and of course your recent actions in New Guinea and the Solomons have made it worse.

So when our leaders talk of this year, 1943, as the year of the grand offensive of the United Nations, I think they're talking sound military sense. This is the year when the gangs, both East and West, get what they've long been asking for. One thing, though: we must remember that in this war we're fighting very desperate men, who can't retire anywhere if they lose, so we've got to be prepared for any possible move of theirs, no matter how crazy it may seem, for there's hardly anything they won't try before they're through. Well, that's how I see it, Jack, Sophie; we're a lot nearer Arizona than we were last year; so – remember us to everybody – and get that tennis court tidied up a bit – and every good wish from us all.

13 January 1943

My Australian Friends

L ast week I talked to some friends in Arizona. This week I want to talk about some friends of mine here in England. But though these friends are living in England, they are not English; they are Australian. Moreover, they spent their childhood and early youth in China. They live and work in wartime England, they were educated and spent most of their later youth in Australia, and they were brought up in China; those facts seem to me to give them a valuable and unusual outlook, and that is why I am talking about them this week. They are brother and sister. Listeners in Sydney, where these two have many friends, will be interested to hear their names: they are Charles and Geraldine Lack. I have just been spending a few days near them. We have had long walks and talks. In the course of these talks, they have said things to me that I think are worth passing on to you.

Now, Miss Geraldine Lack is the headmistress of a large girls' school that has been evacuated from a south coast town, much bombed, to a town further inland. This means that her girls no longer live at home. Some of them live in hostels, but the majority are in billets, that is, lodging with private people. Their life is altogether different from what it was before the school evacuated. It is not as comfortable, of course; it is much less sheltered; it has to be much more responsible and independent. And Miss Lack is very emphatic that this change has been all to the good. In the first place, she says, in spite of the rather difficult conditions – for they have to share buildings with another school and stagger the hours of teaching – schoolwork itself hasn't suffered. The girls are learning just as much as they did, perhaps more, and are equally successful in winning various scholarships to the universities. Outside schoolwork, the gain has been very definite. The girls are kept extremely busy doing extra jobs, most of which, of course, are quite voluntary. To begin with, the older girls look after the younger ones, make themselves responsible for their lot of school life away from home. This is a good thing. It is doubtful, to my mind, whether a girl of seventeen or eighteen can learn anything as valuable in school as this direct and personal kind of responsibility, which fits them better than anything else could for adult life. Then some of the girls, in their spare time and holidays, help the local farmers, doing lighter kinds of work on the land. Others are engaged in helping the pharmacists of Britain, because very important medical drugs etc. can be obtained by distillation and other means from herbs and plants etc. that must be gathered in large quantities at the right time. For example, the nuts of the common horse chestnut, which are found everywhere here in the autumn, are now used for this purpose, and these girls go out and collect them by the thousand. Then again they make themselves useful in various forms of salvage. Thus in these and many other ways they are not only helping the war effort, without cutting short their school careers, but they are also having practical lessons in real citizenship and communal living.

The result, Miss Lack says, is very striking. They are at once more thoughtful and more independent. Miss Lack taught in England for a period before the war, then returned to Australia and came back here in wartime. She finds the difference most marked. Her girls now remind her of girls in Australia. A certain stuffiness, a certain rigidity of mental attitude, a certain delayed development that she noticed before in these middle-class English schoolgirls have now vanished. These wartime schoolgirls are well on their way to being first-class citizens. They are far more interested in the affairs of their country and of the world than they would have been before. The very necessities of wartime, compelling them to discover the links that join them to the rest of the community, arousing for the most part their eager co-operation, have freed them from restrictions that were of no value, have assisted their development, broadened their outlook and enriched their characters. And if this is going on all over Britain then we may expect that the next generation of wives and mothers will demand a better place in a better world than former generations of British women did. So much for Miss Lack.

Now, her brother Charles is a doctor, and, somewhat to his disgust, he has been compelled to remain in a large, scattered country and so far has not been successful, in spite of many earnest applications, in getting himself released in order to join our forces overseas, or to re-join on some epic of medical adventure his old friends the Chinese. He is still in his early thirties and thinks that a much older man could do his job. Though I sympathise with his desire to get away, I'm not sure that a much older man could do his job here, for it involves many visits in the middle of the night, in the pitch darkness of the black-out, to lonely farms at the end of steep, winding lanes or along rather unpleasant coast roads, all in the wildest Atlantic weather, as well as duties as medical officer to an important section of the Home Guard, and of course instant service if there should be local air raids.

His main interest is, of course, in his exacting but satisfying work in medicine, and his talk is often very medical – sometimes a bit too medical for me, who begins to wonder uneasily, after much talk of operations at the last minute on strange fearful growths, what my chances of survival are. In spite, however, of this rather sinister professional talk, like most doctors here, my friend Charles Lack sees himself not, as the older medical men did, as a private practitioner but as a public servant whose fundamental duty is with the positive health of the community he lives in. These young doctors don't merely want to try to cure people when they are sick, but they want to devote the better part of their energy and skill to keeping people well. Thus they cannot help looking further afield than the older doctors did. Their interests are wide because the whole field of public health is wide. They want the people to be properly fed because they know the value of a sound diet and know the evils that can result from a faulty one. They insist that people should be properly housed because they know that families that are badly housed are inviting diseases to themselves and to their neighbours. They demand that the conditions of work and leisure should be such as to give both the bodies and the minds of men and women a chance to function properly. They feel that the doctors should not be expected to patch up the wrecks and ruins of humanity after a callous and greedy industrialism has done its worst for them.

And I believe that these keen, knowledgeable, enthusiastic medical men like my friend will play a great part in the building up of the new Britain and of the new world after the war. They will say, in effect, 'Don't send for the doctor last after most of the damage has been done. But send for him first to make sure that the conditions are right.' It will be difficult for any British government to turn a deaf ear to such demands, and it is my belief that no British government from now on will do it or even want to do it. True, even yet there are demands from the more progressive section of the medical profession about long hours of work, for instance – that have not yet been properly met – but I believe that this is chiefly due to faculty machinery of contact and administration rather than to any wilful disregard of medical opinion. I have great confidence in my friend Charles and his colleagues.

Apart from his professional interests, my friend's greatest enthusiasm is for China and the Chinese. As I said earlier, he spent his childhood and early youth in China, going to school at Chai-fu in northern China and spending more of his holidays in central China, so that he made many long complicated journeys in the country and saw a great deal of it – and its people. Moreover, being young when he was there, and learning early to speak the language, he got to know the people far more intimately than most adults can, and in addition, of course, he made many close friends among Chinese boys of about his own age and came to know their families too. He needs no encouragement to talk of China and the Chinese, but if he did, I should promptly give it to him because for many years now I have been fascinated by all that I have read and heard – and seen in its magnificent works of art – of this ancient civilisation and its people. I am glad that they are our allies and that at last we are beginning to see them as a people in something like a true perspective.

My friend Charles Lack, when he can spare the time, sometimes gives talks on China and its people to the folk of his neighbourhood, and I only wish he – and others with a similar background of real knowledge and sympathy – could be constantly telling the whole lot of us, all the English-speaking peoples, about China. I was asking him the other night what he thought we English-speaking people could learn from the Chinese. His reply interested me profoundly. He said that what the Chinese could best teach us, if we had the sense to learn, was, first, a better sense of values – of what was worth pursuing and worth having, and what was not – than the average Anglo-Saxon has. The Chinese did not worry themselves sick chasing shadows. They were hardly ever hell-bent for power, prestige or the pitiful snobberies. If they desired money, then it was because with it they could buy a few beautiful things that they could appreciate and treasure. They had a fine appreciation of beauty, just as they had a delightful sense of all the domestic virtues.

Then, perhaps because they are members of a very old and wise civilisation, they have, he said, the enviable faculty of living richly in the present – making the most of every here and now – a meal, a meeting with a friend, the sight of a bird, an exquisite passage of poetry. We Anglo-Saxons have a bad habit – I know I am often guilty of it myself – of throwing away or trampling down the present because we are in such a hurry to reach some future happiness – forgetting, of course, that the future happy moment will soon be itself present time and may therefore be robbed of its happiness just because we don't know how to enjoy the present. This enjoyment of the passing moment, my friend said, was of course connected with the Chinese technique of living, which was not largely slapdash like ours but deliberate, controlled, exquisite, deeply civilised.

Yes, we have a great deal to learn from these allies of ours. The contribution that a free and unified China, learning new methods but preserving all that was best in the ancient empire, can make to the post-war world is very great indeed, more especially as much of it related to the happiness of the individual. And fortunately, my friend pointed out, the Chinese and we Anglo-Saxons have one notable characteristic in common, and that is: a profound sense of humour. The Chinese, like the English-speaking peoples, are essentially a humorous folk – unlike the solemn Germans and the conceited, wooden Japanese, we like to laugh – and much of our criticism is conveyed in our laughter. And that is, in my view, a very great kind indeed. With men by whose side we have struggled and fought and with whom we can enjoy a laugh, we can rid the world if its demons, clear the air and start again.

20 and 21 January 1943

Air Raids

Those of you who used to listen to my *Britain Speaks* talks in the autumn of 1940 will remember how, night after night, week after week, I would describe the air-raid nights in London. In those dark and dangerous days, I was talking on this overseas service almost every other night and had certain problems that I made light of at the time but that were quite serious to me. One problem was: how to get sufficient sleep to see me through the next day's work. Another was: how to get to and from the studio to give the talks at all. Sometimes I managed to ride there, sometimes I walked, sometimes I ran. Those were queer times all right. And this week, after an interval of nearly two years, I've been reminded of them, because I've been staying in London and, as you know, the raids have suddenly returned to London. Once again, after a long silence, the sirens have been wailing, the guns have been barking and thudding, bombs have shaken the ground, and fragments of anti-aircraft shells have rained on the streets. Yes, quite like old times, though with some vital differences.

And please don't imagine that because London has been free from raids for such a long period, the country as a whole has been free from them too. It is true there have been no huge systematic blitzings of chosen towns. Armadas of bombers no longer fly far inland and try to flatten a Coventry or burn down a Manchester. The big raids seem to belong to the past. The Luftwaffe has not been able to spare the men and machines lately for such raids. It has in fact completely lost that superiority in mere brute force that it once had. Compared with the massive raids we have made lately, both in Germany and in Italy, anything that the Luftwaffe has done during these past months has been on a pretty small scale. Most of the raiding here has been what we call tip-and-run raiding. A few planes, not always heavy bombers, swoop down out of the clouds, by day or night, choosing districts not too far from the coast, drop their bombs on anything handy, sometimes do a little machine-gunning, and then clear off. This is, if you like, small beer. It reduces the Luftwaffe from a colossal over-shadowing giant, threatening total destruction, to a furious little dwarf, making as much mischief as he can. But that is looking at the matter from a safe distance. After all, it is no joke being among the victims of these small raids, which attack anything and everything. They do not last long, and they do not affect anything but a tiny area, but if you happen to be in that area these raids are very unpleasant indeed while they do last. In fact, during these so-called quiet months, a large section of the country and its people may be said to have been in the front line. At any moment, day or night, something very nasty might happen.

I haven't been mixed up in them myself lately, but during the last six weeks, in two quite different parts of this country, both my wife and one of my daughters have been machine-gunned – without, I'm delighted to add, any ill effects whatever. And I have a daughter who is a dispatch rider in the WRNS – she tears about the place on a motorcycle, often through the pitch darkness of midnight – and she happens to be stationed in a famous town that has never been out of the front line, you may say, since the early summer of 1940. I must admit that she seems to enjoy herself, but then she is at an age when it is more fun to be dramatic than it is to be comfortable and safe, and it doesn't follow that you and I would enjoy it very much.

But there you are – in spite of the lack of any big news of Britain being attacked, the grim old game has been going on – with, of course, this difference now, that for every hundred-weight of bombs that have been dropped here, we've been dropping a ton or two over there, where, by this time, a great many German and Italian citizens must have drastically revised their opinion of bombing as a national pastime. But London, as you know, has been left alone for quite a long time, until this week.

Sunday night, I repeat, was quite like old times. I was staying in an hotel. Oddly enough, the very night I moved into an hotel during the big 1940 blitz it received a direct hit, though by an extraordinary stroke of luck I happened to be out of it at the time, having gone across the road to give one of these broadcasts. The first raid on Sunday came early, just as most of us had finished dinner and were sitting about or standing talking in the large lounge downstairs, just outside the dining room. The sirens went, in the good old style, wailing to high heaven. Nobody bothered about them. That is, of course, nobody among us guests in the hotel, for thousands of other people in the city, on Home Guard or ARP or fire-watching duty, must have instantly jumped to attention and gone straight on duty. But most of us in that lounge, I fancy, imagined that some stray bomber had wandered into the London area. But then, a few minutes afterwards, the guns went into action, and there were some batteries not very far away. Very soon there was a complete devil's tattoo of gunfire, rattling all the windows and almost shaking the whole place. I had an engagement with a friend not very far away, but it wasn't urgent and I decided to wait until at least the worst of the gunfire was over. We're strongly advised to do that, these days, for all that stuff sent roaring up into the air during those barrages has to come down again, and the chances of being knocked out by a fragment of this stuff, which can easily knock you flat, are probably greater than the chances of finding yourself near a bursting bomb. And, as a matter of fact, some people were killed during this raid by shell casings and other fragments from the anti-aircraft barrage. And it was quite a barrage, too. Our anti-aircraft boys were sending up some stuff.

When the raid was over, after an hour or so, I went to meet my friend, and met, with him, an officer we both knew who had just been on duty with a battery; and he told us, with pride and glee, that not only had his boys given a very good account of themselves but that so had the girls too, for now, unlike 1940, there are girls in the ATS attached to many of these batteries, doing various detection and calculation jobs, and most of these girls had had their baptism of fire and had come through it extraordinarily well. The actual presence of enemy planes had keyed them up, and, in spite of the noise and fury and excitement, had inspired them to do even quicker and more alert jobs than they had ever done through hours of practice.

Well, I got back to my hotel, after much good talk on these and other topics, rather late, to find the place very quiet, most people having gone to bed. I went to bed myself, and then, to my annoyance, somewhere about five in the morning, found myself yanked into wakefulness by the wailing of the sirens. Within a few minutes, the guns had opened up again, and now the gunfire was so continuous and furious that I got out of bed and decided to see what was happening. I did what we are always being told not to do, and what I certainly would not make a habit of doing. I turned out the light, then pulled aside the heavy black-out curtains and stared up into the sky. Above the stabbing thunder of the guns, I could hear the same old angry drone of the planes. But the fireworks up there seemed to be on a new and more magnificent scale. One whole section of the sky was brightly winking with exploding shells. There were sometimes so many of them that you couldn't connect this terrific fiery activity with the earth but felt that the sky itself was doing it all, as if it were some liquid coming to the boil and a thousand bubbles bursting in fire and anger. By this time, the nearest batteries had joined in, with the result that all my four windows were protesting and the very room itself seemed to be shaking.

I restored the black-out curtain to its place, switched on the light, put on a dressing gown and a scarf, stuck my feet into some slippers, had a smoke and thought I would see what was doing outside in the corridor and on the landing, from which the sounds of opening doors and talk were coming. Lots of people were coming out of their rooms. The hotel, which incidentally is a fairly large place, has of course a proper air-raid shelter down in the basement, but I had never seen it and didn't feel like trailing down several floors to see it now. A few people, mostly elderly ladies smothered in rugs etc., were going down the stairs, quite slowly, in a calm, dignified manner. Most of the others were hanging about the landing, giving each other cigarettes, yawning and chatting. The talk tended to be about old days and nights of the big blitz or of similar experiences in other parts of the country, much more recently. One woman was saying what it was like in East Anglia. Another described her experiences, which had been tough, in Southampton. There's no doubt that an air raid brings us English out of our shells. As so many foreign observers noted in 1940, we become quite matey and free-and-easy when the whole building we are in is shaking and the sky is raining fire and fury. We speak to people to whom we've never been introduced.

I ought to explain, though, that these people hadn't left their rooms and wandered out into the corridor and landing just to be near somebody else and to talk – though I think that's a bit of welcome comfort – but because it's much more sensible to be out there than in your room, for you are at least free from one of the most obvious dangers of an air raid, namely, flying glass, which, when there is terrific blast about, can cut you to ribbons in a second.

So there we were, lounging out there, chatting and smoking and yawning, the men looking large and tousled, the women looking small and crumpled. Meanwhile, so strange is this life we lead now, somewhere in the night sky, about three miles or so above us, a young man called Wing Commander Wight-Boycott, formerly attached to the CID at Scotland Yard, was setting up a record by shooting down no less than four out of the ten raiding planes destroyed that night. Somewhere up there, while feeding himself with oxygen, this enterprising pilot of night fighters kept seeing Dornier 217s, giving them long bursts and watching them go flaming and screaming down. In one instance, he says:

> *The fire spread along the wings and back along the fuselage of the enemy bomber and lit up the sky so clearly that we could see the black crosses on the aircraft. We watched four members of the crew bale out, one after another, and the aircraft then went down, exploding with a brilliant flash.*

How fantastic this all is! These combats in the night, miles high, between raiding bomber and defending fighter, while far below the citizens trudge to and from their shelters or stand about chatting and smoking and yawning, outwardly cool enough but wondering between whiles whether a ton of explosive might not be already on its way towards them. A strange existence, a fantastic state of things, half crazy, half heroic. And we have the satisfaction of knowing that although we are now playing the grim game harder and better than our opponents are, we didn't start it, never wanted it played this way, and are already shaping in our minds a world in which all these antics will be controlled and finally abolished.

27 and 28 January 1943

Rationing

The last American papers that I've seen contain a lot of comment and speculation about rationing, so I thought we might have a talk about that very important subject. It's important for two different reasons. In the first place, in order to keep the colossal war machine going, you have to cut down supplies and services for the civilian population. In the second place, seeing there are going to be short supplies, you must try to even them out as best you can, so that everybody at least gets a fair share of what is essential. There you have the whole thing in a nutshell. First you have to cut down, and then you have to spread out what's left. It's very sensible. In fact, it's far more sensible than anything that happens in peacetime, when a man on one side of a street may be eating until he's sick and a man on the other side of the street may be dying of starvation. None of us wants to see that sort of thing happening again, and it's my belief that now we've admitted the basic principle of rationing we'll never allow ourselves to return to the old hit-and-miss, run-and-grab anarchy.

Don't mistake me. I've no particular love of skimpy allowances of food – I like my meals – or of official forms and booklets and coupons and the rest. For instance, at present I'm staying in a large hotel in the West End of London. Because I'm staying there longer than five days, they have the temporary use of my ration book. Now, like most Englishmen, I enjoy a good breakfast – I believe it's a question of climate, this breakfast business, because I've noticed that it's only when I'm living in a raw, damp climate that I want a substantial breakfast – but there it is, I like to begin the day with a good meal, whatever happens afterwards. Now, I'll tell you what I had for breakfast this morning in this large West End hotel. I had some oatmeal porridge – *not*, as we all like it, with cream and lots of sugar, but with a pinch of sugar and very thin milk, probably concocted out of dried milk powder. Then after that there was tea, there was toast and scrambled eggs, obviously made of dried eggs. I don't like scrambled eggs much at any time, even when they're made out of good fresh eggs, and they're certainly no treat when they're made out of dried eggs. But it was either that or nothing, so I had that. I'm not grumbling. The breakfast could be eaten and there was enough in it to keep me going, but I couldn't *enjoy* it.

And I think that's a good short description of our food situation here. Our food can be eaten; it's sufficient to keep us going and keep us healthy; but taking it by and large it's of a quantity and quality to keep enjoyment away, to make eating a necessary business and not a pleasure. And that'll do. We can't ask for anything better. And I for one am prepared to go on like this for years and years, long after the war is over, so long as I know that what is being saved, in supplies and services, by the adoption of this system is being devoted to some great creative effort and that we are coming nearer and nearer to social justice.

And that's my point about rationing. Not only is it absolutely necessary for the war effort but also it makes for social justice. It takes most of the sting out of our inequalities. It cuts down, quite drastically, the power and privilege of money. No longer can you have everything you want simply because you have the money to buy it. You can still get some things. Thus you can rent, if you wish, a most large and luxurious apartment. But you can't fill that apartment with butter, eggs, meat, cheese etc.

At this point, somebody will say 'black market'. Well, according to some sensational articles that I've read – though not lately – in overseas magazines about our life here, you could obtain these stores, by paying heavily for them, through the black market. All I can say about that is that even if I wanted to – and of course I don't – I wouldn't have the least idea how to get into touch with the black marketeers, if they still exist, so that I could obtain these supplies, and that I don't know anybody who could put me into touch. I doubt if much of this traffic still exists – because our Ministry of Food and its detectives dealt with it very severely – and even if it does, my point is that as a man who gets about a good deal and knows all kinds of people, I don't myself know where I'd even begin to find it. Now, I've been in countries – and so, probably, have you – where there were certain laws about – well, say – drink. Officially there was no hard liquor in those countries. But unofficially there was plenty, and – this is the point – everybody, including newly arrived visitors, knew where to get it. And that's what I'd call a flourishing black market. And by that test, we certainly haven't got a flourishing black market here. Hardly a ghost of one.

For instance, I'm very fond of bacon. I could make a good meal off fried bacon at any time – and have made good meals – from seven in the morning until six the next morning. Now, we have a small bacon ration, but owing to the fact that I have been moving about so much lately I haven't been able to draw any bacon ration, with the result that I haven't eaten a bit of bacon – not a square inch – for months. Now, if an amiable black marketeer came to my room and showed me a nice little piece of bacon and said I could have it for a pound, I think I'd be sorely tempted. My conscience, which would tell me to have no dealings with the black market, might be quietened by my pointing out to it that I hadn't drawn my legitimate bacon ration for months and therefore I was entitled to some. I don't say I'd fall but certainly I'd be greatly tempted. But nobody does come to me. If I suddenly went bacon-mad, and screamed every morning that I could no longer exist without it, the fact remains that I still wouldn't have the least notion how to set about getting any. So where's your black market now?

No, you can take my word for it that these days our rationing system really works, and that nearly all of us try to help it to work because we realise that it's not only essential to the war effort but that it makes too for social justice. I remember that in the last war, every time I came home on leave I used to hear endless talk about food hoarders. You never hear that sort of talk in this war. Much fewer people want to do it anyhow, and even the ones who do have been mostly circumvented.

I'm particularly pleased too with the workings of our elaborate points system of rationing. Here is a new and better interpretation of the law of supply and demand. Within the limits of the scheme and what the country possesses, you can indulge your tastes, but you have to pay for it – not in money, because the prices are fixed, but in the number of points you're prepared to pay for it. During Christmas, when my family met for the holidays, I sent some of the children out shopping to buy things on points. They returned with, among other things, an enormous round tin containing some dubious kind of meat preparation – incidentally of British manufacture – and when I asked them why they'd saddled us with this doubtful monster, they cried excitedly that it was so big and only took five points. Well, of course it only took five points because there was no demand for the stuff. On the other hand, a small tin of canned salmon, which is in great demand and needs shipping space, costs more than thirty points, making a great hole in the total month's allowance of points. Now, this is fair enough. Most of you are having this points system – if you've not already had it – and I do assure you that, so long as the points cover a wide variety of stuff and they are continually being adjusted to fit the prevailing conditions of supply and demand, the system works very well indeed.

Of course it means that the household budget is a much more complicated affair, and that shopping itself takes more time. Husbands don't notice it much, but housewives do, and have to make some necessary calculations about how the family's allowance of points shall be spent. This isn't so bad when the housewife is at home, but it's tough when she's out at work, as so many of our women are, and one of our headaches here was this business of women out at work finding time in which to do their shopping. In some districts now, in connection with big war factories, there are professional shoppers, who do the job for a small fee. As a matter of fact, the biggest hold-up is in the rather small shops, which are under-staffed anyhow. Here we don't have any of those serve-yourself, pay-and-take-it establishments that I used to see in America, and now, I feel, we could do with a few.

I'll admit that we men feel rationing much less than our womenfolk, who not only have the extra worry and calculating and waiting but are also much harder hit by some forms of rationing. Clothes, for instance. It's true that men's clothes usually take more coupons than women's, but a man who had a fair-sized wardrobe before rationing began can easily get by and, if he is a family man, can spare some coupons for his wife and children. Growing children are the worst off. We men too now have the perfect excuse – I've been looking for it all my life – for not getting new things and for wearing the same comfortable old clothes – No Coupons. On the other hand, we can't enjoy and express ourselves as women do by creating delightful improvisations, turning a dull old thing into some enchanting new thing. I can't imagine what the result would be if I tried any experiments of *that* kind with my clothes.

I noticed the other day in a series of questions from America: 'How do you like petrol rationing?' We have no rationing of petrol now. That stopped last July. Now we have something much more drastic, for you can't have any petrol at all unless you can prove, in your application to the fuel authorities, that you are engaged in work of national importance *and* that the use of a car is absolutely essential. So don't let any listener imagine that his gasoline has been cut down to provide private citizens on this side with motor fuel. Indeed, most private citizens here have now laid their cars up for the duration of the war.

Well, there you are – and what with desperate filling in of application forms for petrol, and registering here and there for the basic rations – butcher's meat, bacon, butter and the rest – and trying to work out how to spend one's points, and then remembering the personal points, without which we can't buy any chocolate or candies of any kind, and then searching for one's clothes coupons, it's a fairly complicated existence. But it cuts down civilian consumption and labour and materials outside the direct war effort. It reduces as far as possible shipping space. *And* it makes for social justice. Nobody shall grab handfuls while other people go without. Take your turn and have only your share. And that's not a bad motto for after the war, either.

And now, finally, a little story, chiefly for the benefit of a few overseas journalists who have stayed in the Ritz for a few days, been entertained right and left, and then have criticised our wartime living. The other day, a pilot officer came to tea with me – a fine big chap with a fund of good talk. During that talk, with the first sweep of his knife he cut in half my week's butter ration and spread it on his toast. A few minutes later the other half went the same way. He didn't understand it was my week's ration, of course, and I was delighted to let him have it. But I'd be very annoyed if I ever caught that pilot officer telling his friends that I was a nice fellow but obviously got more than my share of butter because he'd had plenty when he had tea with me. You see what I mean?

5 and 6 May 1943

Speaking Personally

For the next few weeks at least, I propose to make a change in these talks. Always up to now they have dealt with one particular topic each week. They have been the equivalent in radio of a signed newspaper article. Now – for a time at least – I want to move from the signed article to the signed column – I want these talks to be the radio version of a personal newspaper column, to turn myself temporarily into a columnist of the air. I shall deal with a variety of topics each week, with anything that takes my fancy. There are several good reasons for this change. First, it enables me to talk to you more intimately, and to show you in greater detail the sort of life we're living here. Then again, I've taken a flat in the very heart of central London, in the shadow of Whitehall itself, with Big Ben booming just round the corner, and so I hope to see and hear a lot of things that will interest you. And if I adopt the columnist's method it is much easier to give you a glimpse of all those things. If you don't like the change, tell me so, and I'll go back to the old one-talk-one-topic style, but I'm hoping that you'll enjoy the change as much as I shall.

The best feature of this flat I've taken is the view from the sitting room. It's very high up and overlooks the river. It gives one the best view of the river I've ever seen, except that from Barrie's flat, which was at the top of the old Adelphi building. But it's nearly as good as that. You get a magnificent sweep of the river, right from the Houses of Parliament down to Blackfriars Bridge, and I'm never tired of staring at this noble view. It's surprising too what a lot of traffic there is on the Thames, tugs and barges and all kinds of small vessels going up and down at all hours. What a river! Who called it 'Liquid History'? And what a city! I wasn't born and brought up here, but I have a very deep affection for London. And how beautiful it looks in the early morning and in the evening, when the grey Portland stone takes on a strange luminous quality and seems to shine! You feel that the grand old city has not only a character, a personality, of its own but also – a soul. It has suffered; it has bled; its wounds are still gaping wide; but it has triumphed; and here it broods like some grey, kind old giant. And surely all those young men in uniform, from all the united nations, who come here to London must begin to feel an affection for the noble old place, which belongs not only to England or to the British Commonwealth of Nations but to the whole world, to the whole history of suffering, struggling mankind marching towards freedom and a fuller life. London! The very name sounds like the chimes of a vast old bell. It seems to me the most romantic city in the world now.

I wonder if you realise how extraordinarily cosmopolitan London is now. The streets are filled with the uniforms of all the Allied nations. In a restaurant you hear a dozen different languages. In any bar you'll overhear war stories strange and romantic enough to set up a novelist for life. Going through Soho Square the other morning, I noticed a large motorcar decorated with white ribbons standing outside the old church, where evidently there was a wedding going on. As usual, a group of people had collected outside the church. I had a look at this group. It contained two American Negro soldiers, two Norwegian sailors, a Polish airman, three French women and for all I know half a dozen other nationalities might have been represented there. Again, the other night, at the urgent request of my two children who are still at school but were then home for the Easter holidays, we had a Chinese dinner at one of London's half-dozen Chinese restaurants. I'm very fond of real Chinese cooking and prefer their way of serving a dinner to ours. We went to a small upstairs room in this restaurant, which is itself a small unpretentious place. At one table were two American officers. At another were a young Chinese couple, and the girl was quite beautiful. At another were a Czech airman and his girl. And at the table just behind us there was a Hindu student, a young Austrian Jewess and two English girl students. I have a new play running now in Shaftesbury Avenue, at the Globe Theatre, and when I look in at the theatre, and I have to fairly frequently because I make small changes in the lines and business, it always gives me particular pleasure to notice in the audiences so many American officers and men, and soldiers, sailors and airmen from many different nations. The year the war broke out, I believe I had plays running in seven different capital cities. Now all that's gone, of course, but it looks as if most of those cities had sent representatives here to our theatre audiences in London.

The theatre here is very much in full swing, and in central London alone there are no less than thirty-six theatres giving performances. And there are more concerts than I ever remember in London before. This morning, looking through the advertisements in *The Times*, I counted fourteen advertisements of forthcoming full symphony concerts, to say nothing of all the small recitals. Some of you may remember how, nearly three years ago, I told the story of our campaign to save the famous London Philharmonic Orchestra from being disbanded – a story, by the way, that has just been made into a film. Well, that orchestra is now suffering from playing too much, and badly needs a rest, so great is the demand for good music. Then there's a boom in painting. Art dealers are doing a roaring trade, and they tell me that their clients are putting their names down in advance for the future work of some well-known painters. Many of our best artists, of course, are attached to the various services – as official war artists. Some of the best pictures in the new summer show of the Royal Academy are by these official war artists. I went to the Academy last Saturday afternoon and found it solid with people, much too popular for any chance of seeing the pictures in comfort. The eager demand for books continues, and most good books disappear shortly after they're published, because the demand is so much greater than the supply. The bigger bookshops always seem crowded with customers. All this seems to me important because it proves that this shake-up has done us good here. We're no longer a lazy-minded people. There are signs of a genuine intellectual and artistic awakening in this country. I ran into an American friend the other day. He'd just come from Washington to do an official job here in London. I asked him how this wartime London struck him, and he replied that he found it 'exhilarating'. That was his word, and he chose it carefully – 'exhilarating'. Imagine any American before this war describing London as exhilarating!

Who's the best propagandist in this war? I believe my vote would go to a Russian – Ilya Ehrenburg, author of that massive novel *The Fall of Paris*. But not for the novel but for his war commentaries. I've just written a short introduction to a volume of them that's coming out here, and I've been admiring Ehrenburg's quick, staccato style, hard-hitting and biting wit. For instance, Ehrenburg says of Hitler: 'Although a hardened murderer, he is a vegetarian who is shocked at the suffering of lambs and bullocks. Smoking is forbidden in his presence. This man, who spent ten years in smoke-laden beer-houses, has the nerve to say, "Nobody has ever smoked in my presence."' Or this on Goering: 'Before Hitler came to power, the Berlin Court of Justice deprived Goering of the custody of his child on the grounds that the father was a drug-taker and abnormal. The honest German judges were unwilling to entrust a child to this vainglorious murderer. Hitler has entrusted one hundred million brow-beaten people to Goering.' Or this on Goebbels: 'He began by writing novels. Alas, he had no luck. Nobody bought his novels. Goebbels afterwards explained: "It was all due to Marxist intrigues…" then he made bonfires of twenty million books, taking his revenge on the reading public for having preferred a certain Heine to Goebbels.' And Ehrenburg's war commentaries bristle with words that are like bayonets. Look out for his stuff. It's first-class.

I had a talk the other day with Sir Stafford Cripps, whose job as Minister of Aircraft Production takes him up and down the country, visiting his aircraft factories. Some weeks ago, you may remember, he was criticised for addressing the workers at one factory as 'Comrades'. Now, he tells me, at every place, when he rises and begins 'Comrades', there is an instant, huge and uproarious shout of approval. He was showing me some magnificent photographs of aircraft factory workers, grand types of people, and I was especially interested because I've written a novel all about an aircraft factory. Cripps talks about our aircraft production with great enthusiasm, and obviously feels definite comradeship with the whole vast army of folk engaged in the industry. Which is, you'll agree, very much the right spirit.

Now, here's something I've been wanting to make plain to you. Some of you, I gather, are under the impression that all those of us who talk on the air here are simply so many official mouthpieces. This is quite wrong. Speaking for myself, I can tell you quite definitely that I am nobody's mouthpiece and that I would instantly resent the least attempt to turn me into anybody's mouthpiece. Officials are always glad, as I explained the other week, to supply me with any information I may require about their particular department, and of course they like their part of the war effort to be talked about on the air. But I am an absolutely independent private commentator, and I take my own line. Nobody tells me what to say, and if anybody tried to turn me into a mouthpiece, either he'd go or I'd go. Talks are censored, of course, simply because they mustn't contain anything that might help the enemy, and as you and I are just as anxious not to help the enemy as the British government, we can't complain about this obviously necessary censorship. But do please get it out of your head that talks like these come to you from some kind of propaganda department. They don't. I try to talk to you as I'd talk if we were in the same room together. The only difference is that if you've had enough of me on the air, you can switch me off, whereas I'm awfully hard to switch off when I get going to a room.

My wife came to me yesterday and said, 'I've brought you a present. Hold your hand out.' I did and was delighted to find that she put into my hand a tiny envelope containing one safety razor blade. I'd been using one rather rusty blade for the last month, for there's been an extraordinary shortage of blades here just lately. These young naval officers, chiefly submarine and MTB men, we see about the place, all wearing terrific piratical beards, are now the lucky fellows. Perhaps we shall all end by wearing beards. Women say they dislike beards, but that, I fancy, is because women can't help having a secret and uneasy respect for the bearded male, a respect they don't feel for us smooth-faced fellows. I notice them glancing with admiration and awe at these bearded young heroes from the Navy. I find myself doing it too. These young men look like Elizabethans – the new Elizabethans. And perhaps they are.

23 June 1943

A Different Kind of War

This last week has been a disturbed and anxious week for me, because a member of my family has been having a major operation. It has been successful and the patient is doing well, but naturally this event has prevented me from going about as much as usual. But a man can do a good deal of useful thinking even under these conditions, especially if he has been lucky enough to strike a good rich seam. Now, I happened to see some letters from young Army and Air Force officers – one or two in print, the others in private – that prompted some thoughts I'll now pass on to you. These were serious letters, and the first point I'd like to make is that these young men in our fighting services are in fact more serious-minded than we are apt to assume. It's easy to understand why we make this mistake. There is of course a tradition of easy, thoughtless, swaggering soldiery. And then again young men – and, for that matter, young women – in a mass community rarely reflect the attitude of mind of their more thoughtful members; they descend, so to speak, to the lowest common denominator; the more serious types are also the shyest and most diffident; with the result that they easily produce the impression of an uproarious gang. This in its turn influences our own attitude towards them, so that we tend to offer them our lightest talk and our lightest entertainment, and imagine that their uniforms automatically cut them off from all profound matters. But young men who have been uprooted and know that sudden death may be round the corner may put on a little grin and a little swagger but commonly they have some solemn sessions with themselves, and we are given glimpses of these sessions in the letters they write. Let us remember this when we are offering them hospitality and entertainment. Fun and games, girls and dances, certainly, but don't let us be afraid of offering them diversion and discussion that will challenge their brains and give them a chance of expressing their deeper selves.

The next point is even more important. The sight of these letters from young men on active service confirms a suspicion that I have entertained for a long time, namely, that we make a grave mistake when we assume that this war is like the last and will be similar in its effects. In our more cynical moments, we are inclined to point out that in the last war there was a wave of idealism that ended in disillusion and spiritual defeat. The young men who fought the war came home weary and worn out physically, mentally and spiritually, so that nothing vital and lasting was accomplished. I believe that there is no parallel here – that, on the contrary, in this respect, this present war is likely to move in the opposite direction. For what happened to the young men in the last war? They entered it in a mood of simple faith and fervent patriotism, in an attitude of mind admirably reflected in the early war poems of Rupert Brooke. They left the war disgruntled and disillusioned, writing poetry like that of Siegfried Sassoon. But in this war the young men began by being disgruntled and disillusioned. They hadn't known the illusion of security and steady progress that we knew before 1914; they grew up in the riotous but uneasy 1920s and the grim and sobering 1930s, and security and steady progress was a joke. They came into this war without faith – except the negative faith that Fascist aggression couldn't be tolerated – but it seems to me quite possible that they will acquire and are already acquiring some kind of faith, a sense of enduring purpose, a larger hope, during the war itself. In the last war, we began with something and ended with nothing. In this war, I suggest that these young men, who began almost with nothing, may end with something, a something that will be of immense value to the progressive mind and the progressive cause everywhere. They too will be weary when all the fighting is done, but not too weary to enlist in the great campaign of peace, not so worn out that they cannot hold on to and fight for their own newly acquired faith. Anyhow, that is how I for one read the signs.

Now and again, I read occasional articles in the press – and very mischievous articles they are too – that suggest that our fighting men are either not interested in or impatient with all this talk of landing the post-war world. I can only say that this has not been my experience, after many talks with and letters from fighting men. It is my experience that they are extremely eager to learn and discuss, and that they regard all serious talk of planning as very important news indeed. I have friends who are serving with the Army Educational Corps or are working for our Army Bureau of Current Affairs, and they confirm to a man this experience of mine.

Just received a good long letter from Mr. William G. Smith in Texas, who is a very keen shortwave listener and makes a point of some value to other overseas listeners. He says, 'My BBC listening has kept me far ahead in being able to anticipate developments in so many fields. How little the average American knows of the vast amount of stuff that we have copied from Britain. I refer of course to wartime progress.' This is a good point and it is one I have had in mind since Pearl Harbor, during which time I have tried to show what we were doing here, not only to give you a notion of our war effort but also to prepare you for similar changes in living and social and industrial organisation that were bound to occur in any community plunged into total war. And here you must remember one thing, and by 'you' I mean all overseas listeners. In ordinary times when you come to see us here in Britain, or read about us, you naturally concentrate on those features of our life that are the most widely removed from your own life, with the result that, where Britain is concerned, the emphasis for you is nearly always on the historical and traditional. And Britain is the quaint old island of castles and cathedrals and ruined abbeys and charming thatched cottages, of judges and barristers in wigs and gowns, of Yeomen of the Guard, of royal processions and ceremonies of ancient universities and Inns of Court, and old taverns once frequented by famous literary figures – a charming old tourists' Britain, rooted in the mouldering past. But that has never been more than a phase of the real Britain, which also produced the fastest ships, the fastest planes and the fastest motor cars. In some respects we are irritatingly slow to change – a fact that most of us writers have not been remiss in pointing out over and over again – but it should be remembered that we are also a people capable of improvising quite boldly and quickly on a big scale, when thoroughly aroused, and that one reason why we are able to do this is that behind our screen of easy self-criticism and grumbling, of almost eccentric individualism, we are actually a people with a very strong and deep-rooted sense of communal life, with an immense fund of public spirit and profound patriotism to draw upon, so that in the face of obvious common danger our people waste little time in sectional quarrels but get straight on with the job. I mention that because in many of the letters I receive from overseas listeners which contain the most handsome tributes to our war effort, there is a certain note of bewilderment and surprise, as if the writers were amazed by our suddenly revealed ability to do so much in so short a time. And I suggest that this bewilderment is based on a false conviction of this island and its people, a conception in turn produced by the interest of tourists and easy romances.

And I have sometimes thought that Hitler, whose intuitions are at least a trifle more profound than the information given him by such second-rate rogues as Ribbentrop, has always had an uneasy sense of the fighting power of the British people, about which he now knows a great deal. And so do his generals. One of them, an air general, has written an article on the ethics of aerial warfare. Unfortunately for him and his kind, this article comes four or five years too late. He ought to have written it when Germany was putting in some aerial bombing practice in Spain, when Nazi Germany began to threaten all Europe with its air force, or even when Warsaw, Rotterdam, London, Novgorod and Coventry were being bombed. In September 1940, Goebbels wrote in his own paper, 'England will not have enough blood and tears to satisfy our remorseless desire for revenge. All that England has suffered is only a beginning.' Later in the same year he wrote, 'This is the beginning of the war to the death in the air. Terror was sown on London on Sunday night. This is the first of the great air raids; and they will continue as long as the British government does not lay down its arms...' Now, that was the time when this air general Quade should have published his article on the ethics of aerial warfare. But the ethics of bombing didn't worry him then. It is only now, when bombing turns into a boomerang and he sees the ruins of Cologne, Lubeck, Bremen, Hamburg, Essen, Duisburg, when he learns that the industrial town of Bremen has been completely destroyed, wiped right off the map, that he seriously discovers that he has never cared very much for this bombing. The Nazi ethics of aerial warfare are quite simple and easy to understand: they are that it is right and proper for Germans to bomb anything and anybody they please but that it is a dreadful thing and all wrong for their former victims to do some bombing in return. It is glorious that Coventry should be bombed but a terrible thing that Dusseldorf should be bombed still harder. These hypocritical pretences, these crocodile tears, seem to me to add the final contemptible touch. But this highly organised squealing is of course part of a highly organised propaganda campaign, designed to persuade their own people that it isn't the fault of the German high command that one German city after another is now being laid in ruins; and further this hypocritical stuff is also being put out to try to weaken the bombing offensive and to create some dissension in our ranks. But Goebbels will have to do better than this.

And he should give some attention to his art department too. The *News Chronicle* here has just published a large photograph that recently appeared in a Nazi-controlled French paper. It shows some seamen struggling in oily water, and these, we're told, are British seamen about to be rescued by the U-boat that sank their ship. The caption reads: 'The survivors are rescued clinging to a rubber raft. But it is difficult to haul them on board because of the slippery oil with which they are covered.' Fine! Good dramatic picture. Unfortunately, it's rather too dramatic, because we recognise in these seamen clinging to the rubber rafts no other than Noël Coward, John Mills and other chief actors in Coward's film *In Which We Serve*, and this propaganda picture of U-boat civilities is in fact a poor reproduction of a 'still' – as they're called – from Coward's film. I'm afraid Dr. Goebbels is no longer the man he was now that he has to sit up at night wondering how on earth he will ever make his final get-away.

30 June 1943

British Propaganda

First, I'll answer two correspondents. A listener in Southern Rhodesia wants to know 'Why is it we hear so little of our propaganda war with the enemy?' And from his subsequent remarks, I gather that he feels there is something undemocratic about this 'hush-hush' business. But it seems to me that explaining our propaganda moves would be rather like explaining in advance our invasion moves. I take it that the reason why we don't explain our propaganda to the enemy to our own people is that we should also have to explain its particular purposes, and therefore would be then busy neutralising it. Don't forget that everything put over on the air is accessible to everybody. My second correspondent, Mr. Coleman of Long Island, says that he would greatly appreciate hearing directly from Britain – from 'some ordinary, everyday persons' – with whom he could exchange sensible information about our respective countries and their war efforts. We are attending to this, Mr. Coleman, and hope to have you fixed up pretty soon. This direct exchange is, of course, a capital idea. Let the people themselves get acquainted, and not depend too much upon governments, radio and the press.

By the way, there's a paragraph in the last number of *Collier's Magazine* I've seen, the issue for 18 May, that is worth noticing. It's humorous but has its serious side. It describes how in the mess of one command of the American Eighth Army Air Force in England, a series of fines has been humorously imposed on men using Anglicisms – 'the Anglicisms of American airmen' – I'm now quoting the magazine paragraph – 'who had been somewhat carried away by the glamour of the RAF'. And under the notice in the mess about the fines, it said: 'These English fliers are grand guys. So are we. They've got guts. So have we. England's a swell dump. So is the USA. Be yourself.' Which is good enough. But I must point out that the Americanisation of Britain – thanks chiefly to the influence of Hollywood – has been going on a long time now and has lately reached a new high level. I've sometimes thought that these American soldiers we see in the West End of London must wonder if we British have nothing of our own to offer, for they must notice that there are American plays in our theatres, many American songs and scenes in our musical shows, dance bands playing American tunes with English girl crooners trying to sing with an American accent, and juke boxes grinding out the products of Tin Pan Alley. American humour is prominent both on the radio and in our magazines. American slang can be heard everywhere. I think, in fact, that it's being rather overdone. What I would much prefer to see is a deliberate exchange of what is best and most characteristic of each country. I notice that our distinguished American visitors are still surprised by the boldness of the war planning here, by the power of rapid improvisation shown by a people they obviously regarded as hide-bound traditionalists; and this surprise is clearly due to the fact that the American idea of this country is still rather out-of-date, in spite of all our efforts. But I won't enlarge on this topic. You've all heard me before.

Whatever may be best for America – and clearly it's not for me to say – there can be no doubt whatever of the success here of the Ministry of Food's policy of pegging food prices by granting subsidies. It marks one of the essential differences between this war and the last, and although conditions have actually been more difficult for the nation in this war than they were in the last, it is a fact that we are better fed now than we were then. And we have steered clear of the danger – always a very grave danger – of the deadly upward spiral movement of inflation. If prices begin to rise rapidly then wages must go up, which means that prices rise again, and so do wages, and so it goes on. Our policy here has been to keep the prices of essential foodstuffs down to a reasonable level by pegging them and meeting any potential loss by granting subsidies. In addition, of course, we ensure that each person receives a supply of those essential foodstuffs by rationing them – or, in the case of rather less essential things, by applying the points system. This seems to me sensible not only in wartime but at any other time too. I for one – and I speak as a man who is comfortably off and can afford to indulge his tastes – never want to return to the old grab-what-you-can system. If, for example, there is a shortage of milk and oranges then let the children have milk and oranges first, simply because they stand in most need of them. Necessaries should never be put up for auction, only luxuries. That seems to me a sound principle for any time.

I don't know how it is where you are, but I notice that here the anti-planners, the people who for reasons best known to themselves want to live in a haphazard community, are busy working a rather neat little trick. What they do is to guy the planners by pretending that anybody who believes that we should plan out the future is promising an impossible earthly paradise. For instance, a cartoon in one of our papers – not famous for its progressive views – shows two middle-aged women at some planners' meeting, and one is saying to the other, 'Oh, he isn't as good as last week's man, who promised round-the-world-cruises for everybody.' Now, it's possible that occasional enthusiasts do make large claims and promise far too much, but it's my experience that most of the experts, in various departments of human affairs, who insist upon the necessity for large-scale planning are in fact strictly realistic in their outlook, and usually begin by pointing out that unless we want to plunge this world into a wild chaos, we simply have got to plan, whether we like it or not. I've noticed too that most of these opponents of planning content themselves with this easy satire, and don't explain what kind of a world it's going to be without any planning. They don't, in fact, ask us to take a good long look at the alternative. The appeal is too often merely to our laziness and prejudices.

Think of it for a moment in wartime terms. Of course it's rather a nuisance to have ration cards and points coupons and identity cards, to go to the Employment Exchange and register, to make a return of your employees and so on and so forth, and nothing is easier than to make people join in a grumble about these things, and to denounce the bureaucracy, and to say that we'll have to ask permission to breathe next – all that stuff is very easy. But the same sort of superficial objection could be raised against being compelled to drive on one side of the road, to register a car, to stop at the red light and move on at the green one, to be responsible for having proper brakes on the car and so forth. Yet we know very well that without such regulations, driving would have been impossible and there would have been wholesale slaughter on the roads. Similarly, without all this registering, all these cards and coupons, the war effort would have been impossible, and in the chaos that would have resulted, our enemies could have walked over us. I think the ordinary man or woman in most places is well aware of this, and it isn't he or she who starts these attacks. Of course officials overdo it sometimes – and the ordinary citizen, standing on his democratic rights, does well to stand up and complain. I'm all for that. But that is one thing, and trying to sabotage the war effort – and possibly the peace effort that must follow it – is quite another thing. And let us make no mistake about it. We've got to plan – not to provide everybody with world cruises but to salvage our civilisation. We're fighting the Nazis, Fascists, Japanese, because they don't believe in our civilisation anyhow and are anxious to put a hideous system of their own in its place. Once we've saved the world from them then we've got to go forward and save it from our own greed and laziness and stupidity. And taking cracks at planners is about as sensible as being in a shipwreck and taking cracks at the approaching lifeboat men.

I've had two of my daughters, enjoying short holidays, staying with me, and as their mother is still away, we've done our own catering. Not too badly either. No meat, unless you count one tin of bully that we got on points and converted into corned-beef hash. I make a pretty good kedgeree out of grade 3 salmon, which is light on points. Plenty of peas and broad beans, thank goodness. Our favourite salad is raw cabbage cut into fine shreds and then thoroughly soaked in a good salad dressing. I make the dressing, and as there's no olive oil, I use, as a base, liquid paraffin from the chemist's. No eggs, but the egg powder we get isn't bad for scrambled eggs or a sketchy sort of sweet omelette. As a rule, though, we have to buy our sweet – or dessert – course from the shops – rather stodgy cherry or gooseberry tarts or some sort of custard. Sausages and meat pies are nearly always to be had from the shops, too. If these were normal times, and there was any amount of food to be had, I'm certain these girls of mine would consider this catering business just a bore, but just because it's now a bit difficult and something of an adventure, they seem to enjoy every minute of it, and return from shopping, the string bag crammed with vegetables, beaming with triumph. I did the shopping the other morning and forgot about the paper shortage, with the result that I found myself loaded up in the most disastrous fashion and felt that at any moment the whole supply would fall into the road. Fortunately, at the last place I went to, a big store, a girl assistant took pity on me and found for me a big stout bag in which I could put everything.

This paper shortage haunts us authors. As I suspected it would, my new novel is now out of print, and so are most of my old books. I was glad, though, to give permission for several of my books to appear in a special cheap edition for the men in the forces. Had a good talk the other day with W. E. Williams, who used to run Adult Education in this country, and has now, though still a civilian, been put in charge of the Army Bureau of Current Affairs, known as ABCA. He confirms my view, frequently expressed to you, that the men in the Army want to discuss serious topics and are really concerned about the future of the world. The trouble is, as he pointed out, that they're mostly short of facts. As yet they haven't a solid enough base of sheer information. And that's what he and his enthusiastic corps of ABCA officers are trying to put before the men – facts, facts, facts. It's the opposite of the Goebbels system, which tries one kind of fairy tale after another. His latest is that we're trying to destroy German culture. And this from the man who superintended, with glee, the burning of the books! He must think nobody remembers anything longer than a week.

14 and 15 July 1943

War Becomes Routine

It would be easy to give you a picture of London sizzling with excitement over the invasion of Sicily. I could describe the bright eyes and flushed faces around the loudspeakers, the impatient crowds clamouring for the latest editions of the newspapers, the knots of people along the pavement discussing the last items of news, the tense crowds in Whitehall – and so on and so forth. Unfortunately, this fine vivid dramatic story wouldn't be true. And I believe that when you are dealing with the world's news, truth is far more important than drama, colour, excitement, red-hot stories. My quarrel with a good many wartime reporters and commentators is that they jazz the whole thing up too much. This war doesn't need that treatment. Let the facts speak for themselves. They're fantastic enough. What – for example – could be stranger than the fact that at this moment young men from Lancashire or Devonshire, from Ontario or Saskatchewan, from New Jersey or Alabama, should be fighting among the olive and lemon groves of Sicily? Who could have imagined that five years ago?

Another fact, not strange at all, is that London is taking this invasion of Sicily quite calmly. Those signs of public excitement simply don't exist. These days, I live not far from Whitehall and the huge establishments of the war ministries, and so I am well situated to discover any marked signs of stress or excitement among their staffs. But everything round there has seemed quite normal. You would never guess that anything special was happening. It's the same in the city itself. There's nothing to show that we've just begun one of the most complicated and difficult operations in all military history. Newspapers sell briskly, of course, but then they've been selling briskly for a long time, if only because their circulations are now limited and so there are never any to spare. Most people are probably listening to more of the BBC news bulletins than usual, hoping to catch some latest bit of information. But it would certainly be an exaggeration to say that the news 'electrified' the London crowd, as we are told the news 'electrified' people elsewhere. There's no indifference, but there's no excitement. I would say that the press, which has broken out into big headlines and large-scale maps of the field of operations, tends on the whole to show more excitement than its readers, who are taking it all in their stride.

Though, of course, these are early days, and the real battles have not yet arrived. This fact is stressed as much here as it is, I imagine, with you. Sometimes in stressing it, the military critics and the writers of editorials, I feel, are apt to over-praise the Germans at the expense of the Italians, who can fight well when properly led. And in the last stages of Tunisian campaign, the Italians appear to have made as good a showing as the Germans, if not better. I hope we shall make it clear to the Italians that they are not, in fact, defending their homes against us – for we don't want their homes or anything else that's theirs – but are only risking their lives to defend the Fascist regime that has never brought most of them anything but bullying, high taxation, low wages and a whole way of life that never meant anything to the ordinary Italian people. We should ask them why they should fight for the Germans, whom they dislike, against the British and Americans, who are old friends and good customers.

I want to return for a minute or two to that point about the lack of any particular excitement here. It's rather an important point, for various reasons that I'll show later. We are not, of course, a wildly demonstrative or dramatic people. Our tendency is always to under-play and under-state. This is one reason why Americans – and, let's face it, Canadians and Australians – and the English sometimes fail to understand each other. An American friend of mine, over here on government business, pointed this out to me only the other day. An American gets some job in the war effort – he knows it's responsible and important – and he's eager and excited about it – and naturally he's full of it, wants to show what a man-size job it is, wants to compare notes with other men who are doing similar jobs, and can't wait to talk it all over. He meets an Englishman who is perhaps his opposite number in our war effort, or is at least doing the kind of job the American is interested in, and this Englishman, instead of launching out on the magnitude and wonder of his job, merely mumbles that he's been able to do one or two interesting little things, doesn't bother to mention what they are, says 'Quite, quite!' to anything the American puts in as a lead to further confession, and generally gives the impression of being rather inefficient, bored and probably half asleep. That's the difference we must all make allowances for – otherwise we shall tend to misjudge each other. The man from the new country doesn't – in point of fact – think he is wonderful, and is quite as ready to take criticism as he is to dish it out. On the other hand, the man from the old country is by no means indifferent to his job, and is probably far from being bored and half asleep. It's merely a difference of habitual manners.

Now, let us return to the lack of any great excitement here in London. This is not only due to the fact that we are not an excitable people and like to take things coolly. There is something else, sometimes easily overlooked. It is that people in this corner of Britain have been in fairly intimate contact with great events for some time now. Three years ago, our great ally, France, had collapsed, and the Nazi Army was at Calais, at Boulogne, at Dieppe, at all those places that we thought of as neighbouring seaside resorts, to which we could slip over at any time. For months and months, the gigantic German nailed fist hung over us, almost darkening the sky, its nearest armour only twenty-one miles from our shore. We have watched our cities burn and have seen our friends pulled out of the ruins. One of my daughters, a girl of nineteen, has done duty in the WRNS, month after month, and heard not only the bombs fall but also the Nazi shells whistle over her head. We have seen and heard and felt a good deal in these parts, and that makes a difference.

I lay some stress on this because I think it helps to explain something that puzzles and rather distresses some of the overseas soldiers and airmen who come here. They've left home, these fine lads, often in a great cloud of glory and a fine romantic state of excitement, come ashore here eagerly, and then often tend to feel rather let down. The people are friendly enough, but they seem rather cool and unresponsive. The truth is, of course, that they aren't living in the same atmosphere as our visitors, our very welcome visitors, who see everything bright and new and exciting. These people of ours are mostly right up to the neck in the war effort, with Home Guard, civil defence or at least fire-watching on top of their long day's work; they haven't much time, haven't much energy to spare, haven't much money; they've been through one crisis after another, taken it and dished it out; with the result that although they have the most genuinely warm and friendly feeling for the men from overseas who arrive among them, it's almost impossible for them to respond as some of these men would like them – and expect them – to respond. And I've noticed that the men who've been here for some little time realise this, and indeed begin living in the same atmosphere themselves. And I trust these remarks may help to explain something that may also have puzzled some of you fathers and mothers, sisters and wives, after receiving letters from this side that may have expressed some disappointment. Don't worry. It all straightens itself out. You can bet that all these relations are straight and easy right now in Sicily.

London is full of exhibitions these days. There must be a dozen within half a mile of where I live. In the Underground railway station just across the way is an exhibition showing the average American. The various services keep having exhibitions. There are exhibitions of housing, of suggested reconstructions of London after the war, of town planning and so forth. I must receive an invitation to some exhibition or other by every post. All of which confirms my belief that we are intellectually much more alert than we used to be. Meanwhile, some of the very best exhibitions have been organised by departments that before the war would have been thought incapable of showing the public anything but the door. For instance, one of the best and most successful exhibitions of this war, now being held in the blitzed section of a large store, is an exhibition of all the newest weapons and equipment of our Army, and it is attracting crowds all day long. You might wonder where all the crowds come from, seeing that we are up to our necks in the war effort. Who are these idlers who attend exhibitions or listen to the speeches and the music in Trafalgar Square or stare at the sentries outside Buckingham Palace or hang about Downing Street in the hope of catching a glimpse of Mr. Churchill? Or – for that matter – stroll in the parks, watch the ducks on the lakes, or talk or read sitting in the thousands of little green chairs that we have in these public places? At first sight, it looks as if our Ministry of Labour must have very wide, loose meshes in its net, when so many people – uncountable thousands – have so little to do. But if you observe these crowds more closely, and use your eyes and ears, you soon discover that many of them are servicemen on leave with their wives or girlfriends, that others belong to the huge army of night workers and are enjoying their few daylight hours of recreation, that others again may be having a day or two off from work, perhaps taking their only holiday of the year. And they all get plenty of free entertainment – and, if they can take it, education – in our exhibition-conscious city.

A little story I wanted to tell you last week, but it was crowded out. Our United Aid To China Fund, run by Lady Cripps, has a shop and depot in Bond Street, and a week or two ago, during the special drive to celebrate China's seventh anniversary of her great resistance, a very old retired colonel, in his late eighties, arrived at this depot to give the China fund fifteen pounds. The old man was obviously not too well off; and then he explained that he had obtained this money by selling a special medal that had been given to him, as the best cadet of the year, at the Royal

Military Academy at Woolwich – in 1876. He had enjoyed so much kindness from the Chinese when he served in the East, years and years ago, that he was determined to contribute as much as possible to the fund. This gallant old gentleman's gesture will certainly be appreciated by the Chinese, a people who revere old age and never forget a kindness themselves.

21 and 22 July 1943

Listeners' Questions

First, a few answers to questions. Several listeners, from various parts of the world, have asked questions about our food commitments, and I will try to give you one combined answer to all these. Feeding British civilians is only one part of our food problem, and a great deal of the food sent from overseas to Britain is not meant for the British civilian at all. Thus large armies in the field are terrific consumers of food, and naturally it is the best food. Most of our beef, for instance, goes to our fighting men – as it should. I suppose I average about one modest helping of roast beef per month – and no steak, of course. Then, under our reverse land-lease policy, we supply the American forces in this country with food. Again, in co-operation with the Americans, we are now beginning to plan the invasion of Europe not only in terms of ships, men, munitions, but also in terms of food. As we move forward, the people in the liberated territories will have to be fed, and we shall have to feed them, just as we are giving food to so many Sicilians at this moment.

And what we have done here to produce more foodstuffs has undoubtedly been one of the great triumphs of our war effort. We are now the most highly mechanised farming community in the world, and we are producing more per acre than anywhere in the country. We have some six million more acres under the plough than when the war began, which is an increase of just about 50 per cent. We have nearly doubled our pre-war production of vegetables. Although we no longer import the vast quantities of cattle feed and have ploughed six million acres of grass on which dairy herds grazed, our milk production is almost what it was before the war. It is true that our milk is strictly rationed now, but that is chiefly because young children and expectant mothers now have far more milk than they used to have: they get it at a reduced price, and if necessary for nothing. We have had to cut down heavily on pigs and poultry, which explains why our favourite breakfast dish – bacon and eggs – is almost a thing of the past. Before the war, we made less than 30,000 tons of silage in this country, but last year we made 1,500,000 tons. The harvest this year will be the all-time record here – and this in spite of the fact that most of the young men have been taken from the land. How has all this been done? Chiefly through County War Agricultural Committees backed by a terrific drive from the Ministry of Agriculture. Control and direction have been backed by local knowledge. Men have been told to farm properly or get out. Not a field has been allowed to be wasted. It's not been easy going. The farmers have had to work like blazes. But nearly all of them have said, 'Tell us what to do and we'll do it' – and they've done it.

A fine letter from a Merchant Seaman in the Indian Ocean, pointing out that the Merchant Navy was on the job at Narvik, Dunkirk, Greece, Crete, Tobruk, Hong Kong, Singapore, Java, Penang, Burma, Madagascar, North Africa and now Sicily; and he suggests that the public know little about the Merchant Navy and its men, and that we have not drawn sufficient attention to what they have done. I must say – and I speak out of a great regard for this service – that this isn't my own impression. I've heard and read innumerable tributes to the Merchant Seamen, and more and better arrangements for their welfare are being made here all the time. But I want to assure him that I am passing on his smaller – and more legitimate – complaint to the proper quarters here. Good luck, sailor!

A lady in Malta, wife of a retired Naval officer there, wrote to me the other day, giving me a sketch of her mother's biography – for her mother, who had been a child in the Middle East at the time of the Crimean War and had afterwards gone to India, had had a romantic, picturesque life. And this lady never hinted for a moment that she herself hadn't done so badly in this direction, living on what was up to recently the most heavily bombed island in the world, an island decorated for its superb gallantry and endurance. Not a word of all that. She seems to have taken all that in her stride. And if she's listening to this, I want to assure her that I've already written to her about the other matter.

A listener, an Australian, living in the heat of Nigeria, West Africa, who depends very much on his radio, puts a question that doesn't come into the category of questions I undertook to answer, but as he's so lonely and cut off, I'll try to answer it just the same. He points out that we of the white races have undertaken to educate the Africans, the kind of men who work for him, and then goes on: 'There is a constant stream of natives passing by. They give me a salute, with a happy smile. The tribes live peaceably. They never quarrel. They work together in perfect harmony, never have wars or quarrels' – and then he goes on to ask, in effect, who are we that we should educate them? His point being that they have at least the sense to live in peace and harmony and apparently we haven't. Well, I'll try to answer even that one. There's no doubt that we – of the so-called white races – belong to the most restless, fiercest and probably most quarrelsome division of the human species. Primitive peoples have always found us at once terrifying and bewildering. What is the matter with us? – they wonder. The shortest answer is, I think, that we're suffering from growing pains and they're not. There is in us a deep creative urge, which often, of course, gets twisted and produces more evil than good. But the good is there, and we are fighting now so that the good will have more chance, and that ultimately we can take its benefits – its real benefits – to the remotest plateaus of Africa. The immense power, due to rapid technical progress, now possessed by the white races means, in fact, that the world will be conquered by men's most evil impulses or by their noblest ones. And that, in my view, is what this war is about. Of course, we are on our side aren't perfect. But our way – and our way alone – lies hope, and for men of every climate, creed and colour. Better to be educated by faulty white men than to be enslaved by thoroughly bad ones, and now even the remotest tribes in the furthest jungles have probably no other choice.

A friend who runs education in one of our northern counties sends me an account of a joint Anglo-French youth rally up at Ullswater in the Lake District. Pupils from a French lycée up there met a group of English youths and girls. They danced their respective folk dances, sang their respective folk songs, and three young French people, who had left France less than a year ago, told of their experiences and answered questions. My friend sends me a frank account of the joint rally written by a boy who has recently left school to work in a boot and shoe factory, and this lad puts most things into a nutshell. He writes:

> *I thought the Rally was a great success, I had a very good time indeed and I am sure all the other people did, especially the French, who seemed to be putting all their heart into the dances and the games. The flies were the only thing I didn't like, when we were having tea especially ... The singing was a bit weak because the English did not know the French songs and the French did not know the English songs too well. I think it would be a good idea if the English learnt a bit of French and the words to some of the French songs, in my opinion it would be one step nearer the Anglo-French relationship after the war, as we are the next lot to help in country affairs when the wise people of today are too old to think about running the country.*

And then there's a charming postscript. The boy says: 'I can play a selection of waltzes for old and young. I can't get to any practices on Monday, Thursday or Friday. Anyway, if I can't do anything, I can help behind stage.' And then – in a sudden wild burst of cosmopolitanism – he ends, faultily but indomitably, 'Au revoir'. But even if as yet it's 'Au revoir' instead of 'Au revoir', I feel that the real seeds of a good sound international relationship have been planted there. Better that, a thousand times, than those pre-war banquets at which second-rate politicians from each country mouthed sentiments in which they didn't believe and on which they were never prepared to act. Let's start with the boys and girls, and songs and dances, tea and chatter, on the mountains, this time.

About a year ago, as I believe I mentioned at the time, the Admiralty here appealed for holiday photographs of Europe. It was pointed out then that these photographs – although they might be nothing more than the most casual snapshot – might prove very valuable to our Intelligence departments and might help us to plan our operations with more certainty. At that time, invasion seemed very far away, but nevertheless people sent in their photographs, and holiday snapshots arrived at the Admiralty by the hundred thousand. They were first sorted into districts and then each photograph that looked at all useful was carefully scrutinised by Naval Intelligence officers and civilian experts, who examined them under powerful lamps and with high-powered magnifying glasses, so that no detail should be missed. If the snapshots – or any sections of them – appeared to be of particular interest, they were enlarged. And notes were made of the date on which each picture was taken. The enlarged photographs were then compared with recent aerial reconnaissance pictures of the same neighbourhood, and this comparison often enabled our experts to decide what measures of defence had been taken in these particular districts. Roads near the coast were, of course, of particular interest, and often some light-hearted little holiday snapshot – you know the kind, 'That's George holding up the bottle, and that's Mabel pulling a silly face' – gave us a valuable clue to the type of road and the amount of traffic it would take. And it is a fact that the invasion of Sicily owes something to these holiday snapshots.

Just had a letter from a Dutchman here in London, who begins by telling me that some years ago, about 1938, he saw a play of mine in Amsterdam, and that the scenery for this play was designed by a young Dutch architect he knew called Limperg. This young architect was a quiet, apparently unheroic sort of chap, interested in the social implications of architecture. But he has just been shot by the Germans, along with a well-known Dutch writer, and a scientist, and nine others. What these men did was this: at the end of March, a number of them, in uniforms of the Dutch police, forced their way into the building of the Amsterdam registry and there destroyed with explosives the archives and the card indexes. They did this in order to prevent Dutch workers from being rounded up and then deported to Germany. Twelve were shot, and eleven others – including doctors, students, writers – were sentenced to penal servitude for life. Just a characteristically brief, unpretentious Dutch glimpse of this huge epic of tyranny, murder, slavery and heroic resistance, which has already cost millions of lives and has produced more human misery than any similar event in the world's history. Do you wonder at the scale of our bombing? Every day counts. Every day produces its new tale of misery and heartbreak. What we are bombing are the steel-and-concrete doors of a vast prison and slave market. We are letting in the daylight.

4 and 5 August 1943

Holidays

The impending collapse of Italy, which will have a very marked effect on Germany's other satellites, throws into relief the political aspect of this total war. Though, in truth, the military and political threads, as we saw in North Africa, can hardly be disentangled. An important action may be taken for a purely military reason, but the political consequences of that action may in turn change the whole military situation. And so it goes on, a very complicated game indeed. Now, there are certain difficulties facing us in Europe, and they can already be noticed, though not yet in full force, in the Italian situation. And there has been much speculation and discussion already in the more serious press and among the better-informed people here. Any military commander occupying what was formerly enemy territory and making use of it to prosecute his major campaign doesn't want a civil revolution on his hands or any state of civil chaos. He wants to do a deal, if possible, with a fairly strong authoritarian government, which he can hold responsible for maintaining order in the country and for seeing that the occupied country fulfils its obligations. Politics may not come into this at all; the military commander may have no politics; he is probably trying to get on with his job with the least waste of time and manpower. Even if he sympathised with the objects, he would probably dislike anything like a real revolution, simply because of what would seem to him a waste of time and manpower. On the other hand, if there is a government capable of keeping order and seeing that its demands are promptly met then he is happy to do a deal with that government so that he can return to his main task.

All this is fairly obvious. But – and this is where the difficulties crop up – Continental European politics are very different from our Anglo-Saxon politics, and especially at the end of a period like that between the two world wars. In Europe, you don't get strong centre parties, the parties of moderation, of caution, of careful liberalism. There tends to be a wide gap in the centre, and therefore a gulf between the Left and the Right parties. The result is that the average European Right-wing party tends to be far more reactionary and extreme than the conservatives of Britain and America; and, on the other hand, the European Left tends to be far more violent and revolutionary than the Anglo-Saxon Left. There is, you may say, practically no common ground at all between the European parties. There is hardly anything between them but a mutual deep distrust and hatred. Hence the violent revolutions and counter-revolutions and civil wars. (Note – the histories of our people are by no means free from these terrible chapters, but we had them earlier and so were able afterwards to find more common ground.) A Continental reactionary is a real dyed-in-the-wool black reactionary, while the opposing side are usually not merely pinkish but genuinely Red. On the other hand, the kind of liberal democrat who would immediately and almost instinctively understand our point of view and find it easy to co-operate, though he may actually exist in fairly large numbers in many European countries, is not organised for quick political action.

And now the horns of the dilemma begin to emerge. In the circumstances, it seems easier and quicker and much better from a purely military point of view to do a deal with some fairly strong authoritarian government of the Right. But unfortunately these are the very people who tended to encourage, to welcome and then often actively to support the very thing we are determined to destroy. Thus we may find ourselves knocking down with one hand and building up with another. We may find ourselves travelling round a vicious circle. Moreover, it might be our best and oldest friends who might suffer the most from such a government. For it is a fact, impossible to deny, that the hard core of resistance to Fascism and Nazism has always been found on the opposite wing, among the organised working class and the progressive intellectuals of Europe. That is why Fascism and

Nazism have always made haste to try to destroy these classes, to shatter the trade unions and other workers' organisations and to persecute, imprison, murder or drive into exile all the progressive intellectuals. It is the representatives of these people who have worked with us to destroy these monstrous tyrannies; and most of us have for them and with them a respect and sympathy that we find it impossible to extend to the opposing Continental types – the reactionary aristocratic landlords, the big industrialists who contributed to Fascist and Nazi funds, the undemocratic and highly privileged and suspicious military men and the like. We know, in fact, where our real friends are in these countries, and clearly, expediency or no expediency, we have to liberate them, and cannot stand by while they merely exchange one repressive regime for another not very much better. The matter was well stated in an editorial in this last Sunday's *Observer*, an old and influential newspaper with a very moderate political outlook. The editorial, after giving a sketch of the Italian situation, goes on to say:

> *The British have no wish to create disorder and revolution. But we want to say clearly and unambiguously that we would regard it as a national calamity if this country chose as its political ally in Europe authoritarian reaction and tried to suppress the revolutionary popular forces, as Metternich did after 1815. First, such a policy would not be backed by an overwhelming majority of the British people. The British people are committing themselves through the pledges of all parties to a large step forward towards social democracy – at home. In Britain, social changes have a way of coming about bloodlessly and peaceably. That does not alter the fact that the British people, in their great majority, feel at one with the Continental Radicals and Socialists, and would reject a policy of 'Darlanism' just as they rejected the appeasement of Fascism.*

'Secondly, we are convinced', the editorial goes on,

> *that the future greatness and welfare of Britain depend*

> *on our ability to provide, at this fateful hour, leadership*
> *for Europe. To do this we must range ourselves with*
> *the most vigorous and most genuine political forces in*
> *every country ... The political master-force of our own*
> *century, so dependent upon mechanical resources for*
> *its power, is the democracy of the industrial workers,*
> *specialists and managers. Whoever rejects this force*
> *will find himself continually frustrated.*

So says the editorial writer in *The Observer* – and, as people are so fond of declaring now, I couldn't agree with him more.

In ordinary times, this is of course our great holiday season. The British people, down to the very poorest, like to get away to the sea at this time of year, and of course wherever they live they are never really very far from the sea, a fact that must not be overlooked. This year, with the war making enormous demands on our railway transport – and long-distance road transport of passengers has ceased to exist – the government for some weeks now has been making urgent appeals to the people not to travel and has been warning them that no extra trains would be available and that people who decided to travel after all these warnings did so at their own risk.

In addition, the Holidays-at-Home scheme, by which ordinary towns provide various amusements in their public parks and elsewhere, both for children and for adults, has gone forward in a very big way, as I know rather to my cost because I have found myself let in for making opening speeches at various suburban London parks, or at places just outside, and judging children's fancy dress, and assisting in crowning Holiday Queens, and in fact at all manner of rather hot, sweaty, crowded, though often very jolly, Holidays-at-Home antics. And the people have swarmed to these affairs.

Nevertheless, in spite of these excellent counter-attractions and the solemn warnings of the government, large numbers of people have besieged the railway stations all over the country, waited for hours, sometimes all night, for the chance of packing into over-crowded trains, often then to find that there was no accommodation for them at the other end and that they had to wait in long queues even to get a meal. There was a mournful little story in one of our papers the other day about a man who left London with his suitcase to have a nice week's holiday in the Isle of Man. He spent two days and nights, without a bed or any proper sleep, at Fleetwood, vainly attempting to get a passage in the Isle of Man boat. Then, in despair, he went to Blackpool, and found that he had to spend the night, with his suitcase, on the beach. So then he went inland, to Chester, only to find that Chester couldn't offer him a bed, so that he had to walk about with his suitcase all night there. As a last desperate move, he went from Chester to Bangor, but fared no better there, except that he was able to sleep on the beach again. So, rocking from want of sleep, he crawled, with his suitcase, into the London train, only to lose his suitcase on the way, having spent six nights out of bed.

It's difficult to blame the people for wanting to have a breath of sea air, for they've all been working very hard in their factories and in addition have been doing Home Guard duties or fire-watching or some other form of civil defence and also probably digging up an allotment, and nobody denies that they need a change and a holiday. The government can't ration travel, forbidding people to travel at all unless they have permission to do so, because it would take an army of clerks and interviewers to decide exactly who should and who should not be given permission to take a train. So all that the government could do was to issue these many warnings, in various forms, and to encourage the press to print photographs of packed stations and to tell heart-breaking stories of crowds waiting at one end for trains and waiting at the other for meals.

Two things have impressed me in all this. First, the extraordinary good temper of our crowds, who after months of hard work and extra duties might easily have lost their temper at all this queuing up at stations and restaurants, and shown some anger at seeing their all-too-brief holiday period vanishing while they waited for the holiday to begin. But no – from my own observation, and from other people's reports, they have been amazingly patient and good-tempered. They are indeed an astonishingly tolerant and good-humoured people. The other thing that has impressed me has been the power of organisation exhibited by so many of our people – town councillors, borough employees and the like – in so many of these quite elaborate Holidays-at-Home programmes, in which often tens of thousands of people of all types and ages have to be catered for – with games and pastimes and children's shows during the day, and concerts and vaudeville shows and dancing and competitions at night – for perhaps several weeks on end. Having been, in my capacity as a visitor, partly behind the scenes at these festivities, I've been able to see this genuine organising ability at work in all kinds of places and with all kinds of people, and I've come away with a renewed respect for our ordinary folk, who when they set about it, whether it's fighting or amusing themselves and others, can do a job as thoroughly and efficiently as any people in the world, and with much less fuss and bullying palaver than most others, especially the Germans. I'm no organiser myself, so perhaps I can boast a little about the others.

11 and 12 August 1943

This War and the Last

I cannot accept the view that the war of 1914–18 and this war are really all one war. I mention this because certain people here, remembering last week that on 4 August 1914 we had entered the last war, have been putting forward this view. It is, in my opinion, mistaken and mischievous. The last war was essentially a war of rival and competing national systems. It was the same kind of war that had been fought in the nineteenth century, and in the eighteenth century. It was a war between powers arranged in series of alliances. B. had to come in because A. had been attacked, and A. had been attacked by C. and D. because A. had ordered general mobilisation, which so alarmed C. and D. that they mobilised too and attacked first, and before long E., F., G. and H. had to come in. Does that mean that Germany, in my view, is cleared of all charges of war guilt in the last war? No, it doesn't. And here I'd like to quarrel with the usual method of trying to assess war guilt. It doesn't seem to me a question of which sentry fired the first shot, or, for that matter, which Foreign Secretary sent the rudest ultimatum. It is to my mind chiefly a question of intention, organisation and atmosphere. If you find that one country allows its fighting forces to dominate its whole life, regards military officers as being superior to civilians, talks not with reluctance and regret but with enthusiasm about a coming war, is pouring more and more of its wealth into units and weapons that are clearly meant for attack and not mere defence, then in my opinion if you also find that country is at the start of a war, you may reasonably assume its guilt. The intention of Imperial Germany was to make war on a big scale, sooner or later; it was elaborately organised to make war; and its atmosphere was militarist and aggressive.

But all that's an old story. The point I want to make now is that this present war, though it may be seen as yet another chapter in the huge revolutionary history of our times, cannot be safely regarded as a continuation of the last war or even as any kind of direct sequel to it. This war sprang out of a different world. It had an entirely different character from the last war. It exists in quite a different atmosphere. All the people in it behave differently. For my part, I have never seen this war as a struggle between nations, for nationalistic ends. I see it as a fight to the death between certain power groups, like the Nazis and the Japanese war lords, and the rest of the world, whose people may not have agreed yet about what exactly they do want but know what they don't want, namely, to be conquered and enslaved by these power groups. And I do not believe that there exists in the world, outside the Axis fortress, any large number of ordinary people, people who work for a living, common folks not fancy special people, who do not detest the Axis and all its works and pray for our speedy victory. They know very well that we are fighting for them. Certain countries may have to be technically 'neutral' in this world struggle, but I for one cannot believe in any personal neutral attitude towards it, and strongly hold the view that he who is not for us is against us. And if any man assured me that he was personally neutral in this battle for the soul and body of the world, I would prefer not to remain in the same room with him. And any loose talk of this war being a continuation of the last simply disguises the nature of this war, puts a smokescreen between us and the real vital issues of our time and therefore, I say, is both mistaken and dangerous.

I have been reading, with pride and delight, some tributes here lately to the magnificent 50th Division of the Eighth Army. News of this particular division interests me particularly because it is almost exactly the same sort of division as that with which I trained from its start at the beginning of the last war, and with which I went out to France. This old division to which I belonged, in a very, very humble capacity, was the 23rd, and it consisted of men from Northumberland, Durham and Yorkshire – sturdy, pugnacious lads from the pits of Durham and the Tyne, from the combing mills and dye-works of the West Riding, and from the little farms in the bleak northern Dales. And this 50th Division of the Eighth Army is also made up of battalions from Northumberland, Durham and Yorkshire – the same lads a generation later, and many of them, probably, sons of the men with whom I fought in the mud of Flanders and the chalk of Picardy. And, I tell you, they're the salt of the earth. They're like bull terriers. I'd like some of the people who began yapping that the British couldn't fight to have half an hour with these boys. But what did they do in the desert? What didn't they do? At Gazala, when Rommel launched his last offensive – and the fate of Egypt, perhaps the whole Middle East, perhaps the whole world, hung in the balance – this 50th Division held on to cover the general retreat. Then – I quote the printed record:

> *to save themselves, they struck westward deep into enemy territory, broke through the Axis lines and, swinging south and east, fought for thirty miles before re-joining the Eighth Army on the Egyptian border. Then, later, they held Mersa Matruh for several days to gain precious time for the Alamein line to be strengthened.*

Those were probably the very days when Mussolini was making arrangements – the kind of arrangements he loved making – to make a spectacular and triumphant entry, as the new Caesar, into Cairo. Then, before General Montgomery launched his offensive on 23 October, the men of the 50th Division had already broken into the Axis positions several times on different parts of the front and had brought back numbers of prisoners. Then began the great chase. Two thousand miles to the west, the 50th Division were in the assault on the Mareth Line, and it was they who forced a path through the marshlands and across the great anti-tank ditch. It was twenty-four feet deep, that ditch, with steeply sloping sides, and on the other side was an elaborate defence system of trenches, pillboxes, machine-gun posts and concrete strong-points, and they carried it with the bayonet, after using planks and scaling poles. Afterwards, they forced their way across another great anti-tank ditch in Tunisia, where they were in the centre of the Eighth Army's attack. And finally at Enfidaville the seaward end of the line fell to them, and they mopped up the master race like gathering blackberries. And now they're in Sicily. And Lord knows where they'll be next, but wherever they go, the men on the other side will have to be very, very good to stop them. Those are the lads – if you'll forgive this sudden – and, I think, you'll admit, unusual – outburst of local patriotism.

This is the last talk I shall be giving you for some weeks, because I'm leaving London to stay on a Cornish farm until the middle of September. No, I can't exactly say it will be a holiday, for I hope to work hard down there – probably writing a play – as well as doing some occasional cooking and much washing-up for the family. I've just finished a play, which I've written specially for our Army. It's about six soldiers in the desert and will, I hope, be acted by soldiers who used to be professional actors. It's called *Desert Highway* and really has a religious theme. I'm not afraid of offering our soldiers here a really serious play, as it's been my experience that they like good solid fare, something for their minds to bite on, in preference to the light escapist stuff that was being – and is still being – dished out to civilian theatre-goers. Anyhow, this play is some small gesture of gratitude from a middle-aged dramatist to the men who are defending him and his family.

My last public job in London before going away – and I'm glad it was my last because I've had too many of them – was something of an ordeal, because this last Saturday morning – at the horrible hour, for public speaking, of ten-thirty – I had to open a conference of the Association of Teachers of Speech and Drama, a conference on spoken English. A bit thick, y'know, making a tired man address, at half-past ten in the morning, a whole large room full of people who teach other people how to speak. I said that I suspected that they had asked me to do this job so that they could have enough examples of how not to do it, from *my* speech and mannerisms, to last them for the next twelve months. 'Take care', they would say to their more slovenly and less advanced pupils, 'take care you don't do what J. B. Priestley does. Really, he ought to be ashamed of himself.'

I also pointed out to them that just after the last war a man might have been forgiven for thinking that speech was becoming of less and less importance. The age of great political oratory appeared to have ended. Radio had not then become popular and was hardly known to the general public. And at that time, scores of theatres – many of them fine old places with a grand tradition – were being turned over to the films, and in those days the films were silent. It looked, I said, as if we were about to use our eyes more and more and our ears less and less. But what a change now! Oratory has returned here, in the person of our Prime Minister, who has made some of the greatest fighting speeches in our history. The radio has captured almost every home, and dozens of regular broadcasters are known throughout the country by their voices alone. The films have acquired sound and speech, and the theatre is having a revival and looks as if, after the war, it will play a greater part in our life than it has ever done before. This really is, you know, a most extraordinary and dramatic change.

I also said that I knew they would be sensible enough to draw a sharp distinction between mere slovenliness and insensitiveness in speech and that not unpleasant suggestion of dialect which gives us so many local accents, of which my own Yorkshire accent is a fairly marked example. I talk with a Yorkshire accent not because I don't know any better but because I happen to like the broad vowels of my native county. And although I like to hear people talking with reasonable care and accuracy, I also like to hear speech that suggests it comes from somewhere, that has both a bit of earth and a little atmosphere about it, and doesn't give you the notion that it has really come out of a can. I like Scotsmen to sound Scotch, Irishmen to sound Irish, Welshmen to sound Welsh, North Countrymen to sound North Country, West Countrymen to sound West Country and so on. We English-speaking peoples, who now call to each other from every part of the world, must take care that we do not develop our local accents and localise our vocabulary so that in the end we cease to understand each other; that would be tragic; but on the other hand I hope we shall be able to keep a trace of our local landscape and weather and mannerisms in our speech, and will not soon all talk exactly alike. I enjoy all these varieties of English speech – and we hear plenty of them in London now – and I hope you will always refuse to flatten out and standardise your speech, my dear listener, just as I have always refused to flatten out and standardise mine. And next week, you will hear quite a different voice at this time; and that will do you good. So – happy listening and good luck!

17 May 1945

The End at Last (Home Service)

Well, we're here. One long stage of the journey has been passed. We're like people who've been travelling all night in a railway carriage and at last rub their eyes and see the thin grey daylight round the edges of the blinds, feel the train slackening and begin to move their cramped limbs, yawn, take down their battered suitcases and feel rather weary, a bit empty both in mind and body but still vaguely triumphant.

Distance and darkness have been conquered. Yesterday we were somewhere else; now we're here; we rushed through the long night. Now it's daylight.

Now let's go back and remember. The day of the beginning of the war in September 1939 I never heard that we were at war, for I was motoring up to London from the south coast to do a broadcast. When we arrived at Staines, we heard the first warning; the whole of Middlesex like a frightened, wounded animal suddenly screamed at us; all the nightmare articles I had read about bombing suddenly flashed through my mind. But nothing happened. So we went in. Broadcasting House seemed to be full of bayonets and nurses in uniform, and I have never seen it so conventionally war-like since. It was then in fact playing at being in the last war, a bad habit we had about then.

After that first winter, those months of phoney war I seem to remember as a time of black-out and bewilderment. We seemed to grope around in bags of coal, confused, lost. And behind the darkness like an ebony wall there was, we felt obscurely, something hellish brewing. Cosy little articles about our blockade and Germany's stocks of oil tried to comfort us – and somehow failed. And then in spring we knew why. The tree of Europe, hollowed out by Nazi propaganda, by fear and greed and despair, was shaken violently and countries fell like ripe fruit. Cities blazed, old women were herded with machine-guns. Nazi louts ate butter in the streets, the quislings and collaborators came out smiling. The voice of Paul Reynaud demanding some miracle of help was heard at midnight. London solicitors in striped trousers took small boats to Dunkirk; there were trains packed with red-eyed, sleepless troops. We put on LDV armlets and took a few old condemned rifles to the tops of hills. We were alone and the world thought London had joined Babylon, Nineveh and Carthage, but we knew better; and at last we had a government with some men in it and we stopped talking nonsense and went to war.

In that magnificent summer of 1940, when I spent my days collecting information and my nights broadcasting it to the world beyond the ring of steel around us, I think I never felt better than ever before or since. We lived at last as a community with a common purpose, and the experience was not only novel but exhilarating. We had a glimpse then of what life might be if men and women freely dedicated themselves not to their appetites and prejudices, their vanities and fears, but to some great communal task, and not even the brute threat of war, the menace of the very skies, could remove from that glimpse the faint radiance of some far-off promised land. We discovered our neighbours and found that they were fine people. And their long-legged sons, the lads who used to rattle and roar around in horrible little cars, went up into the blue, and there unimaginably fought, saved us and died.

Then one night, broadcasting to America from a dark window opposite the Cenotaph, I heard the first bombs come whistling down on central London. The blitz began. Tall terraces were pink in the glow of burning warehouses. You went to a shop and it wasn't there. You rang up a house and it had gone. Late one night, a friend just back from the East End told me how he had seen a bomb crater and in this crater, mutely appealing to the heavens, were two hands joined together, a man's and a woman's, oldish, toil-worn hands clasped together, unforgettable symbols of the humblest bewildered suffering folk – and I wish every statesman in the world had a model of them on his desk. And I like to remember that nightclub which got a direct hit when it was busiest. The young men and their girlfriends were shuffling and jiggling on the packed dance floor, singing idiotically 'Oh Johnny, oh Johnny, how you can love' – the very types condemned by social philosophers for years, and yet when the bomb fell there was no screaming panic but the young men fought the flames and the girls tore strips from their evening dresses to bandage the wounded. We were, you see, better people than we had thought.

But as the drama of 1940 changed to the grim tasks of 1941, we told ourselves that we could never be beaten, but we asked ourselves too by what miracle we could ever win. The war might last a lifetime and ships were going down; unknown heroes were struggling against delirium and madness in open boats; and shops were beginning to look bare and contemptuous and there were more and more counters and fewer goods. And then came a hot Sunday in June when we heard that Hitler had gone roaring East, and this brought us a great ally, the lean giant in overalls – Russia – which saw with mounting fury all the great works for which its people had sacrificed immediate comforts, all the dams and power stations and factories, blasted and over-run by the grey hordes of robots. And we said – and the Prime Minister said it and the shop stewards said it – these people are our friends and their suffering shall be our suffering and their triumph shall be our triumph. But already we had another ally in everything but name, and, in December, Japan striking out of the blue at Pearl Harbor brought us another enemy but also another great ally, that could fill the sky with planes and the sea with ships – the United States – and the pattern of common endeavour and final victory was now fixed.

But the news was bad. If you want to remember the low point of the war, turn back to the early weeks of 1942, when everything seemed to be going wrong everywhere. Rommel advancing in Libya, German ships escaping up the Channel, Singapore falling with mysterious ease, the Japs swarming over the Far East like yellow fever, and we seemed to be making every effort and to have packets of men and precious munitions all over the world to no purpose. Here at home we seemed to enter a long,

long tunnel of black-outs and hard, monotonous work and cold and fire-watching and spam sandwiches and standing in railway train corridors, and too many people everywhere; and although the tunnel was suddenly illuminated in places, by the turning-tide victory of Alamein, by the sailing grandeur of Stalingrad later, it remained a tunnel and we seemed to grow old in it.

We came out of it, to more danger but more drama and colour and hope, in June last year. First D-Day, so much bigger and better than we had expected. Then, for us in London and the south-east, the summer of flying bombs, which, a joke at first, soon worked themselves up to a crescendo of strain and destruction. We have learned since what might have been in store for us if our armies hadn't moved with such speed; have seen photographs and read descriptions of the giant emplacements in northern France and the underground factories in Germany, where hordes of slaves worked like gnomes in the hollowed-out mountains to produce rockets and robot bombs. It is like an evil fairy tale, this last sinister chapter in the book of warfare, whose worst devices, in their full force, we avoided only by a final miracle of timing. It is like reading some horror story of machine men, with brains but without hearts and souls, who were so filled with rage because they were not truly human that they were determined to destroy everything. Some of our enemies closely resembled such creatures. Let us take care that we don't resemble them, opening the dark hinterland of our minds to those destructive forces that modern man falls an easy prey to just because he will not admit that they even exist. In the end, we made bigger bombs than they did – and the bullies were trapped, freezing, in the hell of their own invention – but if we did it, it was because we had to; there's no room here for the gloating Shakespeare sang in Arden 'This carol they began that hour / How that life was but a flower' – a statement no Nazi would comprehend. So let us tend the flower. It's for that we've been fighting.

We've arrived – yes – and it's beginning to be daylight, but the scene is grim and ruinous, and the journey must continue. There is still another war to finish. Europe around the smoking wreck of Hitler's mad empire must be fed, must be clothed, must be put together again. The world, which is now one indivisible whole of suffering and despair or hope and human triumph, must be nursed into some feeling of security and growing sanity, a new sanity and not the old mere appearance of it with delusions and nightmares lying in wait. There is much to do – and in our present weariness no doubt we often feel there is too much to do – but what we did in the dark against an overwhelming and cruel threat we can do in the daylight against opponents merely fed by our own weariness and prejudices and desire for ease. For we are, I repeat, a better people than we imagined ourselves to be. And just as once we discovered our neighbours and found them fine people, we can go on discovering further neighbours all over this planet.

We British haven't done too badly along the road. At home here we've done things, often desperate things, our way – and on the whole it's a very good way. We've built machines but never lost ourselves inside them. People have had to be pushed about – and we've all got grievances – but they've been left space enough to be human and individual in, to feel fairly free. The notion that people cannot devote themselves to the community without feeling like ants in an ant heap has been proved to be false. We know now that a man hasn't to be a buccaneer to feel a vital, self-developing individual. The community has much to give as well as to take. It is not the flower but at least it is the soil in which the flowers grow. One of the most astonishing things we did was to create those artificial harbours known as mulberries, and how we did it at once, in a very British way too, with plenty of sharp orders but with plenty of checks and balances too, new kinds of neighbourliness popping up, some grumbling of course, some hard slogging and some touches of humour and romance – and no press gangs, no execution squads, no concentration camps, no supermen ringing for slaves. We have built a vast machine to fight the machines that attacked us, but the flower of life still grew, and sometimes among the very logs and belts the green tendrils curled and the golden and white blossoms opened up to the faint remote sunlight. So, with all the care and compassion at our command, let us tend the flower of life, for it is for that that our brothers and sisters died and we were spared.

Faux Priestley

Imitation may be a form of flattery, but Priestley would certainly not have been flattered by Nazi efforts to copy his broadcasts.

From BBC Monitoring
'Special message for the troops by J. B. Priestley', read by the announcer

6 June 1944

Britons Must Not Expect Post-War Perfection

You and your contemporaries have written so many letters to me telling me how worried, bewildered and dubious you are. To begin with, let me say at once that I understand how your minds are working. I have been through exactly the same development. I began to realise ten years ago that, although I had not taken much interest in politics, politics were taking a great interest in me. I suddenly saw that this was not some elaborate game that was being played in Westminster and Fleet Street – it was our life. Even some of our most intimate personal relationships were in fact being shaped and coloured by politics. We might find ourselves lying half starved in a ditch or trapped in a burning house simply because of politics. You know that now – hold on to it and don't let any smooth elderly person persuade you to leave it to them. It can't be left to them.

Nevertheless, your present mood appears to be self-contradictory. One moment you are crying, 'We must have changes'; the next moment you are muttering, 'But there won't be any real changes.' Today you say, 'We must do it ourselves'; tomorrow you may be saying again, 'They won't do anything and we will have to put up with it.' I regard this contradictory mood as very dangerous. If you persist in it after the war it may lead to some sort of Fascism, which has the trick of converting impatience with politics into bad politics: for instance, young people who got into the habit of condemning Parliament or other elected assemblies as talking shops have several times before now suddenly found themselves saddled with tyrants and their secret police. Or, after veering round the problem in a very vague manner for a year or two, you give it up as a bad job, and then the hard-beat man who knows what he wants and how to get it moves in and proceeds briskly to make slaves out of you.

No doubt you would not have that, but all hell might break loose before you find your way into the daylight. Let us stop vaguely hoping and vaguely despairing, admiring this and denouncing that, for a few minutes, long enough to take one calm look at the situation. What are we in for, we British? Some foreign observers who are by no means unfriendly to us and openly admire our war effort have already declared that we cannot survive this war as a great nation: we save the world but will not be able to save ourselves. They point out that we have not the vast natural resources of our allies; one small, over-crowded island cannot compete with their huge rich continent. We do not own enough of the modern sources of power. We are now a debtor instead of a creditor nation. We are not self-sufficient. We demand a standard of living to which our resources do not entitle us. We have not the requisite economic toughness. Our Dominions will shortly be successfully competing against us. The era that gave us natural leadership is over and done with, and now our fortunes are sharply declining. Very soon, some of these mournful prophets have announced, this island will not be able to support more than about half its present population.

Do I myself agree, accept this dismal stuff? No! It is on the same level as those prophecies just before the war, often coming from these same quarters, that announced that we British were now so effete, so decadent, that we would never be able to resist the Axis. Well, we disproved that – but only, it should be remembered, by making a prodigious effort from May 1940 onwards. Without that effort, we were finished, and I believe that if we relax that effort and refuse to make more changes then the rot will set in, and the dismal prophets may be proved right.

But it depends on us. We are quite wrong, I hope, in thinking our decline to be inevitable. Our war production shows what we can do. We may no longer enjoy a favoured position. We have lost the advantages of our early start in industry and we lack certain resources. But, on the other hand, we have immense resources in experience, skill and character, and our prestige is high. The situation then, as I see it, is difficult, but not quite desperate. If we make the brave and wise choice, we shall save ourselves and perhaps save the world by our example. Far too many people look to tinkering despair in peace as they did in war. If we take the wrong turning, there will be no easy way back to prosperity, and our position will be grave indeed. That is the situation, and, in view of it, I think many of the discussions we hear about post-war reconstruction are rather futile and silly because so many of the people in these discussions seem to imagine that we shall have time and opportunity to lean back and wait until some absolutely flawless system, perfected down to the last detail, is presented to us. If some urgent radical change is suggested to them, some of these people will solemnly point out a little weakness here and there, a few minor hard cases that it might create, and then assume that nothing need be done until sheer perfection arises. It is as if a sailor on a ship that was practically breaking up should shake *(line missing from text)*.

This 'don't talk to me until all the details are perfect' is undoubtedly due to an unconscious dislike of change, though carefully masquerading as progressive criticism. Certainly, a great many of the discussions I have heard even among you younger folk have been dangerously set against an evil background – ample time, complete security. It has been assumed that we are trying to improve upon some fairly sane and comfortable and normal style of life that would go on anyhow, rather as if we had six bedrooms and two bathrooms and were merely trying to decide where to put the playroom and the third bathroom. And this is all wrong. It is a kind of appeasement attitude towards historical fact. We shall shortly be compelled to save ourselves from economic and political disaster. All our future as a people is at stake.

Radio National (Enemy Origin) in English, 9.50 p.m., 6 June 1944

Appendix Two

The Other Side of the Mirror:
German Propaganda

From the start of the war, Britain was bombarded with a steady stream of German propaganda coming from Bremen, Hamburg, Breslau and, after Hitler's invasion, Calais and Luxembourg. There were also two stations which claimed to be transmitting within Britain, the New British Broadcasting Service and Worker's Challenge, which addressed its audience as 'mates'. The government didn't need Inspector Foyle to root them out. Both came from Germany.

All German broadcasts were monitored on a daily basis by the BBC Monitoring Service, which also transcribed German transmissions to their own people as well as to the occupied countries, North and South America and Russia. Each day the transcripts were circulated to Churchill, his ministers and possibly to Priestley, who was well aware of what was being said and keenly interested in German propaganda. He was sternly informed whenever any of his own criticisms of British war efforts or the class system were repeated from Germany.

Most transmissions were point-scoring against the British; their losses always greater than claimed, while German losses were smaller. Germany was in every way superior to Britain. Nothing could stand in the way of its impregnable, 'scientific' war machine; British planes were inferior to German, its Air Force was weaker. Germany had massive supplies of oil and could trade with the whole of Europe, while Britain would be brought to its knees by the loss of its export trade and the threat to supplies and shipping. America would not intervene because Isolationism was strong, but would enthusiastically rob Britain of its reserves and overseas investments.

Their image of Britain was the reverse of Priestley's. Churchill was a dictator who was betraying his people; Britain would be ruined by war, unlike the occupied countries, which were better off under German rule. All this was designed to destroy morale, but it was occasionally more generous in giving the names, addresses and dates of birth of British prisoners in Germany. It even occasionally gave the names of prisoners who had not received parcels or communications from home.

Two stations, New British Broadcasting Service and Worker's Challenge, did more to provoke official fears. Just before Christmas 1939, Goebbels ordered the Nazis' British propaganda to be built round the theme of 'fighting plutocracy', so broadcasts treated British politics as a class war precipitated by a bloated plutocracy which had misled the people into a war to protect capitalism and Jewish finance. This oligarchy had dominated British politics and betrayed its working class since the First World War. They had betrayed Germany by imposing the Treaty of Versailles, which Hitler was trying to reverse.

Churchill himself was imposing a needless war and unnecessary suffering on his country by a dictatorship, quite unlike the benign rule of Hitler, who had no desire to invade or bomb Britain. His aims were limited to dominance in Europe, not the weakening of Britain's empire or the invasion of Britain. With his European aims satisfied, Hitler was prepared to offer peace and a new partnership to Britain. If this was spurned by Churchill, the warmonger, then retribution would fall on the British people. Once the British bombing of Berlin and other German cities began to disturb this German idyll, the stations threatened massive retaliation with a heavy bombing blitz on English cities by the mighty Luftwaffe.

Some samples show the growling of the beast:

Worker's Challenge

If invasion is so near as Churchill says it is then nothing can create this workers' state except a revolution right away. We're prepared to undertake it, and we're working for it, but if we can gain time, so much the better. If the German armies come here, revolution is going to be a little difficult, because so far as we know the workers' weapons don't quite come up to the German standard. But if we make peace, we

*have the chance of settling our own affairs. And settle
them we bloody well will. War means hunger. We tell
you again that in a couple of weeks' time there will be
so little food left that the bosses will try and grab it all.
War means dead women and children. Whose women
and children? Ours and ours. The bosses have got theirs
out of the way already, or are preparing to do so. Why
the hell should a little gang of racketeers expect us, the
workers, to give our blood for them? While they conduct
the war in comfort thousands of miles away, this is a
war waged on the workers of Britain by Churchill and
his gang. Our answer is to declare war on them.*

Germany Calling

*Even after the irresistible might of Germany seems
to have swept all before it, the Fuhrer is so far from
wishing to annihilate England that when he has her
at his mercy he still, once more, proposes peace. But
there must be no misunderstanding on one point.
Should Britain give an official answer and should
that answer merely imply the continued desire to
destroy National Socialist Germany then neither
regret nor human sympathy will prevent the Fuhrer
from discharging his clear duty to his own people, the
duty of freeing them for all time from the menace and
intrigues of international finance, exploitation and all
that Churchill's crumbling, evil disposition, all that
Churchill's old world means. As yet, the Prime Minister
and Dictator of Britain has not replied to a gesture
which has aroused admiration all over the world.
What he will say, if he says anything at all, remains
to be seen, but there is no doubt that the propaganda
machine which Downing Street commands is working
at full blast to destroy all hope of peace. The whole scaly,
grinning crew of hack propagandists are chanting,
'The war must go on.'*

*The majority must realise that when war comes
to Britain, it will indeed mean ruin and ashes, as
Churchill has declared. It will mean more. Thanks to*

his incredibly evil plan of employing the whole adult civilian population on military tasks, it will mean a hideous slaughter without possibility of discrimination. If each town and city is to be defended, it will mean inevitably the death of hundreds of thousands, perhaps even millions, of people who do not know how to bear arms but who have been deprived of their non-combatant status by the dictator who proposes to applaud the massacre from Canada.

These English transmissions used a cast almost as big as the roll call of *It's That Man Again* characters: Professor this, Doctor that, even a 'Paul Revere', but the most regular was William Joyce (his own name, not his invented title 'Lord Haw Haw'). Joyce was a man easily hurt:

As to the nature and quality of British propaganda, an amusing example has just come to my attention on which I am going to dwell, because it is personal to me. For the first time since I have spoken on the German radio, I am going to speak very directly about the campaign of slander and libel directed against me. With indifference, I read in the Daily Mail *and all sorts of other rags, some of them American, stories to the effect that I was an ex-actor, an ex-shipping clerk, an embezzler, a gangster, a sadist in family life, an unscrupulous mercenary, that I was born in several different countries, that I had dishonourably eloped with a girl from Manchester – who, incidentally, was and is my legal wife – that I was illiterate, that I could not read English, and that I was insane.*

All these imputations I disregarded as the mere filth of garbage hacks ... But now comes something quite different ... It is worth taking up not merely as a personal issue but as a fine illustration of how British information is manufactured and from what sources it comes.

The Evening Standard *of 21 March last published an article beginning on the front page and headed 'Girl tells of Haw-Haw as spy in London: he had 300 agents'*

... Had I wanted to spy upon England, I should have hardly proclaimed my admiration for Adolf Hitler as I did. I should hardly have been arrested, as I was several times for my National Socialist activities...

To conclude this personal note, I, William Joyce, will merely say that I left England because I would not fight for international Jewry against the Fuhrer and National Socialism and because I believe most ardently, as I do today, that victory with a perpetuation of the old system would be an incomparably greater evil for Britain than defeat coupled with the possibility of building something new, something really National, something truly Socialist.

Whatever the effects of this kind of propaganda, it certainly lost all credibility as the war went on and Joyce's hysteria grew.

J. B. Priestley titles from Great Northern Books:

Novels

Angel Pavement
Bright Day
Lost Empires
The Good Companions
Low Notes on a High Level
Sir Michael and Sir George

Non-fiction

English Journey
Delight

Biography

Priestley at Kissing Tree House: A Memoir
by Rosalie Batten
J. B. Priestley's Personal Secretary 1968-1984

www.greatnorthernbooks.co.uk